From

The Women's Press Ltd
34 Great Sutton Street, London EC1V 0DX

Catriona Blake was brought up in St Andrews. She has had various occupations, which include working for Women's Aid in London and Scotland, for a housing co-operative and on a community mental health project. Catriona Blake now lives in Dundee and is studying accountancy. She plays lacrosse and climbs mountains at every opportunity. *The Charge of the Parasols* is her first book.

Catriona Blake

The Charge of the Parasols

Women's entry to the
medical profession

The Women's Press

First published by The Women's Press Limited 1990
A member of the Namara Group
34 Great Sutton Street, London EC1V 0DX

British Library Cataloguing in Publication Data
Blake, Catriona
    The charge of the parasols: women's entry to the medical profession.
    1. Medical services. Role of women, history
    I. Title
    362.1088042

    ISBN 0–7043–4239–1

Phototypeset in 10/11½ Sabon by Input Typesetting Ltd London
Printed and bound by Cox & Wyman, Reading, Berks

Contents

Part 4 Rights Which Can No Longer Be Reasonably Denied

Acknowledgments

This book started life as a dissertation for an MA in Social History at the University of Essex. I would like to thank Leonore Davidoff, my supervisor, for her encouragement and scholarly advice. I also want to acknowledge the support of my fellow MA students during this period: Anna Clark, Bob Little and Lillian Stoddart.

Most of the research has been done at the Fawcett Library and the library of the Wellcome Institute for the History of Medicine. My thanks are due to the staff of both libraries, particularly to David Doughan at the Fawcett for his enthusiasm and advice.

I would also like to thank Pat Mahoney and the rest of the Explorations in Feminism collective for nurturing the book and for helping me to find a publisher for it.

Various friends have shown an interest in my work and given valuable emotional support: Annabel Faraday, Joan Ferguson, Liz Kelly, Madge Boothe, Sandra McNeill, and all my new friends in Scotland. Special thanks are due to Janet Martens for over five years of love and encouragement, and to Anne Johnston for similar support in the later stages of writing. They have both helped me to believe in myself and in the 'reality' of the book.

I would like to thank Janet Martens, Liz Kelly, Liz Robinson, Margaret Taylor and Pat Campbell for reading and commenting on the final draft. I would also like to thank Wendy Savage for contributing the foreword to the book.

Foreword

This is a fascinating and vivid account of the way that women had to fight to be admitted to the medical profession, and should be read by all aspiring doctors of both sexes, and those responsible for the selection and training of medical students.

By comparing and contrasting the experiences of women on both sides of the Atlantic over a hundred years ago, Catriona Blake shows how the differing strategies of these early pioneers led to a very slow rise in the number of women doctors in the UK compared with the USA, but also how vulnerable the isolated woman, like Elizabeth Garrett Anderson, was, even though she herself had succeeded. The technique of the dominant group of accepting a token outsider, because they are exceptional, does not necessarily pave the way for the ordinary woman.

The description of the fight of Sophia Jex-Blake and the Edinburgh Seven to be accepted into the University shows all the tactics used by those in power to retain their position. They changed the University rules, resorted to legal action, manipulated the male students and attempted to intimidate the small band of women, even though there was a strong body of support for their efforts to qualify as doctors. The effect of this struggle was important as the public learnt about the issues and fair-minded men were appalled by the way these academics had behaved.

Catriona Blake's work has not only made a coherent and exciting story about the struggle of women but has displayed clearly the way that women have to join together and adopt strategies as a group if they are going to succeed in changing the medical profession.

This account of the early history of women in medicine has

been thoroughly researched and has made the stories of these doctors accessible to women today. I am sure that it will be widely read and enjoyed by many of us who had little if any knowledge of the struggle that women had (and are still having) to become full members of the medical and other professions dominated by men.

Wendy Savage
18 May 1990

Introduction

[Doctors] do not know, and it is impossible from the nature of things that they can know, what unrelieved physical agony is endured by women, as a less torture than submitting to the mental trial of soliciting a doctor's aid.

(From a letter to the *English Woman's Journal*, September 1862, by 'A Lover of Invalids'.[1]

Men have little idea how much prolonged and increased suffering is often borne by their mothers, wives, sisters and daughters, just because they have not been able to consult physicians of their own sex. Nay, death itself has often prematurely cut down women, whose reluctance to seek advice from a man was only overcome by extreme pain when it was too late.

(From a letter to *The Scotsman*, 29 December 1872, entitled 'A Woman on Women Doctors'.[2])

These two quotations illustrate the most important feature of the campaign for women doctors in Britain: the determination that an alternative to male medical treatment of women *must* be found. Throughout the campaign, supporters concentrated on this argument for entry to the profession, detailing over and over again the suffering which women experienced as a result of having to consult male doctors. The message which comes across most clearly from the campaign is the demand for women-only medical care for women. One of the reasons for writing this book was to place on record the clarity of vision of early medical women and their supporters and to contrast it with recent developments such as the closure of the South London Hospital for Women and the Elsie Inglis Memorial Hospital, both of which were products of this vision.

The conviction that women doctors were desperately needed strengthened the determination of women that they must win the right to become full members of the medical profession. In particular, it helped to sustain them during periods of fierce opposition to female entry. During the height of the struggle at Edinburgh University, Edith Pechey, one of the women medical students, wrote to *The Scotsman* to complain about the harassment women were facing from many of their fellow students:

> I began the study of medicine merely from personal
> motives; now I am also impelled by the desire to remove
> women from the care of such young ruffians.[3]

There are clear similarities between the opening up of the medical profession to women and entry to other professions in the early twentieth century: they were all characterised by feminist campaigning, determined resistance from the profession as a whole, the extreme misogyny of individual men, and a final resolution through legislation, marred by continuing obstructiveness by the male professional establishment. These features can also be found today with the campaign for the ordination of women.

However, there the similarities end. The issue of women's entry to the medical profession was not seen by supporters as one of equal rights to employment, despite the fact that the demand for useful paid work was central to feminist campaigning of the 1850s and 60s. The crucial issue for them was the relieving of the suffering of women who were forced to consult male doctors. The whole area of health is uniquely important to women, in a way that law, banking or accountancy are not. It involves the question of control over what happens to their bodies. Every woman is affected throughout her life by the nature and quality of medical care available to her. Supporters of the campaign for medical women did not see it as a test case leading to the entry of women into other professions, and these in fact remained closed to women for another 43 years.

The professions of law, accountancy, banking and so on were not opened up to women until after the granting of limited suffrage in 1918, at which point Parliament had to start to listen seriously to a number of demands for legislative change which women were making. In 1919 the Sex Disqualification Removal Act opened all branches of the legal profession to women, after years of campaigning by feminist organisations and resistance from male lawyers. The Society of Chartered Accountants and other professional bodies were forced to open their doors to women, too, as a result of this Act, although others, like the Institute of Banking, had already done so voluntarily. The final struggle was over entry to the Civil Service. In 1921 a government decision to open every grade to women resolved the matter on paper, but true equality of opportunity was obstructed for a number of years. In 1925 three women graduates were the first to pass the entrance examination to the Civil Service.

As with other campaigns to gain entry to sanctuaries of male power and privilege, the movement for medical women was strengthened by a conviction that they were not asking for permission from men to be let into *their* territory but instead were demanding access to a sphere which they had inhabited equally with men in the past. They drew on the history of medicine in the western world to demonstrate that women had always practised medicine, as village healers and university professors, and that they had been deliberately excluded by men as part of the whole process of professionalisation of the seventeenth and eighteenth centuries. The fact that they were demanding the reinstatement of traditional rights rather than the granting of new ones lent moral force, as well as tactical ammunition, to the campaign.

One of the most striking features of the campaign was the range and nature of the tactics used by men, and by medical men in particular, to try to prevent female entry to the profession. The tone of written attacks on medical women, especially in the *Lancet*, ranged from patronising and dismissive to paranoid, abusive and downright vicious. The following passage comes from an account in the *Lancet* of Elizabeth Garrett Anderson's first year as a student:

The advanced guard of the Amazonian army which has

so often threatened our ranks, on paper, has already
carried the outposts and entered the camp.[4]

A letter in 1869 (four years after Elizabeth Garrett Anderson
qualified as a doctor!) described women's entry to the profession
as 'an outrage on all modesty, and a miserable travesty of our
noble art'.[5]

The suggestion that women should enter the profession seems
to have induced in medical men an apoplexy of extreme fear
and indignation. They accused women of trying to bring about
their financial and social ruin. They condemned women doctors
themselves as physical, emotional and sexual freaks. They per-
sisted in questioning the existence of a desire among women for
women doctors, despite growing evidence that this desire did
exist. Above all, they seemed desperate to defend the profession
against what they saw as pollution by the female sex.

These attitudes of mockery, anger and fear spilled over into
specific tactics used to prevent women's access to educational
institutions, professional bodies, and medical appointments.
Supporters of the campaign accused the profession of 'medical
trades-unionism' and of trying to perpetuate a male monopoly
by underhand methods. While I was doing the research for the
book, the lengths to which medical men had been prepared to
go and the supreme dishonesty of their tactics left me open-
mouthed in amazement. In particular, it was horrifying to see
the blatant use of violence, and the threat of violence, to restrict
women's freedom of movement and to scare them off.

There are obvious parallels to this today, with recent examples
of extreme hostility towards medical women whose perspective
is perceived as threatening by medical and other man. For
instance, Wendy Savage, a consultant obstetrician working and
teaching in the East End of London, had to fight a bitter struggle
for professional survival as a result of the implacable opposition
of many of her male colleagues to her belief in sharing medical
decisions with her female patients. Another medical woman who
has recently found herself with her back against the wall in a
desperate attempt to clear her name is Marietta Higgs, the
paediatrician at the centre of the crisis in Cleveland over the
diagnosis of child sexual abuse. The attack on her professional
integrity has clearly been politically motivated, coming from

those opposed to her insistence that the protection of children must be her first priority.

In writing this book I was also particularly interested in the political perspectives of the women involved in the campaign. I include a close examination of their attitudes towards female independence and male power, and the tactics they used to further their aims. As with most feminist campaigns, there is a wealth of material on tactical disagreements between supporters of medical women on a wide range of issues. To anyone who has been involved with the present-day women's liberation movement, this will be at once familiar and fascinating.

The book is largely an account of attempts by middle-class and upper-class women to gain entry to the medical profession. Working-class women had a direct interest in the campaign, but only as potential recipients of the professional care of middle-class women. Many supporters of women doctors stated explicitly that it was working-class women in particular who would benefit from female doctors, as they had to put up with treatment by young, inexperienced or incompetent male doctors. Early women doctors tended to set up in practice in working-class areas, often working in dispensaries for women. These invariably proved very popular with local working-class women.

Despite the fact that they had a direct interest in women doctors, working-class women did not have the opportunity to be active participants in the campaign. However, we do not know what part they did play in the struggle, as this was not documented. Therefore, their voice is missing from the account of how women gained entry to the medical profession. I have tried to be specific about where I am talking about working-class women, where about middle-class women, and where about women in general. I have not followed the same procedure for men: except where I have indicated otherwise, the reader can assume that 'men' in the text refers to middle-class men.

The first part of the book gives a brief introduction to five key areas which I hope will make it easier for the reader to make sense of the story of the campaign. These five areas are: middle-class women's lives and politics in mid-nineteenth-century Britain, the 'new' feminism of the 1850s, the history of women in medicine in Britain, the nineteenth-century British medical profession, and the campaign for women doctors in the

United States. The major events in the struggle for women doctors are summarised in a chronology at the end of the book (pp. 207–210).

The second part carries the narrative through the 1860s, concentrating on the career of Elizabeth Garrett Anderson, which dominated the campaign during these years. She first entered the Middlesex Hospital as a student in August 1860 and spent the following five years in private medical study. In 1865 she became only the second woman to have her name entered on the medical register and for a number of years after that she was the only woman doctor in Britain. As well as running a private practice, she saw patients at her dispensary in Marylebone, which grew into the New Hospital for Women, the first in Britain to have a female medical staff. Elizabeth Garrett Anderson's approach to the campaign was informed closely by her experiences in the 1860s, during which she pursued her medical studies on her own, received support from individual medical men, and went a long way towards establishing her own professional success. She always believed that the campaign would best be served by individual women carving out careers for themselves and thus paving the way for other women. In this section I also look at: the visit to England in 1859 of Elizabeth Blackwell (the first woman to gain a medical degree in the United States and later the first woman on the Medical Register in Britain), early coverage of the question of medical women in the *English Woman's Journal*, and other developments of the decade, particularly in nursing and midwifery.

Women's concentrated struggle in the early 1870s to gain entry to medical degrees at the University of Edinburgh occupies most of the third part of the book. The mood here is quite different from that of the 1860s, with the beginnings of collective female action aimed at overcoming specific institutional barriers in order to establish for *any* woman the right to become a doctor. The key figure of these years was Sophia Jex-Blake. Her strategy for promoting the cause of women's entry to the profession was influenced heavily by her experience of living among the community of medical women in Boston and seeing the support it received from the local feminist network.

In the spring of 1869 she began to put this particular political vision into action, travelling up to Edinburgh to try to gain entry to the medical degree course at the university. In the late summer she was joined by four other women, and by two more the following year. After a quiet winter the forces of resistance began to muster, and from spring 1870 onwards the women faced increasingly hostile attempts to remove them from the university. The story of the following three years is an extraordinary one of harassment, dirty tricks, and a complete polarisation of the middle-class population of Edinburgh. A pronouncement from the Court of Session in June 1873 finally put an end to the struggle in Edinburgh and women had to look elsewhere for solutions.

The final part covers the rapid successes of the mid–1870s, with the setting up of the London School of Medicine for Women in 1874, partial access to the medical register for women with the Enabling Act of 1876, and the addition of four more women to join Elizabeth Blackwell and Elizabeth Garrett Anderson on the register in 1877. Although the immediate objective had now been achieved, there were still many barriers in the way for medical women.

In the epilogue there is a brief summary of continuing battles over the next two decades, along with happier news of further successes. The struggles faced by medical women in the century following entry to the register could themselves fill another book.

1 'Like Eagles in a Hen-House'

In 1852 Florence Nightingale wrote a series of essays on the rights of women which were privately printed in 1859 under the title *Suggestions for Thought to Searchers after Religious Truths*. One of these essays, 'Cassandra', was a cry of desperation against the suffocating experience of life as an unmarried woman in an early Victorian upper-middle-class family. In this essay she expressed the frustrations felt by many women of her class, married and single, about the boredom, passivity and physical limitations of their lives.

She passionately condemned the supreme waste of women's capabilities:

> Why have women passion, intellect, moral activity, these three – and a place in society where none of the three can be exercised?[1]

She angrily attacked a society in which women were 'never supposed to have any occupation of sufficient importance *not* to be interrupted' and were brought up to see their own desire for intellectual stimulation as selfish.[2] Women were always expected to be available to meet the needs of others and, if they wanted to have any time to call their own, they had to grab this after everyone else had gone to bed or before they were up. Women were not even allowed much independence in the innocuous activity of reading:

> And what is it to be 'read aloud to'? The most miserable exercise of the human intellect. Or rather, is it any exercise at all? It is like lying on one's back, with one's hands tied and having liquid poured down one's throat. Worse than

that, because suffocation would immediately ensue and put a stop to this operation. But no suffocation would stop the other . . . [3]

Constance Maynard, another upper-middle-class woman, echoed these feelings. She described her and her sisters' confinement within the family looking after their invalid mother as being shut up 'like eagles in a hen-house'.[4]

Dependent lives

There was little chance of avoiding the confinement of marriage. Marriage was seen as an inevitable event in a middle-class woman's life. A young single woman was not regarded as an adult: all efforts were concentrated on protecting her from the outside world. An older single woman, undeniably an adult, was a failure, an embarrassment, and often a financial burden on her family. A single woman of whatever age could never enjoy the independence of a single middle-class man and was expected to be always on call for family duties, particularly to nurse sick and elderly relatives.

Major shifts in patterns of work from the eighteenth century onwards increasingly took production out of the home. As a result married middle-class women found their traditional functions disappearing. By the mid nineteenth century their husbands would most likely work away from home and not require their assistance as book-keeper, secretary or partner. They would probably have at least one servant and those household items which could not be produced by the servant would be ordered in from outside. A man who could afford to employ at least one servant and let his wife be a 'lady of leisure' had succeeded in establishing his middle-class status.

However, throughout the Victorian period a small but growing number of single women, and a few widowed and married women, rebelled against the emptiness of their lives and embarked on various forms of independent activity. Most carved out their life's work in the broad area of reforming philanthropy, which became increasingly popular with middle-class women during this period. It was one of the few ways in which these women were permitted to participate in the public sphere. In breaking away, these women often used religion as a justification for a 'socially useful' career.

In the mid nineteenth century Christianity pervaded the culture of middle-class women and provided an ideological framework for their role as wives and mothers. Ironically, as well as often sanctioning the virtual imprisonment of women with only a limited range of permitted activities, Christianity also provided many women with the means to escape the confines of the middle-class home. Both feminists and anti-feminists used religion as a fundamental basis for their political beliefs. Specific ideological strands worked both to restrict *and* to liberate women's lives. Women campaigners often used arguments which were similar to those used to justify the repressive image of the 'angel in the house'.

For instance, feminist arguments about prostitution emphasised the natural weakness of women, the sacredness of maternal functions and, above all, women's moral superiority. Most campaigns for the greater involvement of women in the public sphere were strongly founded in this belief that women were morally superior to men and that therefore only they could truly understand issues like prostitution. Indeed, many feminists tended to see emancipation not as freedom for its own sake but rather as freedom for women to perform their reforming and caring role more widely and with greater effect.

At first glance, it is surprising that so many feminists had a conventional Anglican upbringing. However, a closer look at these women shows that most of them came from families characterised by evangelical piety. They were imbued from childhood with the idea that each individual has a duty to God to undertake some socially useful work in order to spread the gospel. Although evangelicalism also reinforced women's domestic role, it did offer a possible outlet for women in social activism and thereby a means to a certain kind of personal fulfilment.

Radical religious activity also offered opportunities to women. Many feminists active in the mid nineteenth century came from a Unitarian or Quaker background. Unitarian and Quaker women had experience of speaking in public and were brought up to believe in female equality with men. Compared with other women in the Victorian period, they had relative freedom from family opposition and a degree of confidence in pursuing a public career of some kind. It is not surprising that many women active in this period came from these backgrounds.

From the early nineteenth century onwards middle-class women were increasingly involved in philanthropic work on an individual basis and in certain instances in reform initiatives arising out of this work. Through visiting the poor in the local parish, many women gained first-hand knowledge of sickness and poverty. Women's charitable donations rose dramatically in the first half of the nineteenth century, particularly to charities concerned with the Church, children, the sick and servants. Women-only committees ran appeals to raise large sums of money. Through these activities, women gained experience of working with each other and of organising large-scale events.

The pioneer generation

Some women also started to challenge men. In the 1810s Elizabeth Fry began her campaign of prison visiting which was aimed at improving the conditions of women prisoners. She believed that women had a better claim than men to running institutions which housed women and girls. During the 1850s, in the teeth of opposition from the Poor Law authorities, Louisa Twining managed to gain access for women visitors to workhouses to read the Bible and provide small comforts to the residents. Many also challenged the conditions they found there. Women's experience of committees, fund-raising and challenging the male administrators of institutions was to prove invaluable during the campaign for women doctors.

In the early nineteenth century the only paid occupation open to middle-class women not supported by a husband or relative was that of governess. It is estimated that in 1850 there were about 21,000 governesses in work and many more who were unemployed. Compared with others of their class, they were low-paid and had dreadful working conditions. They had no pension and therefore no financial security. They worked long hours doing a wide range of household tasks in addition to teaching. They often had to share a room or even a bed with the children they were looking after. They occupied an extremely isolated position in the household, caught half-way between the upper servants and the family itself.

In 1843 the Reverend F. D. Maurice and a group of other Christian Socialists founded the Governesses' Benevolent Institute in order to improve wages and working conditions and to provide for those women who found themselves too old to continue working but with no savings and no family to turn to. They decided that the best way to improve the situation of governesses was to provide training and raise their status to one of members of a profession with a recognised qualification and standard salary.

In 1847 these same Christian Socialists together with a committee of professors from King's College in London organised a series of 'Lectures to Ladies' for this purpose and the following year Queen's College was set up, with a committee of men, specifically to train governesses. In 1849 Bedford College was founded under the leadership of Elizabeth Reid. This differed from Queen's College in three ways: it was nonconformist rather than Church of England, women were closely involved in running it, and it had the more comprehensive aim of providing higher education for women. At this time such opportunities did not exist elsewhere in England.

These were the first milestones in providing an education for women and girls, a movement which really took off in the following three decades. From the late 1840s onwards, new secondary schools for girls appeared. Lectures were organised in various towns for any middle-class women who were interested in extending their knowledge. Mary Scharlieb, one of the pioneers of the medical women movement, remembered being taken to lectures on science by her aunt in the 1850s. Women greeted these new opportunities with an enthusiasm which was sometimes viewed by men as threatening: there was an attempt to exclude women from a mixed course on electricity in 1844 on the grounds that they were crowding it out.

At the same time as these developments in the education of some girls and women, the liberal intelligentsia were fighting a general campaign over the issue of educating professional men. They wanted to reform completely the mid-century higher education system in order to provide the training required for modern professions. This system would include set syllabuses

containing technical knowledge and expertise and a standard-
ised examination system which would grade students according
to academic merit.

Many men from these reforming, professional middle-class
families strongly supported the movement for women's higher
education and also the campaign for medical women. They were
sympathetic to women who, like them, wanted to establish their
social position through education and a professional career.
They were also often happy for their daughters to acquire the
means of earning an independent livelihood, perhaps because
they often had little inherited wealth compared with other sections of upper-middle-class society.

Florence Nightingale

In the early 1850s, at about the same time as she was putting
her frustrations into writing in her essay 'Cassandra', Florence
Nightingale was finding the means to escape the stifling confines
of the home. At the age of 30 she won a major battle with
her family to be allowed to go to the Institute of Protestant
Deaconesses at Kaiserwerth in Germany, to train as a nurse.
She was horrified by the bad hygiene and incompetent nursing
there but was impressed by the pure devotion of the deaconesses,
who saw their nursing functions within a clearly defined
religious framework. On her return to England she undertook
the job of administrator at the Hospital for Invalid Gentlewomen in London which she tried to revolutionise according to
stringent standards of cleanliness and efficiency.

Then in October 1854 she was asked by the government to
provide nursing services for British soldiers fighting in the Crimean War. She had to do battle with the medical authorities
out there to make them accept the introduction of new standards
and a new hospital regime. She also had to deal with internal
problems among the group of women sent out from Britain, an
uneasy mixture of working-class nurses and high-minded 'ladies'
from nursing sisterhoods. Despite these problems, she succeeded
in achieving a radical improvement in sanitary conditions in the
military hospitals and in 1856 returned to England a heroine.

Throughout the war there were extensive reports of her work
in the Crimea in *The Times* and a major fundraising exercise

was organised through its columns. As well as inspiring an increase in women's contributions to hospitals and nursing institutions, Florence Nightingale became a household name and set an example to the women of England of what a middle-class woman could achieve. However, in common with many pioneering women of this period she preferred to work on her own, and learned to use men to achieve her ends rather than seeking an alliance with other women. Some historians have suggested that her attitude towards other women may have been affected by the intense resentment she felt towards her mother and her sister.[5]

In the years before the beginnings of an organised women's movement in England in the mid 1850s, women in the public sphere were few in number and generally isolated from each other. They tended to do battle with the world on their own, or together with male reformers, rather than seek to establish alliances with other women. They were often outspokenly anti-feminist and expressed their contempt for other women whom they saw as less single minded and strong willed than themselves. For instance, Florence Nightingale unleashed a scathing attack on women in general in a letter she wrote to a friend in 1861. She characterised other women as demanding and selfish, lacking sympathy and concentration, and unable to take in or repeat facts with any degree of accuracy. However, pioneering women like Florence Nightingale and Elizabeth Fry were of crucial importance in inspiring other middle-class women to believe that they too could have a role to play in public affairs. This meant that in the early years of struggle and uncertainty medical women could look to examples of women who had already established themselves in the public sphere.

2 'We Want Work'

By the time the campaign for women doctors got under way in the 1860s a new phase in feminist activity had already started. For the first time this activity could be seen as a *movement*, even though it was still very small and largely knit together by networks of personal friendships. Women were now coming to feminism from a wide range of political and religious backgrounds, although still almost entirely middle-class. They started working together on specific campaigns, in alliances which often cut across political and religious divides.

One of the leaders of the new-style women's movement was Barbara Leigh Smith (later Bodichon), who was from a wealthy, radical Unitarian family. Her grandfather had been a close associate of William Wilberforce during the anti-slavery campaign. Her father was a radical MP who was involved in issues such as the 1832 Reform Bill and the campaign against the Corn Laws. Barbara was the eldest child of his relationship with a milliner 23 years younger than himself. He never married. Like Barbara Leigh Smith, many feminists of this period had strong family links with radical politics which encouraged them to believe that legal reform, as a way to remedy social injustice, was not only necessary but possible.

Barbara Leigh Smith's father believed in educating his daughters and enabling them to be financially independent. He settled an annuity of £300 on Barbara which gave her a degree of independence which was unusual even for a young upper-middle-class woman in the mid nineteenth century. Many prominent feminists of the 1850s, 60s and 70s, including two of the first women doctors, Sophia Jex-Blake and Elizabeth Garrett, had access to considerable family wealth, if not quite this level of independence. Barbara Leigh Smith was also one of the early graduates of Bedford College.

In 1854 she published a pamphlet entitled *A Brief Summary in Plain Language of the Most Important Laws Concerning Women*, which can be considered one of the first publications of this wave of the women's movement.[6] In the section 'Married Women and the Law' she described the legal position of a married woman, by which her body, her personal property and her earnings all belonged to her husband. She had no legal identity, her husband was responsible for all her acts, and his involvement was necessary if she wished to enter into a contract or take legal action. He had complete custody rights over their children, but absolutely no legal responsibility to support her.

In response to this pamphlet 26,000 signatures were collected in support of a campaign for a wife's right to financial independence. The Married Women's Property Bill of 1857 was defeated and legislation giving extensive rights to married women was not passed until 1882. However, some property rights were given to separated, divorced and deserted wives in the Divorce Act of 1857. This Act was crucial in making public the economic and legal oppression of married women. Publicity about some contemporary court cases also exposed the physical and emotional violence which many suffered. These were particularly important in disproving the belief, still widely held today, that this violence is only carried out by working-class men.

In 1855 and 1856 the feminist Anna Jameson gave two lectures called 'Sisters of Charity' and 'The Communion of Labour', which were later published and widely read.[7] Anna Jameson had had to go out to work as a governess from the age of 16 until her marriage at the age of 31. She had lived with her husband for only two years and had later become legally separated. She had started writing articles in the 1840s because of financial difficulties. Her husband ceased to pay her allowance in 1851 and she was excluded from his estate on his death three years later. Her feminism derived in large measure from her personal experience of having to support herself for most of her adult life.

In her lectures Anna Jameson suggested the creation of Protestant religious orders for women to be trained in nursing and social work, a major extension of work already started by the

Quaker Elizabeth Fry and male High Church Anglicans in the 1840s. She wanted to provide a solution for the recently discovered problem of 'surplus women' and also to extend women's moral influence into the public sphere. She had a vision that these single, working religious women would carry the domestic sphere into the public, 'that the *maternal* as well as the *paternal* element should be made available' in institutions such as workhouses, orphanages, prisons and hospitals.[8] The pioneer generation had already focused their individual efforts in this area – Elizabeth Fry in prisons, Louisa Twining in workhouses and Mary Carpenter in Ragged Schools – and these lectures were well received by a middle-class public which was avidly following reports of Florence Nightingale's work in the Crimea.

The individual efforts of reforming women then received a boost with the foundation in 1857 of the National Association for the Promotion of Social Science (NAPSS). This operated as an umbrella group for a number of middle-class reforming organisations, and its yearly congresses, held in cities throughout Great Britain and Ireland, provided forums for a discussion of a wide range of social issues including feminist concerns about employment, higher education, and entry to the medical profession. Individual philanthropic and reforming efforts were increasingly turning into large-scale organised activity, often with the NAPSS as a springboard, for instance with Louisa Twining's Workhouse Visiting Society, rescue work with prostitutes, and the Ragged School movement, which built on Mary Carpenter's work of the 1840s and 50s.

In 1856 the upper-middle-class women brought together by Barbara Leigh Smith's initiative on married women's property rights bought the *English Woman's Journal*. From 1857 to 1864 the *Journal* was the major publication of the women's movement, with Bessie Rayner Parkes as editor. Her father was a Unitarian with radical sympathies, and she had been a close friend of Barbara Leigh Smith's for over 10 years. In 1859 production of the *Journal* moved to offices in Langham Place and these became the centre of the growing women's movement. In 1864 the *Journal* was replaced for a year by the *Alexandria Magazine*. Then in 1866 Jessie Boucherett founded the *Englishwoman's Review* and this took over as the major feminist publication until 1910.

Women and work

Employment for women was one of the major issues taken up by the Langham Place group. The 1851 census had highlighted a new social problem, that of 'surplus women'. The census revealed that 30 per cent of all English women between the ages of 20 and 40 were unmarried, that three million of the six million adult women worked for subsistence, and that two million of these were independent of men. The *English Woman's Journal* highlighted the lack of employment opportunities for middle-class women and demanded the right to follow an independent career. It called for training for (middle-class) women to run institutions catering for (working-class) women, echoing the proposals put forward by Anna Jameson. It also attacked the working conditions of working-class women in various kinds of employment.

It did not, however, tackle the issue of class itself. Middle-class feminists wrote about the sufferings of working-class women but did not question the class system which caused these sufferings. Nor did they believe that their own classist attitudes required change. They shared the prevailing view that class differences were fixed and therefore not open to question. The campaign for the vote was also effectively for the benefit of middle-class women only. In the early days of the campaign male suffrage was very narrow and even after two further measures of franchise reform, in 1867 and 1884, only two-thirds of men had enough property to qualify for the vote. Throughout the suffrage campaign, feminists demanded that women should have the same electoral rights as men. Before 1867, therefore, they were asking only that the vote should be given to a small number of women. They did not see this as a problem: the vote would afford greater scope to the talents of (some) middle-class women and greater protection for working-class women.

In 1859 Jessie Boucherett, Adelaide Proctor and other women from the group at Langham Place founded the Society for Promoting the Employment of Women (SPEW). Jessie Boucherett was the 'odd one out' among the Langham Place group, less well-off than the others and from a solidly Conservative family. She is said to have become involved after seeing the *Journal* on a railway bookstall and travelling to London to seek out the women at Langham Place. Adelaide Proctor had been a close friend of Bessie Rayner Parkes since childhood. When Adelaide died in 1864, Bessie became seriously ill and later wrote a volume of essays which included her recollections of her friend.

The society kept a register of women seeking employment in skilled lower-middle-class occupations, such as book-keepers, shop assistants, clerks and telegraph operators. One of its most important projects was the setting up of the Victoria Press in 1860 to provide women with an introduction to printing, which was considered by the SPEW to be an occupation suitable for women.

By the 1850s it had become more acceptable, even desirable, for middle-class women to do quite extensive unpaid philanthropic work outside the home. Such activities did not constitute an established sphere of male employment and women were therefore not threatening men's jobs. The work had low prestige since it was new, it was not done on any great scale, it involved working with the poor, and it was non-profit making. Also the middle classes were becoming increasingly worried about the recently 'discovered' problem of urban poverty and its possible consequences for social stability. The unpaid social work of middle-class women performed a vital political function without posing any threat to middle-class family status or to male employment.

What was *not* acceptable was a middle-class woman earning a salary in a professional job and achieving a level of independence from men and from family. Work that was considered acceptable for a 'lady' if unpaid was immediately transformed if she accepted a wage for it. Sophia Jex-Blake's parents were horrified to hear that she accepted payment for teaching mathematics at Queen's College in the late 1850s. By and large all middle-class paid work was male, and female paid work was working-class. If a middle-class woman earned a wage, the status of her family and her own dignity were damaged.

In 1857 Barbara Leigh Smith published a pamphlet *Women and Work*, in which she called for greater employment opportunities for women: 'One corresponding cry rises from a suffering multitude of women, saying, "We want work".'[9] In this she reprinted a letter from Jessie Meriton White in which she gave a detailed account of her attempt in 1856 to embark on a medical education. She also included large sections of 'An Appeal on Behalf of the Medical Education of Women' by Elizabeth Blackwell.[10]

In the pamphlet she condemned the idleness which 'tens of thousands' of young women were forced into, on the grounds that women had a duty to God to be useful, and that lack of activity was leading to persistent illness and insanity for many women. In response to the pamphlet, male writers expressed the contemporary fear that women would cheapen the middle-class job market and force men to emigrate. Women were seen as dilettantes rather than as serious professional workers, and therefore as endangering any profession which was seeking to exclude amateurs and establish its status. Many learned societies catering for science-related professions, in particular, closed their doors to women in the 1860s on the grounds that an explicit statement that they were for men only automatically raised their status.

Barbara Leigh Smith was particularly enthusiastic about women entering the medical profession, as this would provide them with a good career and at the same time relieve the suffering of young women patients.[11] Medicine was a particularly attractive career option as it was more prestigious than teaching but, unlike other professions such as law or the Church, did not involve public speaking or the interpretation of male law, secular or religious. The fact that medicine would give women an occupation not sanctioned by religious associations and also a status as experts, as independent professionals with a good income, aroused hostility which did not surface in connection with sisterhoods or teaching. Perhaps the decision to concentrate less on women's right to follow a medical career than on women's right to consult a female physician was a tactical one, given the hostility which had been aroused by campaigns for a woman's right to education and to paid employment.

In early Victorian Britain middle-class women were beginning to break out of the prison of the household and take part in activities in the public sphere. A few women of exceptional strength and determination, like Florence Nightingale, were carving out careers for themselves in the field of health and social welfare. This individualistic pioneer generation was followed by a larger, more explicitly political, group of women who wanted to band together in order to open up opportunities for women in general. This was the background for the campaign for medical women in Britain.

3 Women Healers and Medical Men

Supporters of medical women clearly stated that their demand was not for women to be allowed into a new area of activity but rather for the reinstatement of traditional employment opportunities.[12] In her important essay 'Medical Women', published in 1869, Sophia Jex-Blake declared that what women were demanding was *re*-entry to the medical profession.[13] In a wide-ranging historical survey covering ancient Greece, medieval Italy and Spain, and England from the Middle Ages to the nineteenth century she established that women had always been the primary healers in the community, and she documented women's contribution to medical science. She then demonstrated how women had been systematically excluded from medicine by men over the previous 200 years. She protested strongly against the current male monopolisation of 'all intelligent knowledge of disease'.[14]

Subsequent historical research on women in medicine in Britain has unearthed evidence which substantiates and develops these claims. For example, in 1421 a Parliamentary edict included a clause that 'no woman use the practice of Fisyk' on pain of long imprisonment.[15] This was in response to a petition from male physicians. Women must have been practising medicine in significant numbers and with some degree of independence to have prompted this action. Evidence suggests that, from the Middle Ages on, women constituted the majority of health carers, fulfilling the role of doctor, in diagnosing and prescribing treatment, and the role of nurse, in tending the sick. These roles were not to become separated until the rise of the modern medical profession, which was exclusively male from the beginning, from the eighteenth century onwards. The distinction was rather between *men*, a very small number of physicians and surgeons whose medicine was highly theoretical and protected by a rigid guild system, and *women*, who were independent practitioners serving their own community and who had an empirical approach to medicine.

These women healers tended not to have any formal training, with knowledge and skills passed on from one practitioner to another, often from mother to daughter. They have been characterised as illiterate and unskilled by medical writers from the eighteenth century onwards, and modern medical historians have claimed that the growth of the male medical profession with its scientific approach has brought medicine out of the 'dark ages'. By codifying and extending knowledge, men claim it as their property and seek to exclude others (particularly women) through a process of mystification.

After the mass destruction of hospitals during the Reformation in the sixteenth century, healing took place almost exclusively in the home. Written accounts of the lives of well-off women living in the following two centuries make it clear that curing and caring for the sick was seen as one of the major duties of a woman in charge of a household, and an important area of skill for her. However, with the development from the seventeenth century onwards of professions outside the home from which women were specifically excluded, this function was gradually removed from the household duties of a wife and mother, at least in well-off households.

At the same time, from the eighteenth century onwards, working-class women practising as 'untrained' but skilled midwives were increasingly being dismissed as incompetent by male medical writers. They also faced a threat from the new phenomenon of the 'man-midwife'. 'Men-midwives' were usually working-class men who saw midwifery as a means of gaining entry to general medical practice. The success of these men lay mainly in their monopoly over the use of forceps and other instruments which were increasingly popular for use in childbirth, a monopoly enforced through their membership of the Barber-Surgeons' Company.

In the nineteenth century, with the rise of the general practitioner and the growing acceptance of obstetrics by the male medical establishment, midwifery practice was on the decline.

By the mid nineteenth century midwifery training had deterio-
rated and the reputation of midwives within society as a whole
had sunk very low, with male medical writers in particular
portraying midwives as drunken old women. A few midwives
were in well-paid salaried jobs with charities or in workhouse
infirmaries, and one or two had lucrative private practices with
middle-class patients. However, midwives had generally been
pushed out of all but working-class births and were confined to
normal labour and general nursing and aftercare. Midwifery
work was usually part-time and was supplemented by charring
and taking in laundry.

The Obstetrical Society, which had folded in 1830 after five
years' existence, was reformed in 1857 by a group of London
obstetricians, with membership open to any (male) medical practitioner. Some members were in favour of a system of registration for midwives but many wanted female midwifery practice to be abolished altogether. The danger at this stage was
that *all* childbirth would be in the hands of men unless something were done to improve the training, remuneration and
reputation of midwives.

The demand for hospital nurses in early nineteenth-century
Britain was low: there were only 4,000 general hospital beds in
England and Wales in 1800, serving a population of over nine
million.[16] Furthermore, their work consisted of domestic rather
than medical tasks. Nursing was reformed and emerged as a
skilled occupation with the expansion of hospital medicine in
the latter part of the nineteenth century. Until that time doctors
and their male assistants performed a wider range of medical
tasks than they do today and nurses were virtually confined to
general cleaning and other menial tasks.

As with midwifery, it is difficult to get a realistic picture of
nursing standards in the mid nineteenth century. Those who
wrote most extensively on the subject tended to be reformers,
who obviously had a political interest in representing nurses
in the worst possible light. Florence Nightingale declared that
nursing was done by those 'who were too old, too weak, too
drunken, too dirty, too stolid, or too bad to do anything else'.[17]

What we do know is a little bit about their working conditions: they worked long hours for very low pay, often slept
in cubicles off the wards, and often received alcohol in part

payment of their wages. No specific qualifications or experience were required. They were usually married women with older children, who brought to nursing the skills acquired while looking after their own households. Sisters had usually been upper servants and their role was to supervise the domestic work of nurses. Matrons, also, had little knowledge of nursing itself and functioned mainly as administrators.

So, by the mid nineteenth century women had been relegated to a subordinate and ancillary role in medicine. Nurses and midwives were working-class women performing mainly non-medical tasks for working-class patients. Most of them had no medical training and they had little, if any, control over their own work. It was into this system of medicine with its rigid gender and class divisions, by which middle-class men were professionals and working-class women were untrained ancillaries, that middle-class women were demanding entry as independent practitioners.

4 A Changing Profession

The Victorian medical profession was neither united nor static. The shifting structure of the profession and the conflicts within it had direct effects on the campaign for medical women. The campaign found itself at various stages caught up, sometimes to its advantage and sometimes not, in hostilities between different groups of medical men, and also in conflicts between the profession and the lay world over the establishment of professional independence and authority.

The 1858 Medical Act

In the early part of the century the profession was divided into three 'classes': physicians, surgeons and apothecaries. Although members of these three groups performed similar medical tasks, they did so for different social classes and as a result each had very different status. Only fellows, members and licentiates of the Royal College of Physicians were considered to be gentlemen, or members of a learned profession. Their claim to this status lay more in their possession of an Oxbridge degree and membership of the Church of England than in their professional expertise. Although the medical abilities of surgeons were often as sound as those of any physician, they were seen as having the status of skilled craftsmen, and apothecaries that of little better than tradesmen. Both fell short of independent professional status. Reproducing as it did the class divisions of wider society, the early-nineteenth-century medical profession lacked cohesion. As a consequence it faced major difficulties in its attempts to establish social authority.

The most important single medical development in the nineteenth century was the 1858 Medical Act. This set up a General Medical Council to oversee education and registration and to publish annually from 1859 a register of all qualified medical practitioners in Great Britain and Ireland. This Act was a watershed, as it established in theory the professional equality of all medical practitioners and paved the way for greater professional unity. It also made the exclusion of women an easier task. The Act made no provision to *compel* any of the licensing bodies to examine anyone who applied. The way was laid open, therefore, for the arbitrary exclusion of any individual, or group, from practising medicine in Britain.

The council was made up of crown nominees and representatives of the medical corporations and universities which granted licences and degrees. It was accountable through the Medical Officer to the Government, a post created in 1855. Possession of any one, or a combination, of the various qualifications (see Appendix 1) enabled a medical man to have his name placed on the Medical Register. Most medical corporations had more than one category of member, denoting different degrees of seniority. For example, the Royal College of Physicians, London, included fellows, members and licentiates (FRCP, MRCP and LRCP). Inclusion in the Medical Register allowed someone to practise in *any* field of medicine. One of the problems with the Act was that the 19 licensing bodies had widely differing standards of examination and so there was no uniformity of expertise among those on the register.

The 1858 Act did not make it a criminal offence for unregistered individuals to practise medicine. Such people were prevented only from being employed by the state as medical officers, from recovering fees by legal means, and from using the title 'doctor'. This is an indication of the relatively low status enjoyed by doctors even by 1858. Parliament was not convinced that their level of expertise merited the creation of an exclusive profession.

In the early 1870s, Louisa Atkins, Edith Pechey and Eliza Walker were prevented from gaining a recognised qualification for entry to the register but were able to practice fairly successfully on the strength of a foreign degree. Because of the structure of the profession in Britain, registration was seen by the medical women movement as the final formal barrier to women being accepted equally into the profession, and the removal of this barrier meant immediate victory. The struggle in Britain was sharper but also shorter than that in the United States and entry, once won, was not open to challenge.

The General Medical Council also played an important role in the mid-century changes in medical education. Medical education was shifting from an individual relationship, where the master was employed by the pupil, to a collective arrangement of courses and lectures, with control passing from the student to the teacher. The old system of apprenticeship was seen as lowering the status of the profession, because of the similarity to a skilled trade and because this system made it more difficult to restrict entry to the profession to those from a respectable class background. There were continuing moves within medicine to ensure on the one hand that all doctors had undergone a set course of training in an educational institution and on the other hand that all those entering the profession possessed the requisite class credentials. Medical education was also becoming increasingly complex with the steady introduction of new courses to keep up with advances in medical science and changes in medical practice. However, medicine was only slowly becoming a graduate profession: in the 1880s less than 30 per cent of registered medical practitioners held a degree.[18]

Medical education was also affected by a general reforming movement within higher education which was attacking the assumption that a general training of the mind was all that a professional man needed. This assumption lay at the heart of the traditional liberal education gained at Oxford and Cambridge. Under the influence of new utilitarian ideas, and the demands for professional expertise made by an increasingly complex industrial society, progress was being made in providing what was primarily a technical education for professional men. This was a major stimulus in the foundation of the University of London in 1828, with its courses in medicine, law, engineering and economics.

Internal divisions

By the middle of the century a new distinction between the mass of general practitioners and the London-based consultant elite had been superimposed on the old tripartite division between physicians, surgeons and apothecaries. The consultant elite had greatly increased their power in the early Victorian period through the establishment of medical schools in the voluntary hospitals, with a particularly strong power base in London. There were eleven of these hospitals in London, the older ones founded by endowments and the newer ones by annual subscriptions from wealthy lay people. The consultants now held more and more control over medical education and over medical appointments within the hospitals, thereby holding the key to the careers of a large number of young medical men.

The consultant elite were seen to be out of touch with the needs of other medical men and were reluctant to pursue policies which might weaken their own status and power. The number of general practitioners had grown rapidly in the early nineteenth century in response to the new demand from the industrial and commercial middle classes for medical care for their families. These medical men were increasingly critical of the power of the consultant elite and accused them of 'poaching' their valuable patients in the interests of raising their own prestige. They were dependent on the elite for introducing reform, as there were no general practitioners on the General Medical Council. They were frustrated by the elite's failure to bring about two initiatives which they perceived as crucial to their own survival: first, the limiting of the number of students at medical schools (which was resisted by the consultants who benefited from high enrolment figures); and secondly the improvement of conditions and remuneration of general practitioners.

In 1823 the medical radical Thomas Wakley set up the *Lancet* as a vehicle for his entrenched opposition to the self-perpetuating power of the Royal Colleges and for his accusations of corruption. He wanted a far greater say for the ordinary medical practitioner in the running of the profession and (before 1858) greater protection from competition from quacks. In 1856 the Provincial Medical and Surgical Association was renamed the British Medical Association and continued with the work of representing the interests of the provincial general practitioner. It became one of the most powerful voices in the profession, with membership rising from 2,000 in 1867 to 11,000 in 1886, over half the total number of all medical practitioners.[19] Both the *Lancet* and the *British Medical Journal* (the periodical of the British Medical Association) were consistently opposed to medical women for the whole of the period covered in this book, on the grounds that the entry of women to the profession would sabotage the campaign to improve the status and remuneration of the general practitioner.

Another fracture within the medical profession came with the proliferation of medical specialisms from the 1850s onwards. This period of rapid growth had been preceded by the establishment of obstetrics during the previous one hundred years as a special branch of medical practice. Lying-in hospitals had been set up at a steady rate from the 1750s and in 1830 the Obstetrical Society was founded. Other areas of specialist medical practice were then developed from the mid nineteenth century onwards: 78 new hospitals were founded in Britain between 1860 and 1879. Of these, 16 were lying-in, women's or children's hospitals, compared with seven in the previous 60 years. These ventures were attempts by certain medical men to achieve success and prestige, and as such were viewed with suspicion by the main body of the profession. General practitioners believed that medical specialisation would erode their incomes and the consultant elite saw it as a threat to the prestige of the general hospital as the centre of medical education.

Medical women were caught up in this conflict. Their insistence that they intended to treat women and children *only* stirred up opposition from both sides. They were seen as a dangerous threat by that section of the profession which had created obstetrics as its own particular sphere of medical operation. They were also treated with suspicion by those engaged in *general* practice, who believed they would steal patients from them.

However, the campaign for female entry also benefited from this trend. Medical specialists were greeted with enthusiasm by the lay public in the 1860s and 1870s and attracted large sums of money for the setting up of their hospitals. This was one reason why ventures such as the New Hospital for Women in the early 1870s were given substantial financial support. Also there was greater acceptance than there might otherwise have been from the public for women doctors specialising in obstetrics, gynaecology and women's health in general.

The struggle for professional status

As well as being affected by splits *within* the profession, the medical women movement had a bearing on struggles *between* the profession and the outside lay world. The campaign brought danger to the profession by unleashing already existing opposition in various sections of society towards medical men. Contemporaries were eager to accuse male doctors of trades-unionism in resisting the women, and the resolution of the conflict involved lay in intervention in the internal running of the profession.[20]

One of the important features of this period was the conflict within these large voluntary hospitals between the lay governors and the increasingly powerful medical staff. Medical men were gaining control over hospital appointments and thus freeing themselves from dependence on lay patronage. They were also winning a major say in decisions about the running of these institutions. One focus of this conflict was their attitude towards the patients. Whereas the lay governors were interested in running the hospital as a charitable institution providing free medical care to the 'deserving poor', the medical staff tended to see the working-class patients as raw material for medical research and education.

Another issue over which the lay governors and medical staff vied for control was that of the Nightingale nursing reforms. These were seen by the governors as a means of improving the care of patients and thus promoting the overall philanthropic project, whereas the medical staff saw them as a threat to their control over the medical side of hospital management. The other major area of conflict was of course over medical women. As will be seen in the narrative of the campaign, the lay governors and the medical staff of the large hospitals regularly found themselves on opposing sides.

The attempt to establish medicine as a profession for gentlemen was one issue over which the elite and the rest of the profession were united. The mid-Victorian medical profession was acutely aware of its relatively low status and was doing everything in its power to raise it. The concept of a liberal profession which provided a model for doctors in this pursuit of prestige was fundamentally male-identified. It was based on a 'community' of men, bound together in the public sphere by a system of exclusive associations, journals and clubs. Male professionals shared with other powerful men the identifying characteristics of economic independence and patriarchal authority within the family. Women's demand for entry was by definition in direct conflict with professional aspirations.

Very few medical men had the social prestige of a public school education. It was only younger sons of professional middle-class families who went into medicine, whereas the most successful medical men often sent their sons into the Church or the army. Medicine seems to have acted as a half-way stage between respectable crafts and trades and the higher professions. It was a fairly cheap profession to enter, as it required far less capital outlay than the traditional 'learned' professions of the Church, the army, and the law.

Medical men were anxious to secure an income high enough to support a lifestyle which would put them on a par with their middle-class patients. Even by the 1870s over half of medical men were earning less, and many considerably less, than the annual salary considered adequate for a gentleman to support his family. Many medical men had to accept the less attractive prospect of a salaried post, as an employee of the state in Poor Law or public health, or of charities or businesses. In these posts their income, although steady, was limited and, more important in many ways to a profession vulnerable in its shaky social prestige, they were *employees*, valued more as skilled technicians than as independent experts with professional autonomy.

They were also worried about the problem of overcrowding in the profession. There certainly was competition for medical practice in Britain in this period, particularly in London where there was a high doctor/patient ratio. A survey of medical men who graduated from St Bartholomew's in 1869 showed that 10 per cent were very successful and 50 per cent made an adequate living, while as many as 28 per cent barely survived.[21] However, the evidence on overcrowding does conflict with figures cited during debates over legislation in the mid–1870s, when supporters of medical women quoted statistics which showed the number of medical men falling slightly between 1851 and 1871 at the same time as the population increased by almost 50 per cent. This can perhaps be explained by the fact that there was no medical register in 1851 and so the figure for this year would have been inflated by a number of medical practitioners who were never in fact registered and who therefore would not have appeared in later censuses under the category of the medical profession.

What is clear, however, is that medical men *believed* their professional careers were under threat from too much competition. Both the *British Medical Journal* and the *Lancet* regularly carried articles about medical incomes and overcrowding in the profession. There was an attempt to use collective professional power in the 1860s to boycott organisations which paid low salaries to their medical officers but this attempt failed when it became clear that there were enough unemployed doctors prepared to defy the boycott and accept lower salaries in order to get a job.

In resisting the 'pollution' of female entry, medical men were prepared to go to great lengths to preserve the profession as a male 'club'. They wanted to protect their own career interests and those of the next generation of medical men. Medicine was increasingly seen as a hereditary resource to be handed on from one generation of males to the next, in much the same way that family businesses are handed on from father to son. This line of 'inheritance' often came into arguments used against the medical women movement during the years of the campaign.[22]

In the mid nineteenth century medical men were keen to establish medicine as a science, as one way to raise its status within society. In this period science in general was enjoying a new independence from aristocratic patronage and scientists were increasingly being seen as objective experts who should be consulted on matters of social policy. New professions were emerging which based their claim to status on possession of specialist scientific knowledge, rather than on more traditional sources of authority such as the interpretation of the pronouncements of a divine being. There was also widespread enthusiasm for greater lay knowledge of science and medicine, with the general public attending popular lectures, and reading books and pamphlets on these subjects.

As part of the medical profession's attempt to establish its credentials, scientific papers were given at British Medical Association branch meetings and other local medical societies, and scientific articles were printed in medical journals. A large number of new medical textbooks were printed in this period and prizes were set up to reward medical and scientific merit. Strenuous efforts were made in the field of medical scientific research and in improving medical techniques.

Medical men were also keen to establish a monopoly over this body of knowledge, a crucial step towards professional autonomy. They would then be in a position to resist having their authority undermined by lay interference in judgments over medical and related issues. They could also insist that appointments and promotions should be controlled internally on the basis of professional merit.

Through the energetic development of the institutional trappings of professionalism, doctors were gradually winning the struggle for status. Inevitably, they believed that female entry would only hinder attempts to improve the prestige of the profession. In particular, they believed it would damage medicine's claims to be a science, which they saw as an exclusively male area of intellectual activity. Women doctors would 'soften' the image of the medical profession, dragging it down to the level of the 'semi-profession' of nursing.

The campaign for women's entry to the medical profession was closely affected by what appear to have been the two strongest themes in the history of the profession in the nineteenth century: extensive internal conflict, with shifting patterns of hierarchy, control and resentment; and an increasingly collective effort for the general improvement of the profession's status, prestige and autonomy. Many of the institutions and features of the profession were relatively new, for instance the hospital-based medical schools, the General Medical Council, the British Medical Association and the register. The vulnerability of the mid-Victorian medical profession, as well as the undoubted misogyny of its members, helps to explain the often extreme reaction to the challenge from medical women.

5 Opening Doors in the United States

When Elizabeth Blackwell decided in 1859 to visit England for the second time to find out about the medical women movement there, women doctors were, in her own words, already established in the United States as a 'useful innovation'.[23] In most aspects the American movement was at least 20 years ahead of its British counterpart: the first woman doctor started practising in 1835; Elizabeth Blackwell gained her medical degree in 1849; the first hospital for women was founded in 1857. There was an enormous rise in the number of women doctors in the United States in the second half of the nineteenth century and by 1900 there were 7,000 practitioners, compared with only 258 in Britain.[24] Throughout the campaign for women's entry to the medical profession in Britain, the earlier success of medical women in the United States was of great propaganda value in proving that women could be practising doctors.

The main reason why entry was secured that much earlier in the United States was that there were no formal entry requirements for the American medical profession. Any individual, male or female, qualified or unqualified, could set him/herself up in practice. As a result there was a bewildering range of 'doctors' practising regular and irregular (unorthodox) forms of medicine. Unlike Britain, there was no central registration system and instead membership of a local medical society functioned as an indicator of a doctor's status. Women were excluded from all such societies until the late 1870s.

This meant that women in the United States were preoccupied not so much with legal battles around licences and registration as with establishing women as fully competent members of the mainstream medical profession.[25] The greatest danger to women doctors was that they would be lumped together in the public mind with bone-setters, hypnotists, hydropaths and unqualified midwives. There was a great pressure on women to gain medical degrees so that they could place the letters MD after their names to establish their professional status, a pressure not felt by medical men, who could establish their status in other ways.

The absence of a medical register in the United States also had an effect on arguments for and against women's entry to medical education establishments. It was argued by supporters of medical women that, with no legal barriers to practice, women doctors would undoubtedly become a reality and surely it would be better that they should at least be properly trained. The tactic of complete exclusion from the medical profession, as attempted by opponents in Britain, was not open to those in the United States. There the battle was over the professional status of medical women, not their very existence.

The first woman doctor

Although the absence of registration makes it difficult to differentiate between the early women doctors and other female practitioners, Harriot Hunt is usually cited as the first qualified practitioner. After training with her sister through an apprenticeship to two 'irregulars', she set herself up in practice in Boston in 1835. In her autobiography published in 1856 she described the hostility she experienced from the Boston medical establishment who treated her as a 'traitor, outlaw, felon – beyond their laws'.[26] She was denied access to all professional institutions and was given no help by her colleagues:

If I had had cholera, hydrophobia, smallpox or any
malignant disease, I could not have been more avoided
than I was.[27]

In an attempt to clarify her position as a fully trained medical practitioner, Harriot Hunt applied for a degree course at Harvard in 1847, by which time she had been practising for 12 years. Her application was rejected on the grounds that it was 'inexpedient', a word she described as 'so shuffling, so shifting, so mean, so evasive'.[28]

As in Britain, there is evidence in the United States of a

widespread female suspicion of male doctors in the mid nine-teenth century and an attempt by women to acquire and share medical knowledge in order to counter male medical power.[29] The growing women's movement saw one of its primary goals as the establishment of women's right 'to fully understand the physical laws which govern their own organisation'.[30] A number of successful female physiology societies were founded in the 1840s to teach women about their own health. One of these societies, the Ladies' Physiological Institute of Boston, founded in 1848, had over 300 members, its own library of medical books and anatomical models for demonstration.[31] Lectures were given on physiology, anatomy, menstrual problems and obstetrics, the latter subject seen as particularly important in helping women in childbirth.

There was also growing opposition to medical men taking on obstetric cases. This issue was taken up by the pamphleteer and lecturer Samuel Gregory in *Man-midwifery Exposed and Corrected*, published in Boston in 1848. In this pamphlet, which sold 18,000 copies in six months, he attacked the practice as immoral, describing it a 'a form of fashionable prostitution; a primary school of infamy'.[32] Presumably he saw the woman giving birth as the prostitute and the male doctors as the client. In the same year he set up the New England Female Medical College, the first medical college for women in the world, in order to train female practitioners to take on obstetrical cases.

However, in the long term the college was a failure. It offered a poor standard of medical education and tended to attract only wealthy women who could afford the fees and who were more interested in philanthropic activity than in becoming serious medical practitioners. It also faced hostility from the Boston medical profession. The requirement for students to study for three years under a practitioner often had to be waived because local doctors refused to co-operate. Given the potential feminist support available in Boston, the college could possibly have survived all this medical hostility. However, Samuel Gregory only alienated the local women's movement through his refusal to tolerate any active female participation in the running of the college. The college eventually closed in 1873.

Elizabeth Blackwell MD

In 1847 Elizabeth Blackwell began her attempt to gain a medical degree. She was brought up in Bristol in a nonconformist family which was closely involved in radical politics. Her father, Samuel Blackwell, was a Whig and an ardent follower of William Wilberforce, the leader of the anti-slavery campaign in Britain. Elizabeth recalled how she and her siblings had decided to give up sugar as a symbolic gesture against slavery. In 1832 the family emigrated to the United States when Elizabeth was 11, settling first in New York before moving to Cincinnati. Samuel Blackwell became actively involved in the anti-slavery campaign in the United States and was a close friend of the leader of the abolitionist movement.

Elizabeth and her two sisters, Anna and Emily, were the oldest children in the family, with six younger brothers. As a result they developed 'habits of unconscious independence'.[33] After her father's death, she and her sisters ran a school to support the family and were drawn into the issue of education for women. She talked of her distaste at this point at the prospect of marrying:

I became impatient of the disturbing influence exercised by the other sex. I had always been extremely susceptible to this influence . . . But whenever I became sufficiently intimate with any individual to be able to realise what a life association might mean, I shrank from the prospect, disappointed or repelled.[34]

The school was closed in 1942 and Elizabeth took up a teaching position in Kentucky for three years before returning to the family home in 1845.

She then decided to embark on a medical career. In her autobiography she attributed her initial decision to enter medicine to a friend's declaration on her deathbed that she would have been spared her worst suffering if a woman doctor had been available. Attempts by various medical men to discourage her only made her more determined:

The idea of winning a doctor's degree gradually assumed the aspect of a great moral struggle, and the moral fight possessed immense attraction for me.[35]

An entry in her journal at this time shows that the decision was
also tied up with her feelings about marriage:

> I felt more determined than ever to become a physician,
> and thus place a strong barrier between me and all
> ordinary marriage.[36]

In 1847 she approached a number of medical colleges in
Philadelphia but was rejected by all of them. In her autobiography she reported that she was often met with vague sympathy
but also with an insistence that it would be impossible to allow
her to study. The medical men at these colleges were generally
being faced with the issue of female entry for the first time.
Later in the campaign this mild sympathy from individual medical men turned to collective hostility. A similar pattern could
be seen in Britain. Elizabeth Garrett met with surprise and
mild sympathy from the medical profession in the early 1860s
whereas Sophia Jex-Blake and her companions were faced with
determined, collective opposition from 1869 onwards. At this
stage it was suggested to Elizabeth that she go to Paris disguised
as a man to pursue her medical studies. She rejected this plan,
insisting that what she saw as her moral crusade must be pursued 'in the light of day'.

She then received an invitation from the Dean of the Faculty
of Medicine at Geneva College in New York State saying that
the medical students were keen for her to enrol at the college.
Despite some mild ragging in the classroom, the male students
respected and supported her, and the dean was keen to publicise
the fact that a woman was studying medicine there. However,
she did relate how the students and professors were not sure 'in
what species of the human family to place me'. She was also
treated with great hostility by middle-class Geneva society who
regarded her as either immoral or insane. In her autobiography
she recalled how she used to rush from her rooms to college
every day to avoid the criticism and cold-shouldering.[37] She also
wrote of her horror at witnessing a gynaecological examination
by a male doctor: 'Twas a horrible exposure, indecent for any
woman to be subjected to such a torture.'[38] Despite the social
ostracism she faced, her determination to become a doctor was
further strengthened by this confirmation of the need for women
doctors.

Elizabeth spent some time studying in the Women's Syphilitic Department of the Blockley Almshouse. Most of the women in the ward were unmarried and many had been servants and seduced by their masters. Her comment points to her future involvement in sexual politics: 'All this is horrible! Women must really open their eyes to it. I am convinced that *they* must regulate this matter. But how?'[39]

After graduating in 1849 she visited England where she was well received and invited by various doctors to visit their hospital wards. She was shown round St Thomas', one of the prestigious London hospitals, by the senior surgeon and was even asked to sign the visitors' book as Elizabeth Blackwell MD. She then travelled to Paris to continue her studies. However, she could not find a hospital which would accept a woman and instead had to enter La Maternité, the midwifery college, on the same basis as the other students. While studying here, she lost an eye through infection. Soon after this accident, she wrote to her uncle: 'I certainly esteem myself very fortunate, and I still mean to be at no very distant day *the first lady surgeon in the world*.'[40]

On her return to London she managed to get hold of a ticket of admission to study on the wards at St Bartholomew's, where she was welcomed by all but the Professor for the Diseases of Women. Her treatment at these London hospitals contrasts quite dramatically with the experience of Elizabeth Garrett, Sophia Jex-Blake and other pioneer medical women in Britain in the 1860s and 1870s. She was discouraged, though, by what she saw as the attitude of women in England:

> Prejudice is more violent the blinder it is, and I think that Englishwomen seem wonderfully shut up in their habitual views.[41]

While she was in London, however, she met Florence Nightingale and the two women became lifelong friends.

In November 1950, encouraged by Elizabeth Blackwell's graduation, Harriot Hunt approached Harvard again, reassuring them in her letter that there was no impropriety in her studying there:

> In opening your doors to women, it is mind that will enter

the lecture room, it is intelligence that will ask for food;
sex will never be felt where science leads for the
atmosphere of thought will be around every lecture.[42]

Perhaps because she was by now 45 years old and therefore
seen as sexually 'safe', she was allowed to attend lectures. At
the same time the university also agreed to accept three black
men, Martin Delany, Daniel Laing and Isaac Snowden, into the
medical degree programme. There does not seem to be evidence
of any alliance between Hunt, who was only seeking entry to
some courses, and these black men.

The white male medical students held a meeting at which they
raised objections to the university's decision to admit the three
black men, whom they described as 'socially repulsive', on the
grounds that their own medical degrees would be devalued.[43]
They also claimed that Harriot Hunt was unsexing herself and
must be excluded in order 'to preserve the dignity of the school,
and our own self-respect'.[44] As a direct result of this protest,
Harriot Hunt was approached by 'leading members of the faculty' and persuaded not to attend lectures at Harvard. Harvard
finally agreed to let women into the medical degree programme
on 5 June 1944!

On her return to United States in 1851 Elizabeth Blackwell
applied for the post of physician in the women's department of
a large city dispensary, but was rejected. At this time her sister
Emily applied for a medical degree course but found that the
door which Elizabeth had prised open had slammed shut behind
her.

Elizabeth now opened a surgery in a private flat in New York
and set out to establish her professional position in the face of
hostility from male doctors and from middle-class society. As a
result of this ostracism she had very few patients in these early
days. In a letter to her sister Emily, she gives a vivid picture of
what she went through at this time:

A blank wall of social and professional antagonism faces
the woman physician that forms a situation of singular
and painful loneliness, leaving her without support,
respect or professional counsel.[45]

Elizabeth Garrett faced similar professional isolation when

she set up her practice in London in 1865, and even as late as 1878 Sophia Jex-Blake had a major struggle to establish her professional reputation after she moved to Edinburgh.

Unlike some of the medical pioneers in Britain, Elizabeth Blackwell could not fall back on family wealth. Establishing her professional position was a matter of economic survival and she worried constantly about money. She also faced persistent harassment, including physical and verbal abuse from men when out on call during the night. As she herself hints at in her autobiography, the threat of male violence operated as a strong policing measure to discourage women from pursuing an active public or professional role, 'I understand now why this life has never been lived before.'[46]

The loneliness, financial anxiety, professional insecurity, and fear of male violence which medical women had to face during these years cannot be underestimated. They are vividly described by Elizabeth Blackwell:

I had no medical companionship, the profession stood aloof, and society was distrustful of the innovation. Insolent letters came by post, and my pecuniary position was a source of constant anxiety.[47]

To fill her time she prepared and delivered a series of six lectures in 1852 on the physical education of girls, in which she advocated intellectual stimulation, physical exercise and classes in female physiology for adolescent girls. She criticised the practice of women marrying while very young and proposed instead that their education should continue. In many cases, she claimed, women only chose to marry because of the absence of other options and needed the opportunity to find some purpose in life. This of course is still true to a certain extent today, especially for working-class women.[48] The lectures were well attended, mainly by Quaker women, who with their children formed the majority of her patients at this time. With their help she published the lectures as *Laws of Life in Relation to the Physical Education of Girls* and the work was well received.[49]

At this time she also adopted an orphan girl, Katharine (Kitty) Barry, from the pauper nursery of the immigrant depot in New York, in order to help overcome the loneliness she felt. Kitty became 'daughter, housekeeper, accountant, secretary, and friend to Elizabeth Blackwell for as long as she lived'.[50] In her autobiography she recalled an amusing anecdote about Kitty. When a male doctor came to visit her, Kitty, who was of course used to the idea of Elizabeth's profession, remarked: 'Doctor, how very odd it is to hear a *man* called Doctor.'[51]

A hospital and a college for women

In 1853 she applied again to the city dispensary but was rejected for the second time. Instead she opened a small dispensary for working-class women and children. Pioneer medical women discovered that there was a great demand for their services in working-class areas and found it far easier to establish their professional careers in this setting than in private practice for middle-class women. The dispensary was a great success and the following year she was granted a charter for a hospital.

In December 1855 she gave a lecture on 'The Medical Education of Women'. Among the reasons she gave for wanting to open a hospital were that female physicians would 'save the feelings' of the women patients and that this would 'avoid their being ever injured by the indiscriminate admission of a crowd of students'.[52] In response to this lecture, a committee was formed to raise funds for a hospital. She was joined in this venture by her sister Emily, who had received a degree from Cleveland Medical College, Ohio, in 1854, and by Marie Zakrzewska.

Marie Zakrzewska had practised as a midwife in Poland before emigrating to the United States with her sister in 1853. The year after her arrival she enrolled at the Cleveland Medical College in Ohio and graduated two years later. She faced intense social prejudice as a medical student and in particular had great difficulty in finding a boarding house which would accept a female medical student as a lodger. When she started in practice she encountered problems similar to those faced by Elizabeth Blackwell. When she went out on calls at night, she walked back home either with the messenger or with the local policeman.[53]

In 1857 the New York Infirmary for Women and Children opened, with a female resident medical staff and a male consulting board. It faced widespread opposition and constant worries about its financial position. But it fulfilled two important functions for women: as well as providing a setting in which women could care for women, it provided a badly needed teaching resource for female students. With the increasing emphasis within medical education on clinical training, it was of vital importance that women medical students should have a hospital where they could be guaranteed admission. The practice of obstetrics and gynaecology in a women's hospital also provided a way into medical practice which might otherwise have been impossible for early women doctors.

In 1859 Marie Zakrzewska moved to Boston and was appointed Professor of Obstetrics and Diseases of Women and Children at Samuel Gregory's Female Medical College. In 1862 she resigned from the college after quarrelling with Gregory and founded the New England Hospital for Women and Children, a venture for which she depended heavily on the women's movement in Boston. Feminists had always been important to the medical women movement in publicly articulating a demand for women doctors. They now translated their support into concrete backing for the hospital. The women's movement in Boston played a crucial role in providing moral and emotional support and the setting up of a women's community in which Marie Zakrzewska could live and work. They raised funds for the hospital, helped to run it, and provided many of its patients. This supportive network was formalised with the establishment of the New England Women's Club in 1869. Lucy Stone's *Women's Journal* was outspoken in its attack on the tactics employed by the male medical profession to exclude women. It offered free publicity to the hospital and to women doctors at a time when the *Medical Register of Boston* refused to list the names of female physicians, despite the inclusion of makers of artificial limbs![54]

By the early 1860s more and more medical women were enjoying successful careers. In 1864 Dr Rebecca Lee became the first black woman to receive a medical degree in the United States. Places like the New England Hospital provided a strong institutional base for the movement. But the vague sympathy which met Elizabeth Blackwell in her initial approaches in the late 1840s had now turned to overt hostility from the male medical profession. Medical men claimed that they were worried about the shaky position of the profession and that women would lower its status and the level of fees.

With the absence of a national medical register such as that which existed in Britain from 1859 onwards it was even more vital for the professional survival of women doctors that they establish their status through membership of local medical societies and entries in local registers. Women were excluded from all medical societies until 1877 when three local societies agreed to admit them. The Massachusetts Medical Society, to which Boston doctors belonged, remained closed to women until 1884, 35 years after Elizabeth Blackwell's graduation. By that stage it was clearly ludicrous to continue to exclude women and the change of policy was the result of a need to face reality rather than any change of attitude.

In an attempt to counteract the hostility of the medical profession towards women doctors, Marie Zakrzewska deliberately cultivated the support of a few of the most prominent medical men in Boston. These tended to be men who felt secure enough in their professional careers to come out in favour of medical women. She was also wary of the reputation women had for favouring alternative medicine. Harriot Hunt had openly espoused 'irregular' forms of medical treatment out of a conviction that these would make a far greater contribution to combating female health problems. Elizabeth Blackwell too was critical of traditional medical methods, although she was more cautious in advocating alternative treatment. In contrast, Marie Zakrzewska thought that women doctors could not afford to alienate the profession by criticising male science and believed that they should avoid association with 'irregulars' if they wanted to be accepted as equal practitioners. Nevertheless, important medical innovations were introduced at the hospital: it had the first social services department in an American hospital; it was the only one which offered both obstetrical *and* gynaecological care; and the female medical staff were keen to encourage natural births.

Meanwhile, Elizabeth had been continuing her work at the New York Infirmary, except for a short break to visit England and France over the winter of 1858/59. The next step was to open a medical college for women in New York, as none of the existing male colleges there would accept women students.

However, this move was unpopular with both opponents and supporters of medical women. The male medical profession believed the movement would be forced to admit failure over the question of medical education. Women doctors at the Infirmary who had been educated elsewhere at male colleges were not convinced that opening a college for women was the right move as they felt that women benefited from studying in a mixed setting.

Despite external opposition and internal doubts, the planning went ahead and the college opened in 1868. The women involved in the college took this opportunity to put into practice certain aspects of their alternative medical philosophy: for instance, in an innovative move, a Department of Hygiene was set up with Elizabeth herself in charge. Another key appointment was that of Mary Putnam Jacobi. She had received a diploma from the Female Medical College of Pennsylvania in 1864, spent a year at the New England Hospital, and was the first woman to study at L'Ecole de Médicine in Paris, receiving her degree in 1871. The Blackwells were waiting for her to come back from Paris so that she could start teaching at the college. As soon as she returned she was appointed lecturer in Materia Medica, and made a professor a year later.

The prevailing view in the movement was that the college was an important stopgap measure, providing training and career opportunities for women until they were allowed full access to male institutions. The strategy of separatism was seen as a means to an end, the ultimate goal being the full absorption of women into the mainstream profession, with access to all its male privileges, facilities and opportunities. Looking back on this strategy, Emily Blackwell later remarked:

> We had held open the doors for women until broader gates had swung wide open for their admission.[55]

In 1872 Mary Putnam Jacobi founded the Association for the Advancement of the Medical Education of Women which had as its main aim the raising of standards, still a primary concern for the movement. The same year she gave a paper at Union League Hall entitled 'Our Future Aims' which contained the following passage:

The assistance of the public is invoked to remedy an injustice which the public has tolerated – that of depriving human beings of the right to educate themselves. Every woman in America who has tried honestly to fit herself for the duties of a physician has been crippled by the organised, almost armed resistance opposed to her efforts to obtain an education.

The campaign for women doctors in the United States had had many notable successes in the 23 years since Elizabeth Blackwell graduated from Geneva College. However, the struggle was by no means over.

PART 2

6 A New Interest in Women Doctors

The first documented attempt by a woman to enter the medical profession in Britain came in May 1856 with an approach by Jessie Meriton White to the centres of medical education in London. She wrote letters to 14 London hospitals, stating that she wished, 'with another lady', to attend a three-year course of medical and surgical study. She wrote to the University of London asking to be admitted as a candidate to the matriculation examination which would qualify her to register as a student. She also wrote to the Royal College of Surgeons to ask:

> Can a woman on producing certificates of having attended during three years the lectures and the medical and surgical practice in one of the London Hospitals be admitted to examination for a diploma in surgery and midwifery?[1]

In a letter to her friend Barbara Leigh Smith, she said that her desire to study medicine had started while she was nursing her younger brother.[2] On one occasion she had set his broken leg when his own doctor had been unavailable, and she was later encouraged by this doctor in her attempt to enter the profession. She received introductions from him to various influential physicians and surgeons in the London hospitals, some of whom were sympathetic to her ambitions.

However, during May, June and July she received letters of refusal from the 14 hospitals. All gave vague excuses as to why it would be impossible to admit a woman as a student: there would be 'so many practical inconveniences' and it would not be 'expedient'. Women who wanted a medical education were again and again met with the claim of inexpediency from medical authorities. This deliberately vague but final form of reply was clearly designed to silence women: they would have been able to counter *specific* arguments against female entry, whereas a blanket assertion of impossibility by those who had control over the resources effectively closed the discussion.

She also received a refusal from the University of London on the grounds that it was not legally empowered to admit women as candidates for the matriculation examination, an excuse repeated again and again during the attempt by Sophia Jex-Blake and others to graduate from Edinburgh University. The Royal College of Surgeons answered her question by saying that the college had never admitted 'a female' to examinations and that it considered that 'it would not be justified in adopting such a course'.

In her letter to Barbara Leigh Smith, Jessie Meriton White said that, despite her failure, the issue had excited the sympathy of a number of liberal-minded medical men and she reckoned that if a group of women were to try they would now be admitted to one of the hospitals as students. She called on wealthy feminists to give financial backing to such an attempt 'to further our common cause', having been advised that she could take up the issue in the courts but being without the funds to do so. She was keen to see other women try, and proposed to fund-raise in order to support them. However, nothing further came of this initiative until Elizabeth Garrett followed her example in the early 1860s. Jessie Meriton White's name does not appear in records of the campaign from the 1860s and 1870s – a puzzling absence.

Elizabeth Blackwell in England again

After spending the 1850s helping to establish the position of women doctors in the United States, Elizabeth Blackwell returned to Europe in late 1858 to help further the cause there. She first went to Paris to prepare a series of lectures on the value to women of physiological and medical knowledge, and on the prospects of extending the work on medical women from the United States to Britain. While in Paris she met a French countess who was very keen on the idea of women doctors and who wanted to found a country sanitarium for women based on principles of hygiene, in England or France. According to Elizabeth Blackwell, the countess' desire was based on her horror at 'the moral degradation which she has observed amongst her own acquaintances from the practice of being treated by men in female complaints'.[3]

While in France she presented her testimonials to the General Medical Council in London, which at that time included men who had allowed her to study in their wards at St Bartholomew's during her visit to England in 1850. She was accepted on to the Medical Register on 1 January 1859. A year later a new charter was granted to the General Medical Council empowering them to exclude from the register all holders of foreign degrees. Although the purpose of this charter was not to exclude women from the register, it would have prevented Elizabeth Blackwell earning this status and did create a major problem for the movement for medical women.

She was the only woman on the register until joined by Elizabeth Garrett in 1866, and then one of only two for a further 11 years until Sophia Jex-Blake and three others were granted a licence by the Irish College of Physicians in 1877. Despite the problem of her isolated position, it was of great importance to have a woman on the register at all. She took very seriously the responsibility placed on her by this position and did all she could to use it to further the cause. For instance, in a long article in the *English Woman's Journal* in January 1860 entitled 'Letter to Young Ladies Desirous of Studying Medicine', she advised women on the difficulties they would face. The task of becoming a physician, she said, 'is still an arduous one' and the difficulties 'require perseverance, courage, and self-reliance to overcome them'.[4]

In this article she set out in detail a suggested timetable for study, covering a period of four years. The first year should be spent at home doing preparatory reading under the guidance of a physician or surgeon. In the second year, the student should work as a nurse for six months, and then in a laboratory and in private classes for six months. This should be followed by 18 months in the United States to obtain a college education, with the remaining six months spent studying at La Maternité in Paris.

She advised students to go to a museum to look at bones and to chemists to see chemical substances in their first year. She gave suggestions for books to read. The student should seek help from a medical practitioner on which books were the best to read and ask him to examine her at the end of the first year and give a certificate. She stressed the importance of nursing experience: no one who is committed 'will hesitate to accept the wearisome details of the nurse's duty'. It would give a good first-hand experience of disease and would come in useful when supervising nurses as a doctor. It was, of course, also the only way a woman could gain any kind of hospital training at that time. She warned of the 'immense discomforts' of study at La Maternité but guaranteed that it would be well rewarded.

The article was accompanied by a footnote inviting women to contact her for further advice:

> Communications from any young lady seriously desirous
> of studying the medical profession, may be addressed to
> Dr. E. Blackwell, care of the Editors of the *English
> Woman's Journal*.[5]

She arrived in London in January 1859 and delivered the lectures she had been preparing in Paris at the Marylebone Literary Institution in London. She then repeated these in Manchester, Birmingham and Liverpool in May and received requests to give them in Leeds, Nottingham and Edinburgh too. She was sent many messages of support:

> Mothers beg me for instruction in health. Young ladies
> listen eagerly to the idea of work. Three desired to become
> medical students.[6]

In these lectures she spoke of her belief in a medical system which focused on prevention rather than cure and of the need for a greater knowledge of health and medicine among lay people. This contrasted with the tendency of the male medical profession to mystify medical knowledge and deny patients access to it.

Her arguments were repeated in a lecture she and her sister Emily gave at Clinton Hall, New York, on 2 December 1859 to raise support for their proposed college. The lecture was reported in detail in the *English Woman's Journal* the following May.[7]

The sisters took as their starting point the belief that the improvements they were advocating would only be made by women entering medicine as fully-qualified practitioners:

> The application of scientific knowledge to women's necessities in actual life can only be done by women who possess at once the scientific learning of the physician, and as women, a thorough acquaintance with women's requirements – that is, by women physicians.[8]

In this lecture they demonstrated clearly that this was a crucial period for women in medicine. They explained how there used to be a place for dedicated women as midwives but that now, with advances in medical science, male doctors were trying to exclude even these women. Either women must win a secure place as fully-qualified medical practitioners or they would be pushed out of medicine altogether. They also expressed their belief that the existence of women physicians would improve general knowledge about physiology and health among women:

> For what is done or learned by one class of women becomes, by virtue of their common womanhood, the property of all women.[9]

They stressed the importance of founding a hospital and medical school for women. At this school the lecturers could impress on women students the importance of 'sanitary science' by 'fully imbuing them with the idea that it is as much the province of the physician to aid in preventing as in curing disease'. The value of a hospital and medical school for women would be threefold: it would provide clear public proof of the professional success of women doctors; it would be a 'valuable medical centre for women' in a hostile profession where connections were often the key to career advancement; and it would be an important resource for poor women needing medical treatment.

After delivering her lectures, Elizabeth Blackwell called a meeting to discuss the setting up of a women's hospital in Britain. At this meeting a committee was elected which later produced a circular on the 'Proposed Hospital for the Treatment of the Special Diseases of Women', which was signed by 26 well-known women. The circular described Elizabeth Blackwell's lectures as leading to a 'strong conviction of the necessity for a more general diffusion of hygienic knowledge among women' and stated the need for a special hospital to treat women with gynaecological problems, as their treatment usually involved 'much avoidable moral suffering'.[10]

Influential figures from the radical community in London became involved in the work of the committee, including Russell Gurney MP and William Cowper Temple MP, who were later to be prominent among the parliamentary supporters of the movement for medical women in the mid 1870s. A sum of £1000 was promised for the setting up of a woman's hospital and £5000 for a medical school. This early enthusiasm for the idea of a women's hospital may be partly explained by the fact that the foundation of specialist hospitals was becoming a popular area of philanthropic activity around that time. However, no definite plans emerged and the support remained only theoretical. Although nothing concrete came of the initiative, this was obviously a cause around which a number of influential and wealthy people were prepared to mobilise.

In April 1859 the *Edinburgh Review* published an article on 'Female Industry', in which the author welcomed the changes Florence Nightingale was introducing into nursing. He went on to talk about women and the medical profession:

> There may be more difficulty about the kindred function
> – that of the physician and surgeon; but it cannot long
> be a difficulty. The jealousy of the medical profession is
> to be sure proverbial; but it is not universal. From our
> youth up some of us have known how certain of the wisest
> and most appreciated of physicians have insisted that the
> health of women and their children will never be guarded
> as it ought to be till it is put under the charge of physicians
> of their own sex.[11]

There was a strong and definite assumption at this stage among supporters of the medical women movement that women doctors would only treat women and children. They were keen to avoid any opposition based on arguments of 'delicacy': opposition, particularly from men, within a society segregated by sex would have been much stronger if supporters had not been so clear that women doctors would never treat male patients. The whole focus of the campaign for medical women was on providing alternative medical care for women to avoid the 'moral suffering' caused by having to consult male doctors. The *primary* concern of those involved with the campaign was with women as patients rather than with opening up another occupation to women as workers.

In a letter to her sister in April, Elizabeth Blackwell showed her optimism about the situation in England:

> From the Queen downwards I see signs of favour. On all hands we make converts, and those who are indoctrinated make converts. The whole way in which the cause is regarded by laity and doctors is most respectful.[12]

In August she returned to the United States to continue her medical work in New York. Before she left London she asked three women, including Mrs Gurney, to act as her representatives in the work of promoting the medical education of women.

The *English Woman's Journal*

The issue of medical women was now enjoying a degree of public prominence following Elizabeth Blackwell's visit, and feminists in England increasingly saw this as an important area of campaign. During its seven years of existence, from 1857 to 1864, the *English Woman's Journal* placed the issue of women's health and the medical woman question high on its list of editorial priorities. In particular, extensive coverage was given to the medical women movement in the United States at a time when the campaign in this country had not yet got off the ground. Many contributors to the *Journal* offered a radical analysis of the issues surrounding the question of women and medicine. It its pages there is ample evidence, at least for middle-class women, of a strong desire in mid-nineteenth-century England for the chance to be treated by a woman doctor.

The second issue of the *Journal* printed a letter from Anna Blackwell, Elizabeth and Emily's sister, which gives some interesting insights into their early careers.[13] She described Elizabeth as motivated by 'an earnest desire to be useful to her sex'. Anna said her sister had decided she must get a medical degree before starting to practise 'as a sanction for her own course and a precedent for other women'. It was Elizabeth's personal experience of 'pain and embarrassment' at Geneva which led her to want to open a medical school for women. It appears from this letter that when Elizabeth travelled to Europe in 1849 she would have considered staying there and following a medical career in France, Germany or England but decided she would have the best chance of success in the United States. She believed there was *intellectual* support for women doctors in England but that 'there is a deep-rooted antagonism to its practical admission which it may take generations to modify'[14]

The *Journal* carried advertisements for women-only physiology classes organised by the Ladies' National Association for the Diffusion of Sanitary Knowledge, which had been founded in 1859, and their early pamphlets were reproduced in full.[15] The association seems to have been philanthropic rather than political in character. The work of its middle- and upper-class members consisted mainly of writing and distributing pamphlets on health and hygiene to working-class women. However, it did state that it recognised that ignorance of sanitary science existed as much among the rich as the poor and it saw as an important part of its work the organisation of lectures to educate its own members in matters of health. Despite having only a very limited political content, the association does seem to have been perceived as threatening by the medical profession, with hostile and patronising coverage of branch meetings in the *Lancet*.

In July 1859 the *Journal* carried a review of 'A Letter to Lord John Russell' (a prominent Liberal politician) from Anna Jameson. She had been active in the married women's property campaign and had written and spoken extensively on the subject of the need for training for women in health and welfare to combat the problems of poverty and to provide an outlet for the energies of middle-class women. In this letter, which the *Journal* stated reflected its editorial views, she argued for the need for women to be trained as nurses *and* physicians:

> Every wife and mother, and young sensitive female, knows how inexpressibly painful it is in many phases of suffering peculiar to the feminine and maternal organisation, to consult young inexperienced medical men; many young

women have suffered cruelly, and some fatally, rather than consult a medical man at all.[16]

She said there was now 'an intention of founding a hospital for women and children' which would accept women as medical students. She also pointed out that poor women were more vulnerable to clumsy medical care from young or second-rate doctors.

A review of a book called *English Women and the Age* in the July 1860 edition quoted a section on the 'Practice of Medicine for Women'. Despite the advance of medical science, there was still 'lamentable ignorance' about women's health and this ignorance often led to 'disease, deformity and early death'.[17] This was echoed elsewhere by feminists' claims that female ill-health was not taken seriously by society generally nor by the medical profession in particular. They were increasingly angry that, despite the supposed advances in medical science, little was still known about women's health problems and that medical men were not prepared to share what knowledge they *did* have about female physiology.

There is evidence during this period for a growing consciousness among middle-class women about their chronic ill-health and about their position as a group of semi-permanent invalids. In the United States Catherine Beecher had written in the 1850s about what she had observed of the 'terrible decay of female health all over the land' during her tours in various towns and cities.[18] The majority of women in her informal survey, who were from both 'wealthy circles' and the 'industrial classes', were suffering from some specific illness or general debility. She also noticed that women seemed to expect to be unwell and often classified themselves as healthy on the grounds that they had no major illness when they were in fact experiencing frequent headaches, body pain and so on.

In December 1860 the *Journal* printed a review of 'Letter to Ladies in favour of Female Physicians for their own sex' by Samuel Gregory, who had founded and now ran the New England Female Medical College in Boston. In this pamphlet he gave evidence of the 'grievous shock to female delicacy caused by the presence and attendance of a male practitioner' and called for a revolution which would totally exclude men from obstetrics and gynaecology.[19]

In 1861 a review appeared of a book on famous women from the past written by Mrs Dall and entitled *Historical Pictures Retouched*. It was originally published in Boston and had now come out in a London edition. The review concentrated almost entirely on the section of the book on 'The Contributions of Women to Medical Science'. The author gave details of the lives of 37 women from the past who had treated women and children and practised general medicine. The reviewer emphasised the point that women were not seeking entry to the profession for the first time but rather *re*-entry. Medicine had previously been women's domain until they were actively excluded by the rising male profession.[20]

In addition to the insistence that women often experienced medical examination and treatment as humiliating, direct accusations were levelled against male doctors. In an article in the *Journal*, 'A Physician' recommended that women would treat women and children only and that they would do this better than male doctors. He then added:

> To say nothing of exceptional cases, where medical men
> have abused the confidence of their patients and done
> violence to female modesty and delicacy . . .[21]

The campaign against male midwifery had rested partly on the fear of seduction, and pamphlets about specific cases of sex crimes by doctors on female patients were produced during this period. Catherine Beecher in the United States hinted at cases of sexual harassment of female patients by male doctors – 'facts . . . of a most shocking nature' – and pointed out that these crimes would go undetected as women were too frightened of the damage the publicity would do to their reputation to report them.[22]

There was also widespread suspicion among women that male doctors were experimenting on working-class women. It was during this period that Thomas Radford, doctor at Manchester Lying-in Hospital and well-known anti-abortionist, started carrying out Caesarian operations. Most of the 55 women operated on before 1880 died and all were working-class.[23] Scientific literature of the period consistently portrayed the male scientist as actively 'invading' passive (female) nature in order to learn its secrets. The links between medical science and male sexual violence were to be drawn out more explicitly during the anti-vivisection campaign of the 1870s and 1880s and particularly by Frances Power Cobbe in 'The Medical Profession and its Morality', published in 1881.[24]

In March 1862 an 11-page summary appeared of Samuel Gregory's 'Female Physicians', in which he expanded the views set out in his earlier work and gave information about the college and its graduates.[25] In this summary he reiterated many of the general arguments used in favour of female entry to the profession, such as the potential contribution of medical women to *preventative* medicine, the need for qualified women to lecture to mothers, girls and young women, and the importance of demystifying medical science. He also specifically referred to the urgent need for medical women to attend women in childbirth, despite the prevailing argument that the 'displacement of women' from midwifery was a good thing because attendance by qualified medical men was safer:

> It is a well-known fact that the attendance of male practitioners has often a very embarrassing, disturbing effect, causing disastrous and not infrequent fatalities to mothers or infants, when there was not the least necessary occasion for such a result.[26]

So great was the response to this article that in May a separate section of the *Journal* had to be set aside for readers' letters on this subject. There were two letters from women and two from men, all four in favour of women doctors.[27] Correspondence on the deeply-felt need for women doctors continued to be published in the *Journal* until it ceased publication in 1864. Among these was a letter from a woman who styled herself 'A Lover of Invalids', in which she stated that doctors could never know 'what unrelieved physical agony is endured by women, as a less torture than submitting to the mental trial of soliciting a doctor's aid'.[28]

One correspondent asserted the desire among women for doctors of their own sex but explained that, until qualified female practitioners became available, women would continue to choose to consult men. She claimed there was no shortage of

women to study for medicine and dismissed the objection that
women would be forced to choose lifelong celibacy:

> A female medical student need not 'devote herself heart
> and soul to celibacy'. She might indeed exercise a more
> independent choice, because she would not be driven into
> marriage by the mere longing for some satisfying
> occupation.[29]

She ended her letter with a pointed question:

> Are all women to be shut out from any and every method
> of earning money by honest and intelligent work lest they
> should grow too independent of their natural supporters?

In January 1864 the *Journal* quoted in full a hostile article
from the *Medical Times and Gazette*. This article referred to
the recent opening of the Female Medical College (for training
midwives) and asked whether it was to be a *medical* college:
'We must confess to a decided *a priori* repugnance for the
proposition.'[30] They also said they did not think 'the artificial
cultivation of a breed of masculine women, unsexed as it were,
for the special functions of medicine, would benefit the patients
or society at large'. The letter ended by asking why women
could not be content with being nurses.

The *Journal* gave a spirited three-page response to this article,
refuting the arguments about 'natural' barriers to women studying medicine put forward by 'medical bigots'. It went on to say
that, even if women did feel shocked by the study of medicine,
they would put up with it for the sake of relieving the suffering
of their sisters:

> . . . it is equally manifest that much pain and death would
> be prevented if women could consult promptly capable
> persons of their own sex.[31]

Not all readers agreed that there was a need for women
doctors. In a letter to the *Journal* from 'A Patient', the author
asserted that many women actually preferred the 'tenderness' of
a male doctor as their 'only gentleman friend' and claimed that
only a man could exercise the physical restraint necessary in
cases of hysteria.[32]

The medical philosophy of Harriot Hunt and Elizabeth Blackwell

At the same time as feminists were conducting these critical discussions about the male medical profession, some of the early women doctors in the United States were developing their own alternative medical vision. In particular, Harriot Hunt and Elizabeth Blackwell developed a radical critique of medical and scientific discourse.

Medicine was gradually changing from a science focused on the patient to one focused on disease, with the patient merely a location for the medical problem. Control was passing from the patient to the doctor as the expert who alone was able to interpret the evidence presented by the micro-organic world. Critics feared that the growing emphasis on interventionist medicine would mean that the needs of the patient would be ignored and the promotion of good health neglected.

In February 1860 the *English Woman's Journal* published a biographical article about Harriot Hunt, the American woman doctor, written by Bessie Rayner Parkes. It was based on Harriot Hunt's autobiography, *Glances and Glimpses, or fifty years' social, including twenty years' professional life*.[33] In the article she described Harriot Hunt's work as a 'sanitary physician', echoing the calls from the Blackwells in their Clinton Hall lecture for a 'science of health'. Harriot Hunt rejected regular medicine's reliance on interventionist surgical and chemical treatment.

While in her early twenties, her sister had suffered while in the care of the family doctor, whose treatments included such practices as blistering and the application of leeches. Harriot Hunt says her sister 'had lost confidence in medicine'. She would argue with the doctor but then 'tamely submit to a fresh round of torturing prescriptions'. After consulting an 'irregular' woman practitioner, she made rapid progress. She and her sister then decided to study medicine themselves, and in particular the relation of the laws of hygiene to women's health:

> Setting aside medication, we endeavoured to trace diseases to violated laws, and learn the science of prevention. That word 'preventive' seemed a great word to me; curative was small beside it.[34]

She believed that women's health, in particular, would benefit more from improving common habits of diet, exercise, clothing and so on, and that if each individual looked after her/his body properly, according to the laws of hygiene, there would be little need for surgery or medical treatment. Her treatment of her patients included 'enforcements of dietetic rules, bathing, and so forth'. She refused surgical cases or any cases which had gone beyond sanitary measures. She believed that many female illnesses were social or psychological in origin and therefore that only women doctors, who could understand other women's lives, could successfully treat female patients. She also saw the role of the doctor as being to teach these laws to the public, and she herself gave lectures to hundreds of women on female physiology.

Many of these beliefs were echoed by Elizabeth Blackwell. In her autobiography *Pioneer Work in Opening the Medical Profession to Women* she talked of her strong scepticism of ordinary medical methods, which in this period included cauterisation (burning out diseased tissue with a hot iron), the application of mercury, and large doses of dangerous drugs. But she was equally dissatisfied with the old 'heresies' such as mesmerism and hydropathy. A letter to a friend, Dr Dickson, while she was studying at St Bartholomew's in London in 1850 contains the following illuminating passage:

I am particularly anxious to become widely acquainted with disease. I am obliged to feel very sceptical as to the wisdom of much of the practice which I see pursued every day. I try very hard to believe, I continually call up my own inexperience and the superior ability of the physicians whose actions I am watching: but my doubts will not be subdued, and render me the more desirous of obtaining the bedside knowledge of sickness which will enable me to *commit heresy* with intelligence in the future, if my convictions compel me to it. I hope you will forgive this confession of want of faith . . . [35]

Elizabeth Blackwell's medical philosophy was close to Florence Nightingale's, and the two women built up a strong friendship on the basis of this. Spiritual values and a strong commitment to Christian belief were central to the work they were doing in medicine itself and for women generally. This contrasts with the outlook of younger pioneering medical women like Elizabeth Garrett Anderson and Sophia Jex-Blake, who were both from religious family backgrounds but who, if they had strong religious beliefs, seem to have kept them separate from their political and professional lives.

Elizabeth Blackwell and Florence Nightingale believed that science must be directly guided by ethical, rather than purely utilitarian, considerations. They did not see disease as a localised problem with specific causes but rather the result of a general state of moral, physical and emotional disequilibrium, with mind and body in close interaction. As Elizabeth said, 'I realised that the mind cannot be separated from the body in any profound view of the scope of medical responsibility.'[36] Like Florence, Elizabeth believed that prevention, in the form of sanitary measures and moral improvement, was far better than cure. For instance, she talked of the duty of the physician to advise parents on the moral education of their children. In her autobiography she described the evolution of her medical philosophy:

> When, in later years, I entered into practice, extremely sceptical in relation to the value of drugs and ordinary medical methods, my strong faith in hygiene formed the solid ground from which I gradually built up my own methods of treatment.[37]

She also paid the following tribute to her friend Florence:

> To her, chiefly, I owed the awakening to the fact that sanitation is the supreme goal of medicine, its foundation and its crown.[38]

7 Elizabeth Garrett, Student and Doctor

During the years of Elizabeth Garrett's early career there was no concerted campaign for women doctors. Until four women tried to follow her example and qualify through the Society of Apothecaries in 1866–7 and the campaign in Edinburgh began in 1869, she was a lone figure. She was constantly breaking new ground, with only the support of (some of) her family, some feminist friends and a few individual medical men.

Elizabeth Garrett at the Middlesex Hospital

One of the most important consequences of Elizabeth Blackwell's visit to Britain in 1859–60 was that she inspired Elizabeth Garrett to embark on what was to be the first successful attempt by a woman to train and qualify as a doctor in Britain. Like many other feminists of this period including Emily Davies and Sophia Jex-Blake, who was to be the central figure in the struggle for medical women in the early 1870s, she came from a strongly evangelical family. At the time of her birth her father, Newson Garrett, had been running a pawnbroker's shop in London but by the late 1850s he was a wealthy businessman and the family lived in Suffolk.

Elizabeth Garrett had been corresponding since 1854 with Emily Davis, whom she had met through an old friend, Jane Crow, who had been to school with Elizabeth at the Academy for the Daughters of Gentlemen in Blackheath. The Crow family had moved to Gateshead, where Emily lived, in 1848. Emily, six years Elizabeth's senior, was the most prominent member of the campaign for the higher education for women in the 1860s and 70s. Jane became the secretary of the Society for Promoting

the Employment of Women in 1860. For several years Emily
Davies was a major source of advice and support for Elizabeth
Garrett. During the late 1850s she was looking for some occupation which would give purpose to her life, and in February
1859 Elizabeth and Emily were introduced by Barbara Bodichon
to the group of women at the *English Woman's Journal*. They
subsequently joined the Society for Promoting the Employment
of Women.

In March Elizabeth Garrett went to one of Elizabeth
Blackwell's lectures and stayed in London for a few weeks to
attend two more. In a letter to Emily she explained how she felt
rather overwhelmed:

> She assumed that I had made up my mind to follow her,
> I remember feeling very much confounded, and as if I
> had been suddenly thrust into work that was too big for
> me, while talking and listening to her that evening at
> Blandford Square.[39]

During this time she made her decision to become a physician.
She was greatly encouraged in this by Emily who had herself
been tempted to train in medicine after witnessing the suffering
of poor women and their children during parish visiting, but
had decided against following a medical career because her own
education had been sketchy. In 1861 Emily wrote an article
entitled 'Female Physicians' for the *English Woman's Journal*.[40]
A year later she wrote a paper for the London meeting of the
National Association for the Promotion of Social Science,
entitled 'Medicine as a Profession for Women'.[41]

In the middle of June Elizabeth revealed her plans to her
father and wrote to Emily to tell her about his reaction. At this
stage he was very 'discouraging' and 'said the whole idea was
so disgusting'.[42] She asked him why it was all right for 'ladies'
to be nurses in the Crimea but not for them to train to be
doctors. She told him she had spoken to her mother who seemed
sympathetic. He promised her that he would think about it, and
she told Emily she thought he would come round to her way of
thinking.

In this letter she also revealed her frustration at the inactivity
forced on her by life at home: 'I could not live without some
real work.'[43] In another letter written later in June she said it

would be 'impossible . . . to live at home in happy idleness all my life'.[44] A month later she wrote to her aunt to explain her decision:

> During the last two or three years, I have felt an increasing longing for some definite occupation, which should also bring me, in time, a position and a moderate income.'[45]

In a letter to Elizabeth Blackwell written in January 1861 she gives another interesting insight into her reasons for studying medicine:

> I had not any very strong interest in the subjects, and was led to choose the profession more from a strong conviction of its fitness for women than from any personal bias.[46]

On 28 June she was able to report that her father had declared that he would prefer a woman doctor to treat his wife and daughters if he could be absolutely sure that she was fully qualified. He had brought up the subject at dinner and, when two guests had shown a deep prejudice against women doctors, had been roused to support his daughter's view. A few days later she told Emily that her father had finally agreed to her plan, although declaring himself not happy about it. She was still hopeful of his attitude changing: '. . . he will be reconciled . . . *if I succeed*. This is an all important point . . .'[47]

She consulted the committee of three women which Elizabeth Blackwell had set up before she left England, and was advised by them to test her strength first in nursing. In August 1860 she entered the Middlesex Hospital as a nurse, with support from some of the physicians and surgeons. She received private coaching from them and was allowed into some lectures and demonstrations. She was busy dressing wounds and going round with the medical staff. The house doctor instructed her on his cases when doing his rounds and, according to her, saw it as 'quite natural for me to see and hear anything professionally'.[48] She was even being admitted to the operating theatre and reported that the male medical students allowed her to stand in a good position to observe one major operation. At this initial stage the students seemed to accept her in her unusual position of unpaid nurse and unofficial student, perhaps because she did not seem to be any threat.

Increasingly she was feeling awkward about being nominally a nurse but in fact getting instruction as a student without paying fees. She decided to try to regularise this situation and in October asked to be allowed to register formally as a student and start paying fees. However, the Treasurer of the hospital refused her request on the grounds that it would distract the other students. Garrett said in a letter written at this time that 'he was too much inclined to treat the subject with amused contempt'.[49] She was, however, allowed to stay at the Middlesex as an amateur until the end of the winter session, and to be attached to the apothecary as a pupil.

Her father seems to have been stirred up by the opposition she was facing. He was now completely behind her efforts to gain a medical education and told her to spare no expense in her studies. However, her mother was not happy. In a letter to her daughter in August she accused her of being wilful and causing her pain. She also told her that relatives were saying that she should abandon her studies and return home.[50]

Elizabeth decided to postpone the question of admission until the following October. She also now rejected the possibility of being joined at this stage by other women, feeling that this should wait until she was accepted officially as a student. She said she did not *need* a companion and was worried that the authorities would be less sympathetic to two or more women. She was also anxious about the prospect of opening the college fully to women, in case the wrong type of woman got in.[51]

In a letter written at this time she remarked that a woman is helped by appearing as much like a lady as possible and criticised a friend for looking 'awfully strong-minded'.[52] Throughout her career she was anxious to create an impression of acceptable femininity. She was determined to show the world that she could have a successful professional career and yet still not sacrifice what she saw as the natural attributes of a woman.

In the meantime she was no longer nursing but spending the mornings walking the wards and the afternoons studying with the apothecary. In March she approached Dr Nunn who was in charge of the dissecting room. She reported that he was sympathetic and allowed her entry towards the end of that month. She also related that it was 'not nearly so shocking as I had been led to expect'. She had obviously been told horror stories about it. However, Nunn insisted that she could only be in the dissecting room when either he or his assistant was there because of the 'larkiness' of the other students.[53]

In June the *English Woman's Journal* printed a letter from 'A.M.S.'[54] Presumably 'A.M.S.' stands for 'A Medical Student' and was a pseudonym used by Elizabeth Garrett. She said she had started studying medicine because she was convinced of the fitness of women for medicine, not because she felt specially drawn to it. She said that doctors and students were friendly and that 'the point where all hesitate is in admitting women into the dissecting-room'. She expressed surprise that so few women had come forward for a medical training and invited other women to join her. Surprisingly, no one came forward in response to this invitation.

In May she was allowed into the Materia Medica lectures and the treasurer even accepted fees from her for this course. For the first time she was officially registered as a student and had to sign her name in the college books to say she would behave like a gentleman! When, however, she passed the exams with distinction and was the only student able to answer a particular question, the students petitioned the lecturers that she be prevented from continuing, on the grounds that it was improper for her to attend classes with male students and that it caused them inconvenience.

In an account of this to Emily Davies, she claimed that the petition had come from the less able students who were using the affair in order to be seen in a more favourable light by their lecturers. Furthermore, she suspected that the lecturers themselves would use it as 'a handle for their own prejudices'.[55] As a result of the petition she was told in June 1861 that she could attend no more lectures. Even the offer from her father to make a donation of £2000 to hospital funds was refused.

In a letter to Elizabeth Blackwell in January, she gave an account of events at the Middlesex and assessed the response of the medical profession as follows:

. . . the general feeling seems to be that each doctor is willing to help me privately and singly, but they are afraid to countenance the movement by helping me in their collective capacity.[56]

Indeed, an account of the train of events at the Middlesex published in the *Lancet* in July 1861 shows the male medical profession at its obstructive and patronising worst. The following passage is typical of its tone:

> The apple of discord is to be cast into our hospitals. A lady – 'teterrima causa belli'* – has penetrated to the core of our hospital system, and is determined to effect a permanent lodgment. The advanced guard of the Amazonian army which has so often threatened our ranks, on paper, has already carried the outposts and entered the camp.[57]

The *Lancet* upheld the students' objections and expressed horror at the thought of mixed classes. With high indignation it pointed to what it saw as the 'inconveniences . . . improprieties, and . . . anomalies' caused by Elizabeth Garrett's presence at the Middlesex, and accused her of starting a campaign to disrupt completely the hospital system.

Private study

Over the summer of 1861 Elizabeth approached and was rejected by all the teaching hospitals in London and by all the university examining boards outside London. But in August the Society of Apothecaries agreed to examine her if she fulfilled all their regulations. Although the pecking order of the three corporations was gradually being replaced by a division within the profession between the London teaching and consulting elite on the one hand and the mass of general practitioners on the other, the Society of Apothecaries was still considered the least prestigious of these licensing bodies, with its origins in trade.

At this stage she was given a letter of introduction to George Day, the Regius Professor of Medicine at St Andrews University, who was sympathetic to medical women. He wrote to advise her to spend the winter studying a wide range of subjects: Latin, Greek, history, geography, logic and mathematics. She also

* 'that most hideous cause of war'

attended lectures in London on botany, physics, natural history
and physiology, the last two given by T. H. Huxley, the famous
scientist. In a letter to Emily Davies, however, she expressed
doubts about whether or not she should attend the lectures on
physiology:

> I should not like to injure the cause needlessly, by rash
> eagerness nor on the other hand, by false delicacy, to miss
> knowing clearly anything that needs to be known.[58]

This was the tricky tightrope that had to be negotiated by all
the early medical women.

In April 1862 a motion before the Senate of the University of
London to allow women into medical degrees was lost by the
casting vote. At this point Elizabeth Garrett considered
approaching Florence Nightingale for advice but decided against
doing so because she was preoccupied with her own work and
would either oppose Elizabeth's plans or be indifferent. She was
then invited up to Edinburgh by Sophia Jex-Blake, who was
attending university classes for the higher education of women,
to look into the prospects of a medical degree at Edinburgh.
Sophia Jex-Blake made various appointments for her which she
followed up during her visit in May. They also went climbing
together in the Trossachs. A motion on admitting women was
defeated 18 votes to 16 at a meeting of the Council of the
College of Physicians, Edinburgh, in late June. These two
decisions were reported in the *Lancet* with obvious satisfaction:

> The College of Physicians of Edinburgh and the Senate of
> the University of London have each gone near to
> introducing a sisterhood of medical practitioners. We
> confess that we should have found ourselves embarrassed
> in that fair company, and congratulate the profession on
> escaping from a predicament which would have promised
> sore trials to their gallantry.[59]

While she was in Edinburgh she also approached the Edinburgh Royal Infirmary, explaining her intentions thus: 'I purpose studying medicine with a view to practising as a physician
to women and children.'[60] She was refused, as Emily Blackwell
had been in 1854. The infirmary was later to be one of the
major arenas for the struggle of Sophia Jex-Blake and her com-

panions from 1869–72. She then went to St Andrews to meet Professor Day, before returning to London for the rest of the summer.

A letter she wrote to her father in June from Scotland reveals her acute consciousness of her pioneer role:

> Believing as I do that women physicians of the highest
> order would be a great boon to many suffering women
> and that in order to have them the legal recognition must
> be given here or in England, I think my work is tolerably
> clear and plain, viz. to go on acting as pioneer towards
> this end, even though by doing so I spend the best years
> of my life in sowing that of which other students will reap
> the benefit.[61]

She felt she was not necessarily naturally suited to a medical career but believed she had the qualities needed in order to open up the profession to other women:

> It is a great thing for anyone in my position to be alive
> to the necessity for exercising tact and showing
> womanliness of manner and externals, and I fear that if I
> at all gave up the post, someone less fitted for it . . . might
> take it and disgrace the cause.

Like Florence Nightingale, another pioneer, Elizabeth Garrett was essentially an individualist, often dismissive of other women's capabilities. They must both have been acutely aware of their own vulnerable position and known that their attempts to enter non-traditional spheres would be jeopardised by association with women who did *not* succeed. However, alongside these unattractive attitudes towards other women, Elizabeth Garrett's sense of responsibility and willingness to sacrifice her life to this cause are formidable.

At the summer meeting of the National Association for the Promotion of Social Science in June 1862 Russell Gurney read a paper written by Emily Davies on 'Medicine as a Profession for Women'. In this she declared:

> It is an unquestionable fact – and here I speak, not from
> hearsay or conjecture, but from personal enquiry
> obtained by extended enquiry – that women of all ranks

do earnestly desire the attendance of physicians of their own sex.[62]

Emily Davies attacked those who found the idea of women doctors treating female patients 'an outrage upon propriety' but who at the same time were anxious to have women as nurses 'waiting upon' male patients. With the class prejudice typical of middle-class feminists of this and other periods, she expressed the view that nursing was not a suitable occupation for women as it was too much like being an 'upper servant', but said that the practice of medicine was perfectly acceptable. Moreover, she said, medicine came more naturally to women than to men.

It is interesting that she referred to the medical authorities as acting with 'marked liberality' and identified the major problem as convincing women themselves (and their parents) of the attractions of a medical career. Little evidence exists which can be used to test the accuracy of this assertion. Although women came forward in increasing numbers from the late 1870s onwards, once the major barriers to entry had fallen, it is striking that Elizabeth Garrett received no replies to her invitation to women to join her at the Middlesex Hospital.

At the same meeting of the association Frances Power Cobbe read a paper on female education and access to university exams, following the refusal of the University of London to admit Elizabeth. The association was a useful forum for collecting support for medical women: its membership was drawn from the middle-class radical community; its members debated a wide range of social issues, and, unusually, it allowed women an important role in organisation and public speaking. Elizabeth Garrett herself, however, had doubts about much action coming out of the association, referring to it rather dismissively in a letter to her mother as a 'universal pow-wow about everything'.[63]

In September she took the arts examination at Apothecaries Hall, a preliminary test which all students had to take before embarking on their medical studies, and passed it with credit. She then returned to Scotland in the autumn to attempt to enter St Andrews University. While she was there she stayed in lodgings at 10 Bell Street. In a letter written at this time she referred to the problem of the 'ladies' of St Andrews who regarded her as a 'social evil'.

Professor Day arranged for her to be given a matriculation ticket, enabling her to attend classes, but in November the senate refused to allow her to attend as a student. She went to Edinburgh to consult the Lord Advocate on whether she could challenge the decision on legal grounds but he ruled that women were not allowed full rights of graduation, although they could attend lectures.

The *English Woman's Journal* published a detailed account of this incident and the *Lancet* greeted it with an article restating its views on the natural barriers to women becoming doctors.[65] The Scottish universities thus remained closed to women. It is interesting, given her advice to medical women in the early 1870s to qualify abroad, that at *this* stage Elizabeth Garrett was determined 'not to quit the question of legal recognition in England [sic] by going abroad'.[66]

She remained in St Andrews until May to continue her medical studies privately, at Professor Day's house, and then went to Edinburgh again. She was well received by Dr Stevenson Macadam, chemistry lecturer at the extra-mural school, where many male medical students received a large part of their professional training, but he failed to persuade the other extra-mural lecturers to allow her to study. However, the world-famous surgeon James Simpson introduced her to Alexander Keiller, who allowed her to attend his lectures on the diseases of women and to witness obstetrical cases at the Edinburgh Maternity Hospital.

After returning from Scotland in the autumn of 1863 Elizabeth enrolled once again as a nurse, this time at the London Hospital. She now knew that no medical school would admit her as a student and so she set out to complete her education by paying for the best teaching money could buy. She carried on with private coaching from sympathetic medical men throughout 1864 an 1865, with financial support from her wealthy father. At this stage it was still possible to get a medical education through the old apprentice system of studying with individual medical men, though this option was becoming less possible as it was being replaced by a more formal medical education based on set courses and lectures, and in teaching institutions. In May 1864 the Royal College of Physicians refused by a unanimous vote her application to be examined, after getting legal advice from the Attorney General that they had no power to license a woman.

Elizabeth now had certificates from various private tutors declaring her competence in all areas of the curriculum laid down by the Society of Apothecaries. She next applied to sit the final professional examinations which would enable her to have her name put on the Medical Register and thus practise legally as a doctor in Britain. The society made a final attempt to refuse to examine her but gave way when her father threatened legal action on the basis that their charter referred to 'any person' and thus did not exclude women. In October 1865 she became a Licentiate of the Society of Apothecaries and in September 1866 her name was placed on the register as Elizabeth Garrett LSA. She refused on principle to use the title 'Dr' until she had a medical degree.

The following February *The Times* reprinted an article from the *British Medical Journal* entitled 'Girl Graduates', which contained the following passage about the possible effect of Elizabeth Garrett's success:

> The Temple of Medicine is likely to be besieged by fair invaders entering through the hall of the Apothecaries' Society.[67]

However, this route into the medical profession for women was now closed off. Soon after Garrett qualified, the society passed a resolution which stated that all candidates must have studied in a recognised medical school, all of which were, at that stage, for men only. There were isolated reports throughout the 1860s of women 'doctors' practising in various parts of Britain but they were unregistered and unqualified, and were probably restricted to midwifery cases. Elizabeth Blackwell and Elizabeth Garrett remained the only women on the Medical Register in Britain until 1877.

Elizabeth Garrett in practice

Elizabeth Garrett now proceeded to establish herself as a competent practising physician, to consolidate this limited victory for medical women and to prove that there was a demand from women for doctors of their own sex. At this time she was living with her old friend Jane Crow, who was working as secretary of the Society for Promoting the Employment of Women. Her practice with middle-class and upper-class women grew slowly in the late 1860s and, like many pioneer women doctors, it was a number of years before she felt financially secure. On a lighter note, in her early years in practice she received a visit from Princess Louisa, who was then 21 years old, and who was enthusiastic about her work. Apparently, Queen Victoria was very annoyed when she found out about her daughter's visit.

In March 1868 she attended Lady Katherine Amberley in a premature and difficult childbirth in which one twin died. Lady Amberley was the daughter-in-law of Lord John Russell, the reforming Liberal politician who had been Prime Minister from 1846 to 1852 and again from 1865 to 1866. She was also the mother of Bertrand Russell. Both she and her husband held radical political views. She had become involved in women's rights and was a member of the committee supporting the Married Women's Property Bill. Elizabeth Garrett called in Sir James Paget, the famous physician, for a second opinion three weeks after the birth and he became a useful supporter of her and of medical women in general. Lady Amberley continued to support medical women and in August 1869 contributed £50 for three years for a scholarship for women medical students. Elizabeth Garrett became the Amberley family doctor.

Another of her patients in the early days was Josephine Butler, who was involved in rescue work with prostitutes and the higher education of women in the north of England. She came from a family background of evangelicalism and campaigning for the abolition of slavery and the repeal of the Corn Laws. She herself was virulently opposed to men attending women in childbirth and had had a midwife present at the births of her four children. She believed that male attendance was a 'profanation' of the 'best and purest feelings' of women and attacked the 'tyranny' of the male medical profession in denying women the chance to consult women practitioners.[68] She wrote to a friend to say how much she appreciated consulting a woman doctor:

But for Miss Garrett I must say of her that I gained more

from her than any other doctor; for she not only repeated exactly what all the others had said, but entered much more into my mental state and way of life than they could do *because* I was able to *tell* her so much more than I ever could or would tell to any *man*.[69]

This remark suggests a double threat to the male medical profession from women doctors. Alongside the explicit fear that medical women would simply steal women patients from them was also a subtler underlying threat to the new scientific approach to medicine. With women patients able to talk freely to women doctors about their psychological and emotional state of health. diagnosis would be made partly according to the *patient's* analysis of her condition, with less dependence on medical observation of clinical symptoms. This alliance between women across professional barriers must have been very threatening to a male profession keen to establish the idea that diagnosis could only be made from the isolation and clinical observation of specific symptoms by those who had undergone a set training in science-based medicine, with the patient as passive recipient rather than active participant.

At this early stage in her career, Elizabeth Garrett continued her involvement in feminist campaigns. The group of women who had successfully campaigned from 1862 to 1865 to open local examinations to women then started the Kensington Society, a women's discussion group. Emily Davies was secretary and the membership of over 50 women included Elizabeth Garrett, Sophia Jex-Blake, Barbara Bodichon (*née* Leigh Smith), Jessie Boucherett, Jane Crow and Mrs Gurney. Meetings were held four times a year from 1865 to 1868 for the discussion of political and social issues.

The discussion society led directly on to the first Women's Suffrage Committee. This consisted of Elizabeth Garrett, Emily Davies, Barbara Bodichon, Jessie Boucherett and Rosamund Hill, and was based in a makeshift office in Elizabeth Garrett's dining-room. During the spring of 1866 the committee took advice from John Stuart Mill MP on the best way to start the campaign. As a result they started to collect signatures in favour of votes for women. By the end of May, 1500 supporters had signed the petition and on 7 June Elizabeth Garrett and Emily

Davies went in person to present this petition to Mill in Westminster Hall. This resulted in the first vote on the issue in the House of Commons.

Despite Elizabeth's active involvement in these early stages and her continuing support for feminist issues, she decided not to join the permanent committee. In June 1867 she sent a guinea subscription for the Franchise Society to her sister, Millicent Garrett Fawcett, but asked that her name not be published:

> I think it is wiser as a medical woman to keep somewhat in the background as regards other movements.[70]

However, the 30 names in the section on 'medical and nursing' women on the Women's Suffrage Declaration of 1889 included hers, so presumably by then she felt sufficiently secure in her professional career to be associated with an overtly feminist campaign.[71]

The Marylebone dispensary

In June 1866 Elizabeth opened a dispensary for the diseases of women and children in Seymour Place, in a working-class area in Marylebone, where her friend Llewelyn Davies, Emily's brother, worked as rector. She had a lot of support from leading Liberals, such as the Gurneys, John Stuart Mill, and the Earl of Shaftesbury, who sent a donation to her in October. Harry Varney, who was married to Florence Nightingale's older sister, agreed to join the dispensary's General Committee. Prominent members of the profession agreed to act as consulting physicians and surgeons at the dispensary and she began to win the grudging respect of the medical profession as a whole, although as an exception rather than the first of many. She engaged a male dispenser but had him take on two women apprentices in the hope that they would eventually take over from him.

The dispensary enjoyed general public acceptance partly as a result of fears of a fresh outbreak of cholera in London after the disease had taken hold in Egypt during 1865. The first death in London occurred 16 days after the dispensary opened. The outbreaks of 1831, 1847 and 1853 were remembered with horror by Londoners and the middle and upper classes feared the spread of the disease from working-class areas. The proposal to open a dispensary in a poor and crowded part of inner London was therefore seen as helping to combat the threat to public health.

The decision to set up in practice as a physician for women and children was tactical. Elizabeth could dismiss as irrelevant the possible objection that men would never agree to consult a woman doctor: she had used this argument to justify her decision to become a doctor in a letter to her aunt in 1860.[72] She could also avoid the danger of scandal. Similar decisions were made by most of the pioneer women doctors as a matter of professional survival.

When looking back on the history of medical women in the United States in 1891, Mary Putnam Jacobi described how obstetrics and gynaecology were the 'portals' through which women entered medical practice.[73] However, she also warned against women becoming ghettoised in the area of women's and children's health and being gradually pushed out of general medicine altogether. But in the early years it was clear where the practical and political choice lay.

The decision to set up practice in a working-class area of London was consistent with the growth in middle-class and upper-class female philanthropy from the mid-nineteenth century onwards. Various forms of social work among the poor were undertaken by these women almost as a logical extension of the 'civilising' role of their fathers and brothers in the empire. Once poverty became defined as a social problem worthy of thorough investigation and intervention, it was seen as natural that women would play an important role in 'solving' the problem by going into poor areas to do charity and 'educational' work. They were less directly associated with class control and the exploitation of working-class labour than were their male relatives, and would therefore stand a better chance of being allowed into working-class homes. Since these activities were accorded low status they were seen as more appropriately women's work. During the later nineteenth century this voluntary work by middle- and upper-class women gradually gave way to professional work by middle-class women as trained and salaried social workers, nurses and so on. Elizabeth Garrett's work in Marylebone will thus have been seen by many as appropriate and not odd or scandalous.

The demand for cheap medical care in working-class areas was very great. Working-class families called in the doctor only in absolute emergencies as they simply could not afford the fee. It was often difficult to get admission to hospital because prospective patients usually needed a letter of introduction from one of the subscribers to the hospital. The Friendly societies and sickness clubs organised by the unions covered only the male breadwinner. Mutual help was a major strategy for dealing with sickness in working-class areas, with neighbours helping out at childbirths and sending soup and other food round to the house when there was illness. People also often went to a local woman who would be considered a street doctor.

There was certainly a desperate need for health care for working-class women. Not only did they suffer as middle-class women did from successive childbearing but their health was also affected by poverty, bad housing, insufficient food and often lethal working conditions. Surveys of schoolchildren in the 1880s showed that girls often had damaged eyesight from sewing in bad light, and back problems from carrying younger brothers and sisters around. Working-class women were often unable to breast-feed because of undernourishment. Evidence from the Women's Co-operative Guild in the early 1900s showed that most women suffered from internal uterine disorders and that they viewed these as an inevitable part of being a woman.[74] Maternal mortality rates in the female population as a whole were higher than one in 200 births (compared with one in 60,000 in contemporary Britain) and were undoubtedly much higher for working-class women.

With very little medical care available to the working classes, and to women especially, the dispensary played an important role in the history of medical women. From the evidence of the work of pioneer women doctors in Britain and the United States there seems to have been a great demand for dispensary services among working-class women, with high attendance figures as soon as a dispensary was opened. The Marylebone dispensary was attended by between 60 and 90 women and children each afternoon.

Women doctors had very strong ideas about what they saw as their educative role in teaching working-class women about hygiene and nutrition. Although this programme had its radical elements, in seeking to spread knowledge of health among women as a whole and in developing a style of medicine which included much more than diagnosis and cure, these middle-class women were very obviously reproducing the prevailing class attitudes of the time. They made a valuable *medical* breakthrough in recognising the importance of social and environmental factors in the development of disease and ill-health but failed to make the *political* connection that these social factors were caused by poverty in a rigidly class-structured society.

They firmly believed that the working-class women they saw as patients suffered as they did largely because of ignorance and immorality. The following excerpt from an appeal by Elizabeth Blackwell for funds to enlarge the New York Infirmary is a perfect example of this belief.

> It will be remembered that the poor who resort to a hospital, ignorant, degraded, even vicious, as they often may be, are, nevertheless, not beyond the possibility of moral as well as material aid – that to such a class of women, the practical advice and counsel of educated women might be invaluable in spreading some wiser views with reference to their own health and life, and the rearing of their children, that they should leave the institution, if possible, better in every respect than they entered.[75]

More medical successes

Following Elizabeth Garrett's example, other women entered examinations at Apothecaries' Hall. In February 1867 *The Times* reported that three women, Frances Morgan, Eliza Walker and Louisa Atkins, had passed the preliminary examinations in Latin, geometry and history but assured its readers that it would be a different matter when they were faced with the dissecting room.[76] Elizabeth Garrett took in all three women for clinical instruction at her dispensary.

In May Isabel Thorne, who was later to join Sophia Jex-Blake in Edinburgh, passed the examinations at the Female Medical College, which trained women in midwifery, with a double first in medical and obstetrical classes and started practising as a midwife. Her initial decision to enter medicine, as with many other pioneer women, had been made partly as a result of her own personal experience, as she had suffered from inadequate treatment by male doctors while in China. Following her graduation she wrote two letters to the *Englishwoman's Review* in which she stated that it was better for women to be attended in childbirth by 'their skilled sisters' than by educated men or uneducated women, and gave information about the college which she said was important in opening up further employment opportunities for women.[77] A year later she was among the top six students in the Apothecaries' Hall lists.

It is clear from their manner of reporting that both *The Times* and the *Lancet* saw these successes as evidence of a threat, the first stage in the full medical education of women. The *Lancet* was at great pains to point out that medicine was *not* among the subjects in which the University of London decided from November 1867 to examine women, and that the Society of Apothecaries had no intention of letting women sit their medical examinations.[78] The *Englishwoman's Review* described this exclusion as 'monstrous'.[79]

Louisa Atkins, Eliza Walker and Frances Morgan now decided to pursue their medical studies in Zurich. The University of Zurich had been open to women medical students since 1864. The Sorbonne in Paris opened its doors to women a year later and Berne and Geneva followed suit soon after. A Russian woman, Nadeshda Suslowa, became the first woman to gain a medical degree in Europe when she graduated from Zurich in 1867.[80]

In 1868 Elizabeth Garrett tried to enter the Sorbonne but was faced with regulations concerning residency. She took the matter to the French government, with her application sponsored by the British Ambassador and supported by the Empress. In February 1869 she heard that she had been accepted as a student without having to fulfil the residential requirements. Her decision to go to Paris must have been an attempt to raise her prestige as a doctor, since a medical degree was not necessary for the practice of medicine: less than a third of all medical men had degrees, the rest practising on a licence only. It was at this stage that she withdrew from all suffrage work, and from any social life, in order to concentrate on her studies. Although she was by now a respected figure, she was also very isolated. She passed her first examination in March 1869, and the rest in June, December and the following January. She submitted her thesis also in January and gained her medical degree in June 1870.

Her graduation thesis was on the topic of migraine. She chose this subject partly because she would not have to ask for access to post mortem facilities. Also she wanted to take a subject 'that demanded some insight into the harmony which exists between the main physiological functions'. This holistic view of medicine contrasts with the growing preference in medical research for isolating specific causes of individual diseases. Her conclusion was to recommend simple food, no alcohol, fresh air and exercise, rather than medication.[81]

A small number of other women from Britain, including Sophia Jex-Blake, started medical studies in Paris and Zurich during the 1870s while medical graduation was still closed to women in this country. Although a medical degree from abroad did not automatically admit the graduate on to the British Medical Register, a few women with foreign degrees gained limited acceptance as medical practitioners in Britain in the early 1870s. A European medical degree provided medical women in Britain with an important foot in the door during the years before full access to the profession was won.

Early responses of the medical profession

Elizabeth Garrett's experience as a student was that individual medical men were often willing to show their sympathy for the idea of women doctors by allowing women limited access to facilities and classes. Because they were unable to imagine that any real threat would ever materialise – that women would have the strength to carry through the initiative – the profession had not yet put up the wall of opposition which faced Sophia Jex-Blake and others from 1869 onwards. The concerted opposition of later years would make it impossible for all but the strongest supporters who were also secure in their own professional careers to step out of line.

However, even at this stage, the collective hostility of the profession was clear. Throughout the 1860s the medical profession was generally dismissive of the seriousness of the medical women movement and tended to treat Elizabeth Garrett's efforts and the reports of medical women from the United States as curious, isolated incidents.

In May 1863 the *Lancet* had reported the publication in the United States of a list of 256 qualified and practising women doctors and later reprinted a report from an American newspaper that there were six or eight regular women doctors in Philadelphia whose practice was equal to an average male doctor.[82] Throughout the 1860s, newspapers, periodicals and journals carried various reports such as these about medical women practitioners and the medical education of women from the United States. This means that, alongside debates in the *Lancet* on whether women were handicapped by their 'feminine' weaknesses and so should be excluded from the profession completely, there were concrete examples of women who had succeeded.

However, the *Lancet* tried to dismiss American women practitioners by claiming that most of them adopted 'charlatanic' methods and to discredit the medical women movement in Britain by association.[82] It is also possible to detect a note of slightly paranoid hysteria, in phrases like 'the charge of the parasols' and 'the realms of medicine being threatened with an invasion of Amazons'.[83] In a letter in 1864 Elizabeth Garrett described the response of the profession in this way:

> The *Lancet* sneers. The *Medical Times and Gazette* treats me as a marvellous exception and gives offensive praise.[84]

Many doctors in the United States openly espoused alternative medical doctrines such as homoepathy and hypnosis, and were seen as separate from the 'regulars'. It was true that a number of American medical women were associated with these 'irregulars', an association seen by the *Lancet* as 'ominous' and sufficient grounds for deep suspicion of any attempt by women in Britain to practise medicine.

Medical journals used a patronising tone wherever possible when reporting even the obvious successes of American women. A leading article in the *Lancet* criticised the 'ridiculous nomenclature' of the New England Female Medical College and referred to the graduates as 'ripe fruits' and 'budding blossoms'.

This article and one in the *British Medical Journal* also reported with smug satisfaction the fact that the College's fourteenth annual report indicated falling attendance and financial problems.[86]

The medical journals laboured endlessly over whether women doctors could marry or not. In some articles it was assumed that they, like all women, would want to settle down as wives and mothers and would give up practice, thus making their training a waste of time and money. On the other hand, one correspondent to the *Lancet* said that a professional career would necessitate celibacy for women but that this was a denial of their 'natural functions'.[87] Contrast all this with Dr Emily Blackwell's response when asked by British feminists about the likelihood of women carrying on their career after marriage and having children:

> Granting women want to be doctors, and that medical science has need of women, women must, and will, enter the profession. I think it most probable that women will modify the practice of medicine . . .[88]

There were explicit attempts by the medical opposition to divide women and turn them against each other. The *Lancet* protested that the issue of medical women was only the 'exceptional . . . restless . . . morbid . . . agitation of a few' and medical men claimed there was no evidence to suggest that women wanted to consult doctors of their own sex.[89] Those women who chose to consult women doctors were described as eccentric women who had a pathological aversion to male doctors. Male opponents were constantly attempting to diminish the threat of female solidarity posed by the medical women movement by branding these women as odd, and claiming that their views ran counter to the wishes of all 'normal' women. Most women, they said, wanted to devote themselves to domestic duties in the home, 'despite the crotchets of a few male-minded ladies'.[90] Hostile comments such as these are representative of a shift in late nineteenth-century Victorian England from an attitude of pity towards spinsters as sad, lonely figures whose lives were a failure, to one of hostility towards them because of what was seen as their desertion of their mothering role, and because of suspicion of their independence and their relationships with other women.

Early medical women came in for the usual insults: they were accused of being 'strong minded', 'unsexed', and being 'as remarkable for the masculine qualities of their bodies as for those of their minds'.[91] By extension, if these women were unnaturally masculine, their male supporters must lack virility: in 1869 in response to the beginnings of the campaign in Edinburgh one correspondent to the *Lancet* referred to the women students 'and their effeminate male friends'.[92] These views were still surfacing in the pages of the *Lancet* in the 1870s, with a leading article in 1873 stating that women and men could not be made equal through education but only by creating 'a race of strong-minded, masculine women'.[93]

8 Nurses and Midwives, Seacole and Barry

Nightingale's nursing reforms

At the same time as Elizabeth Garrett's first approaches to the medical profession for a full medical education, major changes were being initiated within nursing by Florence Nightingale. A large-scale fund-raising exercise had been launched to set up a new training centre for nurses. By 1860 £59,000 had been collected and she was able to open the Nightingale School of Nursing at St Thomas' Hospital in London, one of the voluntary hospitals with an attached teaching school and a prestigious consulting staff. Her aim was no less than to transform nursing into a totally new profession for educated women with its own internal organisation and career structure.

Although this 'new nursing' was deeply moral in purpose, it differed from the sisterhoods in which women did their nursing as a *religious duty*, usually under the direction of male clerics. Florence Nightingale's nurses were part of an independent lay order and were following a career which required particular vocational commitment. They were *professionals* rather than religious enthusiasts. With a new and vigorous training programme, nurses now acquired a definite, although limited, body of medical knowledge and skill. Under the new system the matron was herself a trained nurse rather than the glorified housekeeper she had been, and the work schedules of the nurses in all her wards came under her control rather than that of the medical staff on each ward. A separate and self-governing military-style nursing hierarchy was thus established to work in parallel with the medical hierarchy.[94]

Although doctors were in favour of properly trained nurses

to assist them in increasingly complex medical care, they felt uneasy about the control that they were now losing to this self-governing profession and wanted to preserve the nurse in her position as clearly subordinate to the wishes of the doctor. The fact that these new nurses were middle-class posed an added threat to the profession as they were likely to be far less deferential to the middle-class doctors than traditional, working-class nurses. They were happy for the nurse to have new skills but less happy about the acquisition of medical knowledge as this carried with it a measure of autonomy in their work. They were worried about nurses acquiring sufficient medical expertise to attempt to treat medical cases without any input from a doctor and thus practising a new form of 'quackery'.

There was opposition from the medical profession throughout the period of implementation of the Nightingale reforms, from the 1860s and the 1880s. Male medical students protested that the new in-ward nursing training, with its reorganisation of the wards posed a threat to their clinical instruction. Hospital medical staff resisted the introduction of new nursing in the wider context of their power struggle with the governing committees of these hospitals. For example there was a bitter struggle at Guy's Hospital over the appointment of Miss Burt as matron in 1879. During the following year she introduced a number of reforms, attracting support from the Board of Managers but fierce opposition from the medical staff. Eventually victory was won by Miss Burt, and the cause of nursing reform. It is important to remember that the campaign for women doctors in the 1860s and 70s was happening at the same time as other struggles concerning nursing and midwifery which raised similar issues of professional control and the sexual division of labour.

The Female Medical Society

In June 1862 the *English Woman's Journal* published a letter from 'One of the Committee' of the Female Medical Society about proposals for setting up a college for midwives. The letter announced that a circular would soon be issued 'inviting the co-operation of all who feel an interest in the social, moral, and physical well-being of the sex'.[95] The society wanted the profession of midwifery to be upgraded and expanded in order to provide female health care for women. A pamphlet issued in 1864 described its aims as follows:

> This society is formed to facilitate the admission of women into the Medical Profession, by establishing a Female Medical College in London, and to promote the due qualification and registration of Female Practitioners in Midwifery and Medicine.[96]

The society drew on a tradition of opposition to 'man-midwifery' which viewed the practice of male attendance upon women in childbirth as fundamentally immoral, a dangerous attack on female modesty: 'Certain duties now devolve most improperly upon male practitioners from mere default of duly qualified women.' Also, the use of instruments like forceps was seen as harmful to mother and baby and it was believed that the risks of puerperal fever were increased through cross-infection from a doctor's other medical and surgical work. In its pamphlets the society quoted figures which showed higher mortality rates for women attended by men at childbirth.

The Female Medical College opened in autumn 1864 and had 14 students in the first year, with lecturers paid entirely out of students' fees. In opening the college the Female Medical Society set out to establish a course of training and to distinguish between these graduates and unqualified women by means of certificates and registration. They wanted to do for midwifery what Florence Nightingale was doing for nursing: to raise its status through proper training and by recruiting respectable, that is middle-class, women. The college was well received in the pages of the *Englishwoman's Review*. A letter from Isabel Thorne welcomed it as opening up further employment opportunities for women and breaking the monopoly which men were establishing in midwifery.[97]

In his inaugural address, Dr James Edmunds, a consultant who had been largely responsible for setting up the society, spoke of the danger to mother and child if a midwife was forced by lack of training to call in a doctor in the case of a complicated birth.[98] However, the society failed to recognise that the unqualified midwives to whom Dr Edmunds referred were working-class women whose precious jobs would be threatened by the new trained corps of middle-class midwives.

This initiative to supply well-qualified middle-class midwives was not popular with the medical profession. Whereas nursing reform could never alter the essentially ancillary nature of the work of nurses or their subordinate position within the medical hierarchy, midwives effectively acted as independent medical practitioners and were potentially in competition with doctors for part of their practice. Doctors, therefore, wanted to emphasise the supposedly *working-class* aspects of midwifery, such as helping with household tasks just after the birth, in order to lower its prestige.

The medical journals kept a wary eye on the college and the scope of the work it envisaged its graduates would undertake. In 1865 the *Lancet* claimed that it had managed to dissuade the society from trying to train women doctors at the college and persuaded it instead to train midwives, which it agreed was 'a legitimate . . . task'. Another article expressed the *Lancet*'s satisfaction that the scope of the college was not as wide as its title suggested and Dr Edmunds wrote in to reassure readers that it intended to train midwives only. Another protest at the name of the college came in a letter to the *British Medical Journal* in which the author said that it made one think of 'popular superficial lectures to a rustling silken audience' and that to call a midwifery school a Female Medical College was like calling a school for cookery 'the Ladies' Gastronomical College'.[99]

Opposition also came from the 'Ladies of Langham Place' the group of feminists responsible for setting up the *English Woman's Journal*. These feminists promoted nursing but *not* midwifery as a suitable profession for 'gentlewomen'. Nurses lived either in middle-class homes or in lodgings in the hospital itself. The profession of nursing was therefore seen as less hazardous to middle-class women than that of midwifery, which mainly involved visiting homes in working-class areas.

The society seems to have had an ambiguous attitude towards the movement for women doctors. Pamphlets issued in 1864 and 1866 clearly refer to training women in midwifery *and* 'the treatment of the diseases of women and children'. However, at the Annual General Meeting in June 1866 the society's president, the Earl of Shaftesbury, urged that students should not enter a wider medical sphere, and, despite the remarks two years earlier,[100]Dr Edmunds stated that graduates of the college always passed on difficult cases to male doctors. Yet in his address to the college a year later he declared that the society supported attempts by Elizabeth Blackwell, Elizabeth Garrett and Mary Walker to achieve 'perfect equality' in medicine but confined its own aims to midwifery practice.[101]

To confuse matters even more, at its third Annual General Meeting in 1867 the society clearly dissociated itself from the campaign for medical women by issuing this statement:

> This society is not concerned with the advocacy of 'women's suffrage', female army surgeons, or even female general practitioners, much less with the admission of ladies to medical classes which are attended by young men.[102]

Its position was eventually clarified in a statement contained in the report of the Ninth Annual Session in 1872–3:

> It has been decided that, in order more precisely to define the scope of the Society's teaching operations, the College shall henceforth be designated THE OBSTETRICAL COLLEGE FOR WOMEN, and it is hoped that it will work hand in hand with the Medical Profession.[103]

In the light of the society's caution in supporting medical women, and of subsequent warnings from medical women against women being ghettoised within obstetrics and being bought off with a special, inferior diploma, it might have been expected that Elizabeth Garrett and others would have had mixed feelings about the college. The only hint of this that I could find was a short note correcting a previous report that she excluded Female Medical College students from her dispensary and stating that she let them see the midwifery practice but not the medical and surgical practice.[104]

It may well be that the society was frightened off by medical opposition from its open support for medical women and its original aim of training women in medicine as well as in midwifery. Articles in the *Lancet* show that the medical profession would let the society go just so far in its aims and no further. However, despite the evident caution in some statements of the society's aims, subsequent events made it clear where their political allegiance lay. In 1874 the college was disbanded and members of the Female Medical Society transferred their support to the newly opened London School of Medicine for Women.[105]

Mary Walker's visit

In autumn 1866 Dr Mary Walker of New York visited Britain. A cautionary article in the *Lancet* acknowledged that Mary Walker's career was no 'passing whim' and hoped that she would be well received by the British medical profession, although expressing doubts than any woman here would follow her example. They also reported her views on female dress: she criticised current fashion as a danger to women's health as they placed all the weight of a heavy dress on the hips.[106] She herself wore dresses which hung from the shoulders. However, she came in for heavy criticism in the *Englishwoman's Review* for a lecture she gave while in Britain for saying very little about her own medical experiences and instead laying herself open to ridicule through 'an elaborate defence of Bloomerism', that is, the promotion of trouser-wearing by women.[107]

The lecture also gave a taste of what was to come later in the struggle as it was severely disrupted by 'an uproarious mob of medical students' and the police had to be called.[108] As well as being vocal in their opposition to the campaign for women doctors, male medical students gained a reputation in the 1870s and 80s for disrupting public meetings of radical campaigns such as the anti-vivisection movement. Members of the Ladies National Association were physically attacked by medical students in Glasgow in the early 1870s.

The Delhi Female Medical Mission

At the same time as arguments were raging over the existence in Britain of a desire for women doctors, a number of articles were bringing to the notice of the British reading public the situation of millions of women in India who received little or no medical care because cultural beliefs made it impossible for them to be examined by a man. Various initiatives were launched in response to these reports in order to provide Indian women with alternative medical care. They were all run by white organisations from Britain and the United States and were imperialistic in their aims and practice. They wanted to import white women's knowledge and expertise into India in order to provide medical treatment for native women, and at the same time to 'civilise' them and convert them to Christianity.[109]

In 1867 the *Englishwoman's Review* carried a report of the Delhi Female Medical Mission, which aimed to relieve the physical suffering of Indian women in sickness and to bring Christianity into their homes. The Female Medical College was a direct influence in this: Dr Edmunds was given as the contact for the project and one of the stipulations was that women must be well educated and have a good knowledge of midwifery. They hoped to attend Indian women in 'zenanas' (women's quarters where they lived separately from men), to open a dispensary for women, and to train Indian women as midwives.[110] The *Englishwoman's Review* carried reports of similar projects during the late 1860s and early 1870s.[111]

Female education

During the late 1860s there were a number of important developments in the education of women and girls. In 1865, through the efforts of Emily Davies and her supporters, the Oxford and Cambridge Local Examinations were opened to girls. The following year there was an unsuccessful attempt to persuade the University of London to accept women students. Emily Davies rejected their offer of special examinations for women as she believed this would lead to a separate and inferior higher education for women.[112] In 1867 she and her committee started their campaign to set up a women's college at Cambridge, which resulted in the establishment of Girton.

1867 also saw the opening of the first session of the Edinburgh Ladies' Education Association and the North of England Council for the Higher Education of Women, which brought together local associations already active in various northern towns. Both organisations ran various series of lectures in literary, historical and scientific subjects to large groups of middle- and upper-class women, given by university teachers and designed to prepare the women for examinations. Large numbers of women seized on this chance to study with enthusiasm and commitment. In April

1868 the *Englishwoman's Review* published the text of a lecture given by Professor David Masson to the Edinburgh Ladies' Educational Association. It was reported that this lecture was attended by 400 women and that there was not enough space for the audience.[113]

In 1867 James Stuart gave a series of lectures on science in four northern towns to a total of 540 women. He provided them with suggestions for preparatory reading and set a short test for them to send back if they wished. Some 300 tests were returned. In an article he wrote in 1869 he said that women were both eager for a scientific education and at least as able as men.[114]

Mary Seacole, Jamaican 'doctress'

Whereas in Britain at this time women were restricted to performing mainly ancillary medical tasks, there was a strong tradition in Jamaica (then part of the British Empire) of 'doctresses'. These black women were independent practitioners who performed a wide range of medical tasks including treating tropical diseases and undertaking surgical work and midwifery cases. During the Crimean War one of these doctresses, Mary Seacole, gained a considerable reputation in Britain for her activities at the front, a living example of the potential capabilities of women in medicine. In her autobiography *The Wonderful Adventures of Mrs. Seacole in Many Lands*, published in London in 1857, she gave an account of her life from her childhood in Jamaica through to the part she played in the Crimean War.[115]

She was born in Kingston, Jamaica, in 1805. Her mother was a free black woman who ran a boarding-house and her father was a Scottish army officer. The family was comfortably well-off. Her mother was one of a number of doctresses who practised traditional Caribbean medicine which was based on a knowledge of herbal medicine brought from Africa. As well as treating tropical diseases and other illnesses, she also had skill in tending wounds. A number of the naval and army officers who stayed at the boarding-house were there to convalesce.

In her autobiography Seacole describes her mother as 'an admirable doctress' and 'in high repute'. She says that as a child she naturally developed an interest in her mother's activities: 'I had from early youth a yearning for medical knowledge and practice which has never deserted me since.'[116]

She relates how she pretended her doll had whatever disease was prevalent in Kingston at the time and 'cured' it. After extensive travelling and a brief marriage which ended with her husband's death, she returned to Kingston to run the boarding-house. She was now a respected doctress in her own right and found her skills in great demand, particularly during the cholera epidemic of 1850.

However, she found her life in Kingston restrictive and so she spent some time travelling in Latin America. In various towns where she stayed she had to deal, often single-handedly, with outbreaks of cholera and yellow fever. Her medical techniques were very close to those used in western medicine right up until the discovery of antibiotics in the twentieth century. During this time she even performed an autopsy on a small child who had died of cholera, out of a keen desire to find out more about the disease. She used 'simple remedies' made from herbs which grew locally. As she says in *Wonderful Adventures*: 'So true is it, that beside the nettle ever grows the cure for its sting.'[117]

She also undertook a good deal of surgical work, attending to knife and gunshot wounds. On one occasion she stitched up the ears of a boatman which had been split in a fight. After her return to Kingston in 1853 she was asked by the medical authorities to manage the nursing arrangements at a military base during an outbreak of yellow fever.

By the time of the outbreak of the Crimean War in 1854 she had established a considerable local reputation for her medical skills and gained a wide range of experience in treating tropical diseases, attending to surgical cases, and supervising medical care in a military setting. When news of the medical crisis in the Crimea reached Mary Seacole in Jamaica, she decided to go to London to join the nurses going out to the front:

> Need I be ashamed to confess that I shared in the general
> enthusiasm, and longed more than ever to carry my busy
> (and the reader will not hesitate to add experienced)
> fingers where the sword or bullet had been busiest, and
> pestilence most rife . . . I made up my mind that if the
> army wanted nurses, they would be glad of me . . . [118]

However, despite her considerable medical experience, which could probably not be matched by any woman living in Britain at the time, and the references she brought with her from a number of doctors, the authorities turned down 'the offer of a motherly yellow woman'. She showed little anger at the racism she faced here, putting this refusal down to natural ignorance of her skills.

Instead she decided to pay her own way to the Crimea and 'establish a mess-table and comfortable quarters for sick and convalescent officers'. In order to be able to carry out her intended plan of independent medical work she invested 'a great portion of my limited capital' in medical supplies. She first spent six weeks in Balaclava, sleeping on board ship at night and tending sick and wounded soldiers on the wharf during the day. Of this period she wrote:

I did not forget the main object of my journey, to which
I would have devoted myself exclusively had I been
allowed . . .[119]

She then set up 'The British Hotel' two miles from Balaclava where she offered good food, accommodation and a range of supplies. She also travelled around with her medicines and treated men on the battlefield. After the assault on Redan, when the British army was repulsed with enormous casualties, she reported:

Several times I was ordered back, but each time my bag
of bandages and comforts for the wounded proved my
passport.[120]

She soon built up a formidable reputation based on her medical skills, the dispensing of otherwise scarce medical supplies, the provision of nourishing food, and her obvious courage and commitment to caring for others. She often gave her services and dispensed supplies free of charge. In her autobiography she reprinted a number of letters of testimony she received from patients of all ranks, and asked that anyone doubting her story should read the accounts in the papers of the spring of 1855. She also quoted an article written by the war correspondent of *The Times* which appeared in 1857:

I have seen her go down, under fire, with her little store
of creature comforts for our wounded men; and a more
tender or skilled hand about a wound or broken limb
could not be found among our best surgeons.[121]

As with the popular reputation Florence Nightingale gained
for her role in the Crimean War, it is not clear what connection
there was, if any, between the career of Mary Seacole and the
campaign for medical women in Britain. I could find no references to her in papers relating to the campaign but presumably it
must have been of some significance that a woman was achieving
considerable fame among the British public not just for *adminis-
trative* achievements like those of Florence Nightingale but for
providing a range of complex medical services, that is, for actually treating patients.

The extent of her reputation in Britain became clear after the
war ended abruptly in March 1856. She had made a substantial
financial loss as she had been forced to leave stock and equip-
ment behind and by November found herself in the bankruptcy
court. A number of letters to *The Times* from well-wishers paid
tributes to her and suggested that a fund be set up to reimburse
her for her losses in the Crimea and to enable her to set up in
business. A poem about her appeared in *Punch*. By February
1857 her debts were cleared and she decided to write her autobiography. This was published in July, recommended by the *Illus-
trated London News*, and reprinted within 12 months.

In July 1857 a Grand Military Festival was held to raise funds
for her. Almost 1000 performers took part and it was packed
out for four nights. Mary Seacole was herself given rapturous
applause by the audiences and a report in *The Times* stated,
'Few names were more familiar to the public during the late
war than that of Mrs. Seacole.' Unfortunately, the extravaganza
had been badly planned and she received very little money from
it.

She spent the rest of her life in Jamaica and London, with
endless visits from ex-patients who owed a great deal to her
medical and nursing skills. A portrait of her at this time suggests
she may have been awarded the Crimean Medal, the French
Legion of Honour, and a Turkish medal. She was recognised by
royalty: a leaflet about the Seacole Fund shows the Prince of

Wales as one of its patrons and refers to Queen Victoria's 'approbation of Mrs. Seacole's services'. She also acted as masseuse to the Princess of Wales in 1873 and was a guest at Marlborough House. She died in 1881, leaving a considerable fortune in her will.

The strange tale of James Barry

On 21 August 1865 the *Manchester Guardian* reported the recent death of a medical army inspector who had been found on her death to be a woman. [122] This was James Barry who in 1812 at the age of 15 had entered Edinburgh University dressed as a boy to study medicine. Her origins are obscure and her real name is not known.

She joined the army as a surgeon and achieved some fame for her views on medical and political reform. She was a proponent of preventative medicine, insisting on new standards of hygiene and cleanliness as the best protection against disease. She did not refuse to treat the poor, as many doctors did, and also made efforts to spread an understanding of disease to the general public. But she was given little recognition for this pioneering work and clashed with Florence Nightingale in the mid 1850s when the latter received public acclaim for a similar programme of medical reform in the Crimea.

She spoke publicly against slavery and campaigned for better conditions for those in lunatic asylums, saying that conditions in asylums were bad enough to make anyone insane. With these political views she earned the enmity of many administrators of institutions and other powerful men, and was posted to the tropics, far from Britain, in order to neutralise her political activities. She also had a reputation as a 'lady-killer'!

It seems that her achievements as a doctor were rather lost on her death in the midst of the scandal of discovering that she had been a woman. There are clear parallels between her career and those of the pioneer generation of women doctors, with her emphasis on preventative medicine, her desire to share knowledge of medicine with patients, and her involvement in campaigning politics. It is surprising, therefore, to find that there do not seem to have been any references to her in the campaign for entry to the profession in Britain in the 1860s and 70s (except for the oblique reference to 'female army surgeons' in the Female Medical Society statement quoted above). For instance, Sophia Jex-Blake made no reference to her in the historical survey in her 1869 essay on medical women.

Nor were there any references to Mary Seacole. At first sight the complete silence of campaigners seems baffling. They must surely have known about these two important medical women. News of the scandal surrounding James Barry's death reached the national papers. Mary Seacole's achievements were reported in *The Times* throughout the Crimean War and she attained a certain popular fame in London during the years after the war. The explanation lies perhaps in the anxiety of campaigners to avoid any association with scandal or with women active outside the medical mainstream. Racism may also have been a factor in Mary Seacole's career being ignored.

Despite the fact that they were themselves venturing into uncharted territory, women like Sophia Jex-Blake were still, of course, products of their time and their class. I cannot see them hailing either an independent black woman healer, who had cared for soldiers at the front, or a woman who had lived her life as a man as pioneers of the medical women movement. The determination of campaigners not to let anything jeopardise their efforts to gain acceptance for women doctors meant that they denied the lives and struggles of other women who chose, or had to take, a different route to a similar goal.[123]

9 The First Women Medical Students

In the course of 1869 the focus of the campaign shifted to Edinburgh and to the dynamic figure of Sophia Jex-Blake. Her parents were evangelicals and she had received a heavily religious upbringing. She had been a headstrong child and suffered from heart trouble because of her excitability. She was sent to boarding school and in 1858 at the age of 18 she decided she wanted to go to Queen's College to study. She was opposed by her parents but is supposed to have won them over by going into a fit of hysterics. She was delighted to be there: 'I am as happy as a queen. Work and independence! What can be more charming?'[1] She was also happy to be immersed in a female environment: 'I believe I love women too much ever to love a man.'[2]

She was soon offered a salaried post at the college teaching mathematics. Her parents objected strongly to her being *paid* for working, although she herself could not see why things should be different for her simply because of her sex. In the end she went along with her parents' wishes and declined payment for her teaching. She also taught book-keeping for the Society for Promoting the Employment of Women. In December 1860 she rented a house with her close friend Octavia Hill. However, their relationship was a stormy one and broke up the following October. It took a long time for Sophia to get over the separation, and she was plagued by bitter feelings of a great loss: 'We might have done *anything* together, we two.'[3]

She was filled with enthusiasm for earning her own living, for improving the standard of teaching in girls' schools, and for working together with other women to promote women's rights. In 1862 she went to Edinburgh to continue her education and, after corresponding with Elizabeth Garrett about the prospects for a medical education at Edinburgh, invited her up to see for herself. At this stage she was seen by the small circle of feminists as 'one of the band' and was being urged by Emily Davies and Elizabeth Garrett to study for an arts degree.[4]

Throughout the early 1860s she was working on a vague plan to open a college for girls and went to Germany to study the state of girls' education there. She persuaded an institute in Mannheim to take her on as a teacher, and wrote to her mother of her 'intense exaltation and delight at literally *earning my bread* – something like "My First Penny", you know.'[5]

Sophia Jex-Blake's visit to the United States

In May 1865 she went to the United States to study women's education there. She stayed in Boston with Dr Lucy Sewall, who had been inspired by Elizabeth Blackwell and was now resident physician at the New England Hospital for Women and Children, which was run entirely by women for women and children. Through Lucy Sewall she made contact with the community of medical women in Boston and saw the extensive practical and emotional support given to them by local feminists, particularly through the New England Women's Club and Lucy Stone's *Women's Journal*. She described her time in Boston in a letter to her mother:

> But can't you understand how refreshing it is to slip into
> the bright life of all these working people . . . It reminds
> me of the full colour and life of the old London times
> when all we working women were together.[6]

She was able to observe the fruits of a campaign for women doctors whose strength owed a lot to the backing of the local women's community, and this may have affected her approach later on to campaigning in Britain. Whereas Elizabeth Garrett's role model had been Elizabeth Blackwell, who had experience of opening up the medical profession through her own solo efforts, Sophia Jex-Blake's role model was Lucy Sewall and the women's community in Boston.

In 1867 she published a book called *A Visit to Some American*

Schools and Colleges.[7] However, she was becoming convinced of the need for women doctors and attracted to the idea of following a medical career herself. She confessed that she was 'getting desperately in love with medicine as a science and as an art'.[8] She decided to stay on for a while in Boston with Lucy Sewall and to help her with her work at the hospital.

After returning to England accompanied by Lucy Sewall, to talk things over with her parents, she decided to enrol as a medical student, first at the New England Hospital and later at the Massachusetts General Hospital. She and a friend, Susan Dimock, then tried to enter Harvard University. In their letter of application they quoted Harvard's own declared intention to open the doors of the seats of learning to all seekers after the truth. However, they were refused on the grounds that there was no provision for women students. In March 1868 she joined Elizabeth and Emily Blackwell in New York where they were setting up the Women's Medical College of the New York Infirmary. In the autumn she enrolled as a student at the college.

'Medicine as a Profession for Women'

In November she returned to Britain because of her father's death and spent the winter of 1868–9 at home with her mother. In January she approached Josephine Butler, who had been actively involved in setting up public lecture courses for women through the North of England Council for the Higher Education of Women, and who was very interested in the possibility of opening up the medical profession to women. She had received medical treatment from Elizabeth Garrett. Sophia described her as 'the head of the non-Davies party among the women', a reference to the debate currently simmering among feminists over whether or not to accept offers of a special examination system for women at Cambridge University. Emily Davies was determined not to accept the offers because this would inevitably be seen as inferior. Sophia summed up the opposing approach in a letter to Lucy Sewall: 'Mrs Butler and I say, "Take all you can get and then ask for more," don't you?'[9]

When Macmillan, the publisher, suggested to Josephine Butler that she edit an anthology of essays about feminism she decided she wanted to include an entry on medical women. As a result,

Sophia Jex-Blake wrote an essay entitled 'Medicine as a Profession for Women' which was included in the book, *Women's Work and Women's Culture*, published in 1869. This essay was reprinted in 1872 along with an account of the struggles at Edinburgh in her book *Medical Women: A Thesis and a History*.[10]

In this essay she included a detailed historical survey of medical women to prove that women had traditionally been seen as the healers in society.[11] She cited extensive evidence to show that before the eighteenth century it was mainly women who were responsible for healing. This primary involvement in health care was gradually eroded by the development of the voluntary hospital, the rise of the male medical profession, and a growing division between (male) doctoring and (female) nursing. She attributed the rise of 'man-midwifery' to the introduction of the forceps and referred to the establishment in that period of a male monopoly over scientific knowledge of anatomy, physiology and medical treatment. She accused 'learned men' of preventing others from gaining access to their knowledge.[12]

In a letter to Josephine Butler about the essay one male reader remarked particularly how this section showed that the exclusion of women from medicine was 'a modern usurpation by the male sex'.[13] Josephine herself commented to Sophia on the way the historical section had particularly struck her:

It gives one strongly the impression while reading it, how much the present male monopoly of the profession is an innovation.[14]

This consciousness of deliberate exclusion from the medical profession gave a radical and uncompromising edge to arguments for entry. It made women determined not to be bought off with an offer of limited entry: they were asking for no favours from men but rather demanding the reinstatement of traditional rights.

Sophia Jex-Blake's views on the history of women in medicine were held by other women too. An entry in 1853 in the diary of Margaretta Grey, Josephine Butler's aunt, is a good example:

I have always regretted that [women] have suffered the whole of the medical offices, with the knowledge and applications of simples, which used to lie in the province of mothers of families, to pass out of their hands, and that the practice of midwifery, so obviously appropriate to women, should be given up by them. Medical men in want of occupation lay claim to this as a province of theirs and decry all household dabbling in medicine as derogatory to science.[15]

Sophia Jex-Blake's essay also explored the idea that the desire for women doctors might come from women seeing medical examination by a male doctor as a physical invasion. She pointed out that all patients would of course prefer attendance by a qualified doctor. So long as women were excluded from proper medical training and qualifications, this meant that even women patients might continue to prefer to be treated by men. This did not necessarily mean that they would not, above all, prefer a fully-trained woman doctor.[16]

However, she and the campaign could not afford to do anything to alienate potential support from the profession and she stopped short of accusing medical men of incompetence or misconduct. In fact she was at pains to defend the behaviour of 'the gentlemen of the medical profession' and emphasised that women doctors were needed only because of women's feelings of modesty, and not because of the behaviour of medical men. It is clear from other remarks made in this essay and elsewhere that Sophia Jex-Blake in fact believed that many women suffered at the hands of incompetent and inexperienced medical men.

Another argument she used in favour of female entry was that women doctors would greatly increase medical knowledge about women. The ignorance of the profession on the subject of women's health and female diseases throughout most of the century would shock the modern observer. For example, well into the twentieth century it was believed that the 'safe period' for sexual intercourse was in the middle of the cycle, exactly, as we now know, at the time of ovulation. Specific training in the medical care of women was inadequate. There was a good deal of debate during the 1860s and 70s about possible changes in medical education to include more on obstetrics, gynaecology and midwifery. However, midwifery was not made a compulsory part of the medical curriculum in Britain until 1882, and as late as 1905 a committee reported that regulations on required clinical practice in midwifery for medical students were not being observed.[17]

Sophia Jex-Blake started making enquiries about possibilities for the medical education of women at universities in Britain, and Josephine Butler wrote to a number of university professors on her behalf. One reply she received was from David Masson, Professor of English at Edinburgh. He and Sir James Simpson, the famous surgeon, were keen to see Sophia Jex-Blake try for a medical degree at Edinburgh but were not optimistic about the prospect of success. Sophia also went to Elizabeth Garrett for advice but was told bluntly 'Frankly, I think you not specially suited.'[18] Elizabeth Garrett and Sophia Jex-Blake, the two foremost figures in the struggle for entry to the medical profession in Britain, had very different personalities and were to have a number of public disagreements on a variety of issues in the years to follow.

Along with other professional women, Elizabeth Garrett was anxious that in order to avoid damage to the cause, only those women who would be sure of succeeding should be encouraged to try a career. In her early days at the Middlesex Hospital she had written to Emily Davies about what she saw as the dangers of opening a medical college to women, in case the wrong kind of woman decided to enrol. She thought it was better in her position as an unrecognised student to be on her own. When another woman showed an interest in joining her, she expressed doubts that her nerves would stand up to it.[19] The need to prove women equally competent meant not only were pioneer women under intense pressure to be successful themselves but that they felt the need to police other women and, if necessary, to make sure some women were excluded.

All the possible routes to a medical degree seemed impassable. Elizabeth Garrett had herself been rebuffed by Edinburgh and St Andrews; Sophia Jex-Blake was advised that there was no point in attempting to persuade the medical board or senate at Edinburgh; and, although there was a good deal of sympathy at various colleges of London University, any move to admit women to medical study was blocked by the medical elite at the London teaching hospitals. Josephine Butler summed up the problem of medical opposition when she wrote in a letter to

Sophia, '. . . the MDs will be the obstacle. They hang together so.' She continued with the advice that Sophia should try for a degree at Edinburgh or else on the continent, and was full of encouragement: 'I wish you were an MD. You would have plenty of patients at once – myself among the number.'[20]

Sophia decided to follow up the possibility of a medical degree course at the University of Edinburgh. She was now 29 years old, the same age that Elizabeth Garrett had been when she qualified four years earlier. In her book *Medical Women* she said she chose Edinburgh because of its reputation for freedom from ecclesiastical influence and other constraints. The choice may also have been influenced by the fact that she had already attended lectures for women in 1862 in Edinburgh. Also Edinburgh had a flourishing Ladies Educational Association. The association had been founded in the autumn of 1867 with the object of securing a university education for women and, in the meantime, to establish 'a high-class lecture scheme'. In its first two years of existence, a total of six hundred women attended lectures on English literature, experimental physics, and logic and metaphysics.[21]

The approach to Edinburgh

In February Sophia Jex-Blake wrote to Lucy Sewall and told her that her close friend Ursula Du Pre wanted to study medicine too but was prevented by her mother's 'great prejudice and very bad health'.[22] In March she travelled north on her own, carrying introductions to certain men who were to prove to be among her staunchest allies during the following years. Among her introductions was one to Sir James Simpson who had long been sympathetic to the cause of medical women. In the late 1850s Emily Blackwell had received a testimonial from him in which he agreed that:

> It is evidently a matter of the utmost importance that
> female physicians should be fully and perfectly educated.[23]

However, he was now very old and died the following spring without being able to do much to help. Alexander Russel, the editor of *The Scotsman*, gave her a great deal of support, both on a personal level and through the pages of the newspaper, during her four years in Edinburgh. Later he married one of the women medical students, the widowed Mrs Evans. The other important link she made was with David Masson, who had written to Josephine Butler in support of medical women. He was already involved with the movement to promote higher education for women, having given a lecture to 400 women for the Edinburgh Ladies' Educational Association in April 1868. He gave unconditional support to the cause and fought hard within the university itself for women's right to a medical education.

David Masson gave her a letter of introduction to Professor George Balfour, Dean of the Medical Faculty, and she wrote to him formally asking for entry to the medical degree course, referring to 'the increasing demand for the medical service of women among their own sex'.[24] Professor Balfour agreed to allow her to attend some of the summer classes and to bring her case before the faculty as a whole. There seemed to be no problems with her attending lectures at this stage. Some of the professors' wives offered to accompany her to classes and the male students said they would welcome her. This was in marked contrast to the reception she and her companions were to have in the following three years.

Throughout this time she was corresponding regularly with her two friends, Lucy Sewall and Ursula Du Pre. Ursula had been prevented from joining Sophia and had to content herself with hearing all the details by letter: 'Tell me everything that happens so that I may not lose the thread of your history.'[25] However, in August she went up to Edinburgh on a visit, to Sophia's great joy. Later that year she wrote, 'If only I could be with you!'[26]

In April the issue of medical education for women was raised at the University Court, one of the governing bodies of the university which had on it six representatives from the university and two from the city of Edinburgh. The other two governing bodies of the university, which also played crucial roles in the struggle to gain entry, were the Senate, made up of the professors from each faculty, and the General Council, membership of which was open to all graduates of the university. On this occasion the University Court declared they were not opposed to the medical education of women in principle but were forced

to postpone the matter indefinitely because they were not prepared to make special arrangements for one woman. The wording of this resolution implied that they might look favourably
on an application from a group of women.

Robert Christison, the only medical professor on the court,
was the bitterest opponent of the women throughout the campaign in Edinburgh and no doubt used his influence in this early
attempt to block Sophia Jex-Blake's entry. He had graduated
from the university in 1819 and had been a professor there since
1822. He was by now a respected member of the profession
and later, in 1871, he was made a baronet. Sophia Jex-Blake
described calling on him in these early days only to be told 'that
the decision was entirely decided in his own mind, and that it
was useless for me to enter upon it.'[27]

She also described her approach to Andrew Wood:

> I asked Dr Wood to favour me with five minutes'
> conversation, to which his reply was that he would rather
> not, and turned on his heel and pursued a conversation
> with other persons in the room.[28]

Laycock, another professor in the faculty, declared his early
opposition, saying that he 'could not imagine *any decent woman*
wishing to study medicine – as for *any lady, that* was out of
the question'.[29]

The lukewarm response of the University Court was also
influenced by the submission of a petition from 180 male medical students. They claimed that the attendance of a woman at
classes would force the professors to modify their lectures, leaving out anything which might offend, and that consequently the
mass of students would suffer. The university authorities were
worried about the possibility of student disturbances, and this
factor worked against the women on this and future occasions.
A report in the *Englishwoman's Review* the following January
suggested that the petition had not originated with the students
themselves and, in the light of future occasions when opponents
within the faculty made use of student hostility for their own
ends, it is quite possible that Professor Christison, at least, had
a hand in its production.[30]

In 1869 the *Lancet* was full of letters from outraged Edinburgh graduates, calling on graduates and undergraduates to

resist the threat. One correspondent wrote that the admission of women to degree courses would 'degrade the university, and sacrifice our interests'. Another condemned the university for not 'upholding its professional dignity'.[31] The reputation of each medical school was of great importance to its graduates in the scramble for career advancement in a highly competitive and prestige-conscious profession. This meant that, when women tried to gain entry to any college, hospital or university, the protest from the medical profession was led by male graduates of that particular institution. One letter to the *Lancet* ended with the following call:

> I hope, in conclusion, that all such graduates of the
> Edinburgh University as are anxious to see maintained
> the old *prestige* [author's italics] of their school, will stir
> in this matter.[32]

This was to be a common cry from 1869 onwards. The male medical profession were now less concerned about the specific danger that women would seek to work as unqualified practitioners and more worried about women gaining full professional status. Doctors and medical students began to concentrate their protests on the supposed devaluation of medical qualifications as a result of female entry.

In April Sophia wrote to her friend Lucy about tactics:

> I am sure you are right about women being fitter to
> understand women. I will put in some more about that.
> Do you know whenever it comes home to me personally
> I am more and more amazed how women *can* go to men
> for uterine treatment. I think that, sooner than go to any,
> I would come across the Atlantic again to you . . . I wish
> Dr. Cabot or some leading doctor would publish a
> pamphlet or something expressing his strong belief in the
> '*need* of women doctors for young girls'. This is the point
> that hits the public hardest, I think.[33]

On David Masson's advice, Sophia Jex-Blake now set out to persuade the university authorities to agree to matriculation (enrolment at the university) on the following terms: that she could find other women to join her as students and that she could arrange for enough professors to give separate lectures to them. She herself was already preparing for the matriculation examination. The required standard in Latin was quite high but she welcomed this 'because it will keep out ignorant and silly women to a great degree'.[34]

She advertised in *The Times* on 28 July[35] for interested women to contact her and was soon joined by Isabel Thorne and Matilda Chaplin, Edith Pechey and Helen Evans. Edith Pechey, the youngest of the five at only 24, was the daughter of a Baptist minister who had an MA degree from Edinburgh. Isabel Thorne and Matilda Chaplin had studied at the Female Medical College. Isabel Thorne had been practising as a midwife since her graduation from the college in 1867, and had also taken the preliminary examination at Apothecaries' Hall. She had been on the point of going to Paris to continue her medical studies when Sophia Jex-Blake's advert appeared. A year later the five were joined by Mary Anderson, Elizabeth Garrett's future sister-in-law, and Emily Bovell. In her book Sophia refers to herself and the other six women as 'the so-called "Septem contra Edinam" ' ('Seven against Edinburgh').[36]

Edith Pechey's initial reply to the advertisement in *The Times* contained the following passage:

> Before deciding finally to enter the medical profession, I should like to feel sure of success — not on my own account, but I feel that failure now would do harm to the cause, and that it is well that at least the first few women who offer themselves as candidates should stand above the average of men in their examinations.[37]

From now on the university could no longer claim that it would be 'inexpedient' to make special arrangements for one woman. The strongest argument against allowing women to study medicine which now remained was that mixed classes would harm moral standards and the interests of the male students. In an attempt to remove this objection Sophia Jex-Blake contacted the professors to try to persuade them to teach the women students in separate classes, but met with a disappointing response.

The new proposals to allow matriculation passed the Medical Faculty, Senate and University Court in July and the women proceeded to work towards the entrance examinations. The proposals were finally approved with a large majority at the General Council meeting on 29 October, and by the Chancellor on 12 November. Later that month they were incorporated as regulations in the University Calendar (its constitution). All five women matriculated easily; four of them were among the best seven candidates out of a total of 152 men and women. They also had their names entered on a register of all medical students kept by the General Medical Council. The five were now the first women undergraduates at any British university.

Sophia's brother wrote to her to say how pleased he was about the news from Edinburgh. His letter gives an interesting insight into the response from a man who was not motivated to support medical women from any particular commitment to feminism:

> I am very glad that you are on the medical rails. They are
> real and solid and really lead somewhere. There is more
> specialty about them than in the somewhat vague
> education line. They belong to an old strong well-paid
> profession. They tend to the alleviation of intense human
> misery; and that for a large number of delicate cases
> women when properly trained are the right physicians I
> have felt for years and feel increasingly.[38]

While the university had formally agreed in writing to 'the education of women in medicine', the authorities were very careful to make the distinction between women studying for the profession and those studying out of amateur interest. This strongly suggests that they envisaged that certain women would be educated to be full medical practitioners.

However, the extent of this commitment was to be fiercely challenged in the next three years. In 1884 a history of the university was published, written by Alexander Grant, who had been the Principal of the university during this period.[39] In it he claimed that the number of medical students had been unusually low over the winter of 1869–70 and that this was why many of the medical professors had agreed to give classes to women, as they had time on their hands. He also claimed that the professors who refused were those who had large practices and therefore had no need of the extra income. It appears to have been 'expedient' for some of these medical men to allow women access to a university medical education.

The winter terms

There was extensive coverage in the autumn issues of the *Lancet* of the events in Edinburgh, most of it hostile and the rest patronising and trivialising. There was a recurring insistence that the claim that women wanted to be able to consult women doctors was unfounded: 'Women hate one another, often at first sight, with a rancour of which men can form only a faint conception . . .'[40]

In December the *Lancet* reported an article from the *Philadelphia Press* in which medical women were assumed to be an established fact. Commenting on this assumption, the *Lancet* declared, 'To us, in London, who see only rare examples of the species, this is very droll.'[41] The report then proceeded to debate the relative merits of proposed terms of address such as 'doctrix' and 'doctress'. The *Lancet*'s attempt to dismiss medical women as an amusing irrelevance contrasted with a calm letter from Elizabeth Garrett in September in which she stated that the Edinburgh decision had now settled the question of the medical education of women and announced the award of two scholarships each of £50 for three years, to be competed for in the following June.[42]

Successive letters to the *Lancet* declared that women were constitutionally unfitted for the hard work and responsibilities of medical practice and women doctors would have to remain unmarried because no man would allow his wife to work.[43] It was said that the problem of 'surplus women' should be solved not by introducing unfair competition into a male profession but by arranging for these women to emigrate. A review of John Stuart Mill's *On the Subjection of Women* in the *Lancet* in October declared that, if women were allowed into male occupations, there would be unemployment among men and fewer marriages.[44]

It was generally believed that middle-class men of all occupations were already being forced to leave the country to find work in the colonies because there was no suitable employment for them in Britain, and this was one of the strongest arguments used against any extension of middle-class women's employment opportunities.[45] Since all women's work was traditionally low in status and remuneration, the contemporary fear was that the entry of women would substantially cheapen the male middle-class job market.

There was a strong belief among medical men that *their* profession in particular was underpaid and overcrowded and they feared that women would steal valuable patients and undercut fees, especially in obstetrics and gynaecology. During her initial applications to medical schools in the United States in 1847, Elizabeth Blackwell had come across the following reply from one professor: 'You cannot expect me to furnish you with a stick to break our heads with'.[46] At least two doctors in Edinburgh complained that the women medical students would ruin their sons' chances of a professional career.[47]

During the first winter at Edinburgh a meeting was held on 17 January in support of women's suffrage. Many professional men who were present were strong supporters of the women medical students: Sir David Wedderburn MP, Duncan McLaren MP, Professor Masson and Professor Kelland. A few of their enemies were there too, for instance Alexander Grant and Lyon Playfair MP. The Edinburgh Committee for Women's Suffrage, made up entirely of women, included Mrs McLaren as president, Agnes McLaren (who was later to take a medical degree herself) as one of the secretaries, and Elizabeth Pease Nichol, who played a prominent part in one famous scene involving the women medical students.

The Times reported that the separate classes laid on for the women students by Sophia Jex-Blake cost the women four guineas each, or more if the classes were too small.[48] They had to guarantee 100 guineas for each class in the first year and Sophia had to borrow a great deal of money from her mother to pay her own fees and to help out her less well-off companions. The financial burden of seeking a medical education was always to be an important factor in the campaign. Success for the campaign was dependent on the personal wealth of individual upper-middle-class and upper-class women, particularly Sophia Jex-Blake herself.

They were still faced with the problem of getting enough lecturers to give separate classes, and had to deal with the virulent hostility of much of the medical profession. However, they were treated with courtesy by those teachers who did agree to lecture to them. They were able to work steadily through the winter without being distracted by any major battles and did well in their examinations in the spring. All five women got prizes in botany and four of the five were in the honours list in chemistry and physiology. This academic success could only be matched by about 30 of the 140 male students.

The Contagious Diseases Acts

During the winter of 1869/70, at the same time as these five women were embarking on a medical education at Edinburgh University, a major feminist campaign was launched to fight the Contagious Diseases (CD) Acts. This legislation set up a system of state regulation of prostitution under which women in certain areas could be designated 'common prostitutes' by the police and made to undergo compulsory periodical medical examinations, with the threat of a prison sentence if they refused. The fight against this intervention in the lives of prostitutes and other working-class women is one of the most important chapters in late nineteenth-century feminism.[49] It was also of particular significance for the campaign for women's entry to the medical profession.

The first Contagious Diseases Act, passed in 1864, aroused relatively little opposition as its measures applied only to certain military and naval centres. The only public protest in the early stages came in 1863 with a series of letters to the *Daily News* from the feminist Harriet Martineau, in which she condemned the state regulation of prostitution. The scope of the legislation was extended by subsequent Acts in 1866 and 1868 and opposition to the legislation grew accordingly. In 1866 a group of Baptist and other nonconformist ministers approached the government to warn about the effects of the Acts. In 1867 M. Berkeley Hill, a specialist in venereology and secretary of the extensionist association, approached Daniel Cooper of the Rescue Society of London to enlist his support in favour of the Acts and to invite him to join in agitating for extension to cities in the north of England. Alarmed by this approach, Cooper organised a meeting of rescue societies in London who went on to produce a series of pamphlets in the following two years *against* the Acts. The societies also distributed a 'Memorandum of Objections' to members of both Houses of Parliament, and to members of the Church of England clergy and nonconformist ministers. However, this had little effect and the 1869 amendments further extending the legislation went through.

At the same time there was an organised campaign *in favour* of the Acts. An association was formed to press for the extension of the Acts to more civilian areas. It had many local branches, and members included the Vice Chancellors of Oxford and Cambridge and many men high up in the Church of England hierarchy. The association relied heavily on the *British Medical Journal*, the *Lancet* and local medical organisations for its publicity. Powerful medical men, such as Sir William Jenner, Sir James Paget, Henry Acland (Regius Professor of Medicine, Oxford University) and the Presidents of the Royal College of Physicians and the Royal College of Surgeons, gave evidence in favour of extension to the House of Lords Select Committee in 1868.

Although many individual medical men, particularly general practitioners in the Midlands and the north of England, were involved in campaigns against the Acts, it seems that the medical establishment was firmly in favour. However, those medical men actively involved in the extension campaign tended not to be from the London elite but rather were reforming doctors and those with direct experience of working-class health problems. They were often also in the National Association for the Promotion of Social Science and very close on other political issues to their feminist and civil libertarian opponents over the Acts. They also included some supporters of medical women.

In September 1869 two Nottingham doctors, Charles Bell Taylor and Charles Worth, took the issue to the annual Social Science Congress in Bristol. Their papers against extension were opposed by M. Berkely Hill and by Paul Swain, who spoke of what he saw as the successful application of the Acts in Devonport where he was a hospital doctor. According to the local paper, the ensuing debate was a 'bear garden'. Women were excluded from this particular session of the congress, although Elizabeth Blackwell was allowed to attend on account of her medical status. Eventually the audience, made up mainly of doctors and clergymen, voted two to one in favour of the National Association for the Promotion of Social Science launching a campaign to protest about the Acts. The next day a meeting was held and the National Association for the Repeal of the Contagious Diseases Acts was formed.

As women were excluded from this meeting too, a parallel organisation, the Ladies National Association, was formed. One of the women who had attended the congress was Elizabeth Wolstenholme, a headmistress from Manchester. In December she made contact with Josephine Butler who had been deeply involved in rescue work in Liverpool. By the end of December a general committee was established and a 'Ladies Protest' appeared in the *Daily News* in January signed by 124 feminists and women Quakers. In this they condemned the Acts for infringing the civil liberties of women, punishing women for male vice, and setting up a system of prostitution, protected and sanctioned by the state.

Radical working-class men were also active in the campaign against the Acts. Although there is little documentary evidence, it is clear that there was a general suspicion of doctors among the working classes. In 1888 five prostitutes were murdered in Whitechapel, giving rise to the mythical figure 'Jack the Ripper'.[50] Because of the sexual mutilation of the bodies, one popular theory was that the murderer was a mad doctor. This belief revealed the anger felt within working-class communities towards (middle-class) doctors, which was heightened during this period by the profession's proposals for compulsory vaccination.

Although working-class women attended meetings in the early days of the campaign, Butler was disappointed that this involvement was short lived. There had been a general decline in the participation of working-class women in radical politics in the mid nineteenth century, compared with the days of Chartist and Anti-Poor Law agitation of the 1830s.[51] Also the aims and organisation of later Victorian campaigns such as that against the CD Acts were defined and controlled by middle-class radicals. Although middle-class women campaigners did encourage prostitutes to protest against the Acts and provide legal services to them, the relationship between these groups of women was shaped by class differences. Similarly, in the campaign for medical women, there was both strong female solidarity, against the activities of middle-class professional men, *and* class condescension from middle-class women towards working-class women.

There was a small but active medical campaign for repeal, with approximately four per cent of all doctors in 1872 signing a petition against the Acts.[52] These came mainly from the Midlands and the north. Nevertheless, the medical profession were in general fully in favour of the Acts and remained the strongest opponents to the campaign for repeal. This is not surprising, given their vested interests in the Acts as a source of professional fees, their general opposition to feminist issues and, indeed, the hostility towards them from campaigners. In a letter to a friend written in 1875, Josephine Butler wrote the following about her own experience of medical antagonism:

> The only really *vicious* and *unfair* and *stupid* opposition
> I have met with in all the meetings abroad has been from
> *English doctors* who come to the meetings with large
> bundles of the *Lancet* under their arms. Stupid geese![53]

Campaigners pointed out that the system created by the Acts provided a large number of lucrative jobs for male doctors. In particular they attacked the increasing scope for prestige and remuneration in the expanding profession of state medical officers, which they saw as an ominous alliance of state power and medical professional control.

Hostility towards male doctors from middle-class women rose to new heights during the campaign against the Acts. The involvement of doctors in carrying out state regulation of prostitutes was seen as a vast conspiracy aimed at the medical supervision of women's lives. Feminist campaigners accused male doctors of seeking to cure women of venereal disease only to return them to the 'sexual market' to satisfy men's sexual demands. The language used in campaign literature and in private letters makes it clear that they saw the compulsory medical examination of prostitutes as a violation of women's bodily integrity, bordering on sexual assault. They talked of 'medical lust of handling and dominating women' as a major motive for the examining doctors, and referred to the speculum used by doctors to examine women as a 'steel penis'.[54]

The Shield, the weekly journal of the Ladies National Association, used words such as 'tyranny' and 'inquisition' to describe the examinations. The tone of this extract from an article which appeared in an issue of *The Shield* in June 1870 is typical:

> Encouraged by the temporary success of their secretly hatched and stealthily developed plot for the sanitary supervision, alias the enslavement, of the women of the country, some medical men are now propounding still more daring schemes.[55]

Such views are made more explicit in this passage from one of Josephine Butler's letters to a male friend in 1872:

> It is coming to be more and more a deadly fight on the part of us women for *our bodies*; if these doctors could be forced to keep their hateful hands off us, there would be *an end* to laws which protect vice and to many other evils.[56]

The logical conclusion to seeing the gynaecological examination and treatment of women by male doctors as a form of sexual violence was that women had to be allowed full entry to the medical profession. In a letter to *The Shield*, Maria Firth, who was active in midwifery campaigns, described 'man-midwifery' as 'the root of the tree from whence these unscriptural Acts have sprung'. The unnatural intrusion of men into the medical care of women was accepted only through the 'immoral teaching of doctors'. She attacked male medical intervention in childbirth:

> [They] consider that the often slow, but sure, physiological process of labour, may be mended by the common use of instruments, invented by their so-called scientific skill, as if men could improve on the handiwork of the Almighty![57]

She called on all women involved in the campaign, particularly wealthy women, to insist on being attended by women in childbirth and to support the medical women movement.

The Shield attacked the male medical profession for providing scientific justification for male promiscuity, and echoed Elizabeth Blackwell in stressing the importance of female access to medical and scientific knowledge as a crucial weapon in challenging medical men's use of their scientific authority 'to support indecent and immoral legislation'.[58] *The Shield* highlighted the contradictions in what medical men were saying: on the one hand they resisted female entry to the profession largely on the grounds of decency; on the other hand they were calling for the extension of the medical examination of prostitutes, under which system hundreds of women were being degraded.

Medical women and the CD Acts

The historic session at the Social Science Congress in September 1869 on venereal disease was attended by Elizabeth Blackwell who had returned to England in the summer. She felt her pioneer work in the United States was ended, with women's colleges established in Boston, New York and Philadelphia, and women now accepted into some men's colleges. She set herself up in practice in London and began to devote her energies to the medical women movement in Britain.

As a student, she had worked in the women's syphilitic department of the Blockley Almshouses in Philadelphia and wrote the following in her diary:

> The world can never be redeemed until this central relation of life is placed on a truer footing. I feel specially called to act in the reform, when I have gained wisdom for the task.[59]

She had since then written a good deal on the sexual oppression of women and on one occasion stressed to her sister Emily that 'the relation of the sexes' was 'particularly our duty'.[60] As a result of attending the Social Science Congress she wrote how 'my eyes were now suddenly opened, never to be closed again, to that direful purchase of women'.[61] She devoted much of her later life to feminist campaigns around prostitution, in particular against the Contagious Diseases Acts.

In 1881 she gave a lecture entitled 'Rescue Work in Relation to Prostitution and Disease' to an audience of women, in which she set out in detail her accumulated wisdom on this subject. She declared that all legislation on venereal disease must be based on the two fundamental principles of 'equal justice, and respect for individual rights'; it must respect 'the right of an adult over his or her own body' and cannot interfere with this right by enforcing medical examination and treatment. However, she believed that there was scope for legislation in order to stop one individual harming another. She suggested a law which would make it a criminal offence for one person to have sexual intercourse with another person if they have venereal disease. This would be a radical departure from legislation such as the CD Acts in that it would penalise women *and* men for passing on the disease rather than punishing prostitutes *only* for simply having the infection.[62]

The closed session at the congress was one of many occasions on which women doctors were the only women permitted to discuss 'delicate' issues in public. In 1876 Elizabeth Blackwell was unable to find a publisher for a manuscript entitled 'Counsel to Parents on the Moral Education of Their Children' until she changed the title to *The Moral Education of the Young, considered under Medical and Social Aspects*, to make it clear it was a *medical* work and that she was discussing these issues as a doctor rather than as a woman.[63] In the International Association for the Total Suppression of Vivisection, women were strongly discouraged from becoming involved in campaigns in public. The executive committee was exclusively male, but an exception was made for Anna Kingsford, again on account of her medical degree. Her companion and biographer, Edward Maitland, said that she, 'though a woman by her sex . . . was a man by her mind and her profession'.[63]

In so many situations women, except possibly older married and widowed upper-class women, were totally excluded from debates over moral issues unless they could claim a professional status. Thus, in breaking the male monopoly on medicine and science, women were also posing a fundamental challenge to the moral and political system under which *all* women were excluded from discussing such issues. Women doctors could now speak on behalf of women in a wide range of debates. Indeed, many women saw entry to medicine and to other professions not just as an end in itself but also as a better way to exert the moral influence of women to bring about social reforms.

Despite the obvious links between the campaign against the CD Acts and the campaign for female medical care for women, Elizabeth Blackwell was the only woman doctor active in the repeal campaign in Britain. Florence Nightingale was very hostile to the Acts from the very beginning but, as with her response to other feminist struggles, she was not enthusiastic about the campaign against the Acts. In contrast, many women doctors in the United States were deeply involved in campaigns against regulation in various states and sent letters of support to Josephine Butler. In a paper given in 1877, Dr Caroline Winslow explained how American women doctors were combining 'the moral and beneficent feminine element of character with the stern and inflexible laws of science' in campaigning against restrictive legislation in the United States and were amazed to hear that women doctors in Britain 'should so lack moral insight' as to support the Acts.[65]

Most medical women in Britain believed the Acts were a necessary evil. Elizabeth Garrett, in particular, was outspoken in her support of them. In January 1870 the *Pall Mall Gazette* published an article she had written entitled, 'An enquiry into the Character of the Contagious Diseases Acts of 1866–69'.[66] She saw many prostitutes who had become very ill because of their work and felt that compulsory hospital treatment was the only answer. In doing so, she alienated the Langham Place circle of feminists, her former political allies.[67]

Medical women were, of course, also reluctant to be too closely associated with a political movement which was implacably hostile to the medical profession. Some of those involved in the repeal campaign in Britain, for instance James Stansfeld MP, supported women doctors, despite knowing that they would be on the other side over the Acts. At the height of the campaign in Edinburgh Josephine Butler was asked whether her name could be added to the list of supporters of the women students. Despite the fact that she had been a keen supporter of Elizabeth Garrett and Sophia Jex-Blake in their medical careers in the 1860s, her reply was far from encouraging:

> You are welcome to use my own and my husband's names if you think they will do your cause any good. We cannot conceive that they would, and, on that ground alone, we should be as glad that you should not use them. It had better be left to Miss Jex-Blake's judgment.

All the world knows that we are on opposite sides on one

of the most vital questions of the day, and that the Medical ladies have no sympathy with the efforts being made to get rid of the scandal of a great State system of legalised Prostitution, and therefore it appears to Mr. Butler and me an inconsistency that our names should appear in any such adverse connexion, deeply as we desire the prosperity of the medical women movement.[66]

Sophia Jex-Blake replied, 'I shall most gladly avail myself of your permission . . . to use your names.'[67]

Most of those involved in the women's movement were equally wary of any association with a campaign which was arousing so much violent opposition and was so outspoken on matters of sex and morality. Women active in a wide range of political campaigns, such as girls' and women's education, women's suffrage and anti-vivisection, made a similar decision deliberately to dissociate themselves from the campaign against the CD Acts. It is interesting to see the range of responses to this dilemma from Elizabeth Garrett, her sister, and her cousin: Elizabeth believed that the Acts were a necessary evil; Millicent avoided the problem by not taking a stand on the issue; and Rhoda openly supported both the campaign against the Acts and the suffrage movement. In 1871 the London-based suffrage campaign was split in two by the issue, with the Central Committee of the National Society having links with the campaign against the Acts and the old London National Society insisting that all members stay completely free of any connection.

10 The Height of Battle in Edinburgh

The Hope affair

To return to the campaign in Edinburgh, in March 1870 the women students faced their first major rebuff. Edith Pechey came top in her year in the chemistry examination and should have been awarded the Hope Scholarship, which carried a cash prize and gave access to laboratory facilities. However, she was told she was ineligible and the prize was instead awarded to the male student who came second. It is ironic that the scholarship had been set up by Professor Hope from the proceeds of lectures in chemistry he had given to women in Edinburgh 50 years before in the face of considerable opposition. Furthermore he had lectured to James Barry, the army surgeon discovered on her death to be a woman. The faculty also refused to issue any of the women with certificates of attendance for the classes they had completed.

An alternative interpretation of the Hope incident comes in an account of the campaign at Edinburgh written by Frances Hoggan (*née* Morgan) in 1884.[70] She graduated from Zurich in 1870 and then joined Elizabeth Garrett at the New Hospital for Women. In the early 1870s she married George Hoggan, who had been a naval officer and had then decided out of personal interest to study for a medical degree at Edinburgh. He was at Edinburgh University at the time of the Hope affair and said the women students had been given *privileges* to study there but had no rights. He said they were ineligible for any prizes as they had only been attending a private class given by the chemistry professor, although this, of course, was only because they were not allowed into the main classes. He also went on to say that the greatest opposition to the women came in those classes where they were allowed to compete directly with the men, a comment which seems to condemn the behaviour of the male rather than the female students!

Frances Hoggan stated that it was 'want of tact or patience' which caused problems for the women students and that they would have aroused less opposition at Edinburgh if they had carried on their early 'policy of unobtrusively working on, claiming no distinctions, and sedulously and quietly avoiding all occasions of rivalry between the sexes, which led to such marked success at Zurich . . . and in Paris'. Elizabeth Garrett also was increasingly concerned with the tactics of the women students and especially unhappy about what one historian of the medical women movement has called 'Sophia's indiscretions'.[71] She believed it was tactically advisable to seek a medical education, through the side door, as a *favour* from men to women rather than fighting for it as a right. Sophia Jex-Blake was temperamentally and politically opposed to this mode of operating: she wanted women to have the unchallengeable right to enter the medical profession by the front door.

The women appealed against both decisions. The Senate agreed to issue the certificates of attendance but not to reconsider the issue of the scholarship. As a result the university was heavily criticised in the national press, with *The Times*, the *Spectator* and even the *British Medical Journal*, among others, accusing it of gross injustice.[72] Sophia Jex-Blake quoted a bitingly clever parody of the medical paranoia from the *Daily Review*:

> . . . now it seems that the inferior sex are winning *our* scholarships over our most sacred heads. This is a matter which must be looked to. We will stand a great deal, but this is going a little too far; we must agitate. . . . We must have an Act for the repression of women . . . We must have a bill for the protection of the superior sex.[73]

The story of the Hope affair apparently also circulated through foreign universities and many people in Edinburgh were anxious about the damage this would do to the university's reputation.

The affair marked the beginning of the real campaign to remove the women from the university. There were accusations that they were studying medicine for indecent motives. At a meeting of the Edinburgh University General Council, reported in *The Times* in April, one of the professors in Edinburgh declared that no decent woman could possibly want to enter medicine and talked of the danger of a 'Magdalene' (a prostitute) coming to study. The women students, however, had the last laugh. A letter appeared in *The Times* the next day from 'An Inquisitive Woman' in which the writer queried what the danger might be:

> First, the idea of Magdalenes prosecuting medical studies seems to me a novelty, as they are not supposed to intrude elsewhere in Europe. Is there any special attraction for them in the Scotch Universities?[74]

The ready wit of this response suggests it might have been written by Sophia Jex-Blake.

With the launching in January of that year of the Ladies National Association, the women's organisation dedicated to campaigning against the Contagious Diseases Acts, men were beginning to express publicly the fear that medical women would use their professional status for political purposes. For instance, at the same meeting of the Edinburgh University General Council a speaker referred to the tendency of female doctors in the United States 'to become political and social economists rather than practical physicians, and in that capacity to discuss questions of morals'. This point, too, was picked up by 'An Inquisitive Woman'. She insisted that women's voice must be heard on these issues and that they had a right to influence legislation, especially over the issue of 'the moral pollution of so many thousands of their own sex'.[75] Despite the low profile which most women doctors and medical students kept over radical political issues such as the campaign against the CD Acts, women's access to professional knowledge and power were perceived by men as particularly threatening.

With medical opponents now overtly and actively campaigning against the women students, some of the professors started to withdraw their promises to lecture separately to them. In an attempt to find an alternative solution, David Masson proposed to the General Council that they be allowed into the ordinary classes with the other (male) students but the motion was defeated by 58 votes to 47 on the grounds that mixed classes were morally wrong. Commiserating with the women students, Masson commented, 'Christison . . . seems determined to get rid of you.'[76] Once again it was made clear that they were there on sufferance, not on equal terms with men. The issue of mixed classes was discussed at length in the national press in April and May and various suggestions were made about separate classes, separate colleges and separate diplomas. Elizabeth Garrett wrote to *The Times* on two occasions to reject these suggestions, pointing out that women refused to be fobbed off with an inferior education and useless qualification, and instead wanted full access to the profession.[77]

The issue of mixed classes

Opponents of medical women maintained that mixed classes were a 'violation' of the relations of the sexes and thus a threat to the whole social system. They claimed that the female students would be in moral danger and that the education of the male students would be adversely affected. A letter to the *Lancet* from 'Old Morality' referred to the impropriety of women training in men's wards where certain male diseases should not be witnessed by women, 'involving as it does a knowledge of vice and its practices'.[78]

However, the medical profession faced a dilemma in its opposition to mixed classes. Supporters of mixed classes returned again and again to the contention that discussions of even the most delicate subjects in front of an audience of men and women were quite acceptable, provided they were of a scientific nature. Medical men, who were desperately keen in this period to raise the prestige of the profession by insisting that medicine was a *science*, could not very well refute these arguments without weakening their own position.

Supporters of medical women pointed out that these same male students would later have to treat women with gynaecological and obstetrical problems, with the help of female nurses. They were ready to agree that the study and practice of medicine might involve unpleasant experiences which would shock women's feelings but they refused to accept this as an argument for excluding women. They believed that the facts of nature were sacred and that any unpleasantness was neutralised by the 'purity' of scientific knowledge. Theoretically, there should be no problems with men and women mixing in the dissecting room, in consultations or in scientific debates, where they met as fellow professionals.

Many supporters pointed out that other women were present in hospital wards at the same time as male medical students and that this never seemed to cause any problems. Sophia Jex-Blake received a letter while she was at Edinburgh from a woman who had trained as a surgical nurse. She had performed duties in female and male wards and attended operations with students present. She considered that she had 'enjoyed exactly the same opportunities that people profess to be so much shocked at your desiring to obtain in Edinburgh'.[79]

Also they believed that any feelings of embarrassment were justified by the resulting benefit: the relieving of the far greater unpleasantness suffered at present by all women attended by a male doctor. In an article written in the early 1880s, Mary Putnam Jacobi contrasted the 'superficial ideas of delicacy' used against co-education with the 'legitimate feelings of delicacy' of women who wanted to consult women doctors.[80]

Much of the writing on medicine as a profession for women was dominated by this debate over mixed versus separate classes. Supporters of the medical women movement were split on this issue. Many women insisted that there was little wrong with women and men studying together, as they were more concerned that exclusion from existing classes would mean that women students would be faced with far greater expense and would have to make do with inferior facilities. Other women stated publicly that separate classes were preferable. This latter view was probably influenced by the notorious behaviour of male medical students and their lecturers, behaviour which often amounted to sexual harasssment.

There is a wealth of evidence to show what women medical students had to face in mixed classes. Elizabeth Blackwell stated that her determination to open a women's medical college came directly from her experience of pain and embarrassment while studying alongside men at Geneva College.[81] Elizabeth Garrett attributed the problems she faced at the Middlesex Hospital to 'the vulgarity of other people'.[82] In late 1869 the *Lancet* carried a report from Philadelphia of women medical students being insulted during clinical teaching by male students and lecturers, 'who believe that the effectiveness of their own lecturing is dependent upon a plentiful seasoning of coarse jokes'.[83] It also printed a letter from a doctor suggesting that the women should simply be allowed 'to labour side by side with the funloving, masculine students'. If they carry on with their studies, he said, 'Nature . . . has made some mistake respecting them.'[84] Another correspondent queried Elizabeth Garrett's suggestion that daughters of medical men should seek a medical education by saying that medical men would not let their daughters study if they remembered 'the moral atmosphere of the dissecting-room'.[85] A medical student wrote to *The Scotsman* in December about one Edinburgh lecturer who went 'a long way beyond the requirements of scientific teaching – into the regions of "spicy" but indelicate narrative' and was greeted with cheers by the students.[86] In a similar vein, in an article in the periodical *Nineteenth Century* Margaret Lonsdale claimed that doctors opposed nursing reform because the 'presence of refined, intelligent women in the wards imposes a kind of moral restraint upon the words and ways of both doctors and students.'[87]

Had there been the option of an equal number of places for female and male students in separate but equally well-equipped and staffed courses, this would no doubt have met with women's unanimous approval. Faced with the certainty that this option would never be offered as long as men controlled medical education, they had to determine their stance on mixed classes on largely pragmatic grounds. Thus we find women on the one hand pushing for equal entry to male medical schools and on the other trying to build a system of separatist medical education. In both cases, they were clear that the sexual harassment of women students and objections to mixed classes on the grounds of morality were male devices used to exclude women from male privileges and from the public sphere in general.

At the same time as this debate was raging in Edinburgh over the issue of mixed classes, a member was thrown out of the Obstetrical Society for 'malpractices of a nature too cruel and abominable to allude to here' towards female patients. According to an article in the *Pall Mall Gazette* in April, statements read out during the debate were met with a good deal of laughter from the audience of society members. A letter to the *Gazette* from 'Medicus' stated that the incident would only further convince women of the need for women doctors. He was criticised in the *Lancet* for supposed inaccuracy and for raising the issue in a general circulation paper: the proper place for debate on *medical* issues was in a *medical* journal.[88]

For and against women doctors

Articles in *The Times* and the *Englishwoman's Review* in April called upon women to send petitions to Parliament to disprove the claim that women did not want women doctors, with an address from which petition forms could be obtained.[89] By May women were already sending in petitions to the House of Lords to prove the demand for women doctors among the 'wives and mothers of England'. Even the Female Medical Society seems to have been encouraged by the new political atmosphere to come out strongly in favour of women doctors, despite its previously cautious support for medical women. At a meeting of the society in May 1870, attended by a small number of members, mainly women, a resolution was adopted which stated, 'All medical degrees and licences to practise medicine should be open to candidates without distinction of sex.'[90]

A number of letters from women to newspapers and journals in the second half of 1870 were quoted extensively in an appendix in the 1886 edition of Sophia Jex-Blake's book, *Medical Women*.[91] These letters catalogued the 'number of wretched, broken-down sufferers from chronic disease', as a result of refusing to be treated by a male doctor or, even worse, in front of a crowd of male medical students. In January 1871 the *Englishwoman's Review* reported that in the 1870 session 80 petitions had been submitted to the House of Lords and 106 (with more than 6000 signatures) to the House of Commons.[92]

The medical journals at this time showed that the profession was increasingly worried that the campaign for women doctors was now threatening to disrupt the sexual division of labour within medicine. At the moment men held the positions of authority, responsibility and power, and women performed subordinate ancillary roles. In a letter to the *Lancet* in June a doctor claimed that women were 'sexually, constitutionally, and mentally unfitted' for the hard work of a physician or surgeon'.[93] In reply, Sophia Jex-Blake pointed out that nursing and midwifery involved far more strenuous labour and, with characteristic sarcasm, suggested that the real reason behind this attempt to divert women from professional practice lay in the doctor's reference to the 'least remunerative' area of medicine:

> In the last adjective seems to lie the whole suitability of the division of labour according to the writer's view. He evidently thinks that women's capabilities are nicely graduated to fit 'half-guinea midwifery cases' and that all patients paying a larger sum of necessity need the superior powers of the 'male mind of the Caucasian race'. Let whatever is well-paid be left to the man; then chivalrously abandon the badly remunerated work to the woman.[94]

She refused to be drawn into arguments over women's intellectual ability and asked instead that women be tested according to the same standards as men and either accepted or rejected on the basis of this.

In the following years, articles and letters in the *Lancet* returned repeatedly to this theme of the proper sexual division of labour within medicine. It was stated that 'women's sphere of usefulness in the healing art should certainly be limited to the carrying out of the desires and implicitly obeying the dictates of . . . medical men'.[95] Doctors claimed that woman's role was as helpmate, to 'sustain, succour, revive' men.[96] They rejected the argument that, if women could be nurses, they could also be doctors:

> In the one character she is as awkward, unfit, and untrustworthy, as she is at home, capable, and thoroughly worthy of confidence in the other.[97]

One report suggested that women were perfectly suited to certain routine jobs in public service, which men find 'so irksome'.[98] In trying to channel women into nursing and midwifery, medical men claimed that women were perfectly suited to caring for others but were not able to 'master the secrets . . . of nature'.[99] In her biography of Edith Pechey, Edythe Lutzker includes this quote as typical of the views of opponents to medical women:

God sent women to be ministering angels, to soothe the
pillow, administer the palliative, whisper words of
comfort to the tossing sufferer. Let that continue woman's
work. Leave the physician's function, the scientific lore,
the iron wrist and iron will to men.[100]

As for nursing, the power and authority of the (male) doctor
was becoming firmly established, with the growth of professional confidence and the strengthening of the scientific medical model. Nurses were confirmed as the 'domestic servants' of
medicine under the strict control of doctors. They were therefore
forced to turn to the only possible source of power – internal
control over their own profession. In order to establish the
principle of self-regulation and guard against interference from
the medical profession, they had to exaggerate the differences
between what they saw as the two distinct professions of doctoring and nursing, curing and caring. Thus they effectively confirmed the sexual division of labour within medicine by which
men held the intellectual power and overall control and women
were relegated to a subordinate, low status position.

The profession made explicit its sexist assumptions about
access to scientific knowledge in a leading article in the *Lancet*:
in August 1875:

Obstetrics has only comparatively recently been rescued
from the midwives and the 'sages-femmes', and is just
beginning to enjoy a scientific reputation as a result of the
labour of many intelligent and enlightened observers. Shall
we, then, again consign it to the dark regions from which
it has just been snatched.[101]

It was not only women who posed a threat to these medical
men. They saw medical science as the domain of white men
only and felt deeply threatened by any attempt by anyone else
to enter it. In the letter to the *Lancet* where it was claimed that
women were 'unfitted' for medical work, the correspondent
argued that the main feature of the Caucasian (i.e. white) race
was the power of its male members of scientific discovery. In
the United States black men were trying to enter medical schools
at the same time as white women were and they met with a
similar level of opposition. Medical men in Britain and the

United States saw the profession as a white, male preserve and were fighting to keep it that way.

The first approach to the Royal Infirmary

In Edinburgh a temporary solution was being worked out. The professor of natural history agreed to continue giving parallel lectures to the women but the professor of botany said he was too ill to do the same. In order to gain access to classes in this subject, the women students then approached the extra-mural school. The school provided lectures to medical students outside the university to prepare them for the licence examinations of the Royal College of Surgeons, Edinburgh, and the Royal College of Physicians, Edinburgh. In 1855 regulations were introduced whereby up to four extra-mural classes could count towards university graduation. This was after a protracted legal struggle between the Town Council and the Medical Faculty which reached the House of Lords.

In July the nine extra-mural lecturers formally agreed that women should be allowed into the existing classes (for male students). The extra-mural lecturer in botany agreed to let them attend his class, although he had to deny reports that he was modifying his lectures for their benefit. The lecturers in anatomy and clinical instruction, Handyside and Heron Watson, refused to give *parallel* lectures to the women but instead accepted them into their existing classes. In October a fresh attempt to gain access to classes at the university itself was narrowly defeated, by 47 votes to 46, at the General Council. The vote was heavily influenced by a decisive interjection from Professor Christison, in which he declared that Queen Victoria opposed mixed classes.

In the summer term the women students had again demonstrated their academic ability and their determination to study hard. Four of the five were on the honours list in chemistry and physics and all five were on the list in botany. Out of 140 men, this was matched by only 31, 25 and 32 students respectively.

In October it was reported in the *Englishwoman's Review* that a Mrs Leggett, the widow of an army officer, was attending lectures and studying in the dissecting room at a hospital in Dublin.[102] The following April she passed the preliminary examination at the Apothecaries' Hall of Ireland and enrolled as a medical student. However, by January 1874 the hospital had decided that it could not provide a medical education for women.

The seven women who were now studying at Edinburgh then approached the Royal Infirmary, referred to by Sophia Jex-Blake's biographer as 'the very stronghold of the enemy,' in order to secure clinical instruction.[103] Both Emily Blackwell in 1854 and Elizabeth Garrett in 1862 had made attempts to gain access to the women's wards but without success. Professor Hughes Bennett and Professor Heron Watson, who both lectured to the women at the extra-mural school, wrote to the board of managers to say that there were no problems associated with mixed classes. The women students also sent a letter to the board indicating that they had permission from three of the infirmary doctors to enter their wards for clinical instruction. The women said that there was no need for special arrangements and that they only needed formal permission to enter the infirmary.

Like the newer of the large teaching hospitals in London, the infirmary depended for its income on annual subscriptions from local firms and wealthy lay people. It was governed in the first instance by a board or committee elected annually by the subscribers to look after their interests. Although they were broadly sympathetic to the women's request, the board was under pressure from the medical staff at the hospital. The women were opposed by 16 out of the 19 members of the medical and surgical staff on the grounds that separate instruction would be necessary and that this either reduced the beds available to the male students or subjected the patients to two rounds of students per day. Once again Professor Christison played a major part in drumming up medical opposition. The board deferred the matter, and the women, frustrated, sought legal advice.

It seems that here, too, questions of morality and expediency were not the full story. Dr Littlejohn was quoted as saying that he foresaw the ruin of his son by women doctors.[104] Similarly, Dr Wood protested that he had too many sons to provide for to agree to the medical education of women.[105] They, and many others, believed that the interests of the next generation of males had to be protected from the potentially damaging effect of the entry of women into the profession.

This of course worked doubly against women: with a profession knit together by male family connection and friendship bonds and with careers reliant on personal introduction, women were out in the cold. I do not know of any women doctors in this early period who were themselves daughters of medical men or whose careers benefited from any such connections. Medical men's concern for their daughters extended only so far as their determination that their female relatives would never be allowed to enter the profession.

The 'riot' at Surgeons' Hall

As soon as the board decided to defer the decision, the attitude of the male students changed dramatically. From now on the women had to face the added burden of overt harassment. The tactics of the students included:

> shutting doors in our faces, ostentatiously crowding into the seats we usually occupied, bursting into horse laughs and howls when we approached – as if a conspiracy had been formed to make our position as uncomfortable as might be.[106]

This harassment reached its peak in the infamous 'riot' at Surgeons' Hall in mid November, described in the following passage from Sophia Jex-Blake's account of the years at Edinburgh:

> Various small circumstances had led us to anticipate something unpleasant; and on the afternoon of Friday, November 18th, 1870, we women walked down together to Surgeons' Hall. As soon as we came in sight of the gates, we found a dense mob filling up the roadway in front of them, comprising some dozen of the lowest class of our fellow-students at Surgeons' Hall, with many more of the same class from the University, a certain number of street rowdies, and some hundreds of gaping spectators, who took no particular part in the matter. Not a single policeman was visible, though the crowd was sufficient to stop all traffic for about an hour. We walked straight up to the gates, which remained open until we came within a yard of them, when they were slammed in our faces by a number of young men, who stood within, smoking and

passing about bottles of whisky, while they abused us in
the foulest possible language, which I am thankful to say
I have never heard equalled before or since. We waited
quietly on the step to see if the rowdies were to have it
all their own way, and in a minute we saw another fellow-
student of ours, Mr. Sanderson, rush down from Surgeons'
Hall, and wrench open the gate, in spite of the howls and
efforts of our half-tipsy opponents. We were quick to seize
the chance offered, and in a very few seconds we had all
passed through the gate, and entered the Anatomical classroom, where the usual examination was conducted in
spite of the yells and howls resounding outside, and the
forcible intrusion of a luckless sheep, that was pushed in
by the rioters. 'Let it remain,' said Dr. Handyside; 'it has
more sense than those who sent it here.' At the close of
the class the lecturer offered to let us out by a back door,
but I glanced round the ranks of our fellow-students, and
remarked that I thought there were 'enough gentlemen
here to prevent any harm to us.' I had judged rightly. In
a moment a couple of dozen students came down from
the benches, headed by Mr. Sanderson, Mr. Hoggan, Mr.
Macleod, and Mr. Lyon, formed each side, and,
encompassed by them, we passed through the still
howling crowd at the gate, and reached home with no
other injuries than those inflicted on our dresses by the
mud hurled at us by our chivalrous foes.[107]

The Scotsman, however, did report that one woman was struck
on the back and another pushed off the pavement by the demon-
strators. According to an eye-witness report in the *Daily Review*
three days later, quoted in a footnote by Sophia Jex-Blake, the
'mob began to collect long before four o'clock, and no action
was taken by the police until after five . . .'[108] The following day
a crowd of young men again gathered at the gates of the college
but were kept at bay by the students sympathetic to the women
and had to satisfy themselves with 'vent[ing] their spite in
remarkably bad language'.[109]

Four students were fined and severely reprimanded by the
university authorities and notices were put up on the university
walls that any student brought before a police magistrate would

be dealt with by the Senate as having committed a university offence. There was general suspicion that the university professors themselves were implicated in the incident, whether they simply made it clear that they opposed female entry and approved of any measures taken to stop the women or actually helped to organise the 'riot'. One sympathetic student, Robert Wilson, wrote to Edith Pechey about what he believed lay behind the disturbances:

> May I venture to hint my belief that the real cause of the riots is the way some of the professors run you down in their lectures. They never lose a chance of stirring up hatred against you. For all I know they may have more knowledge of the riotous conspiracy than most people fancy.[110]

In January, an Edinburgh paper quoted a local doctor as saying that young men will often act in order to please their teachers and therefore the harassment did not necessarily indicate the students' views.[111]

According to Sophia Jex-Blake, most of the medical students involved in the 'riot' were from the university rather than the extra-mural classes and had been summoned by a missive put round the university classrooms. She further alleged that Professor Christison's assistant, Mr Craig, had helped to organise it, with the professor's tacit approval.[112] She made it clear that the 'riot' had nothing to do with objections to the classes at the extra-mural school but had happened at a time when opponents needed strong arguments for the exclusion of women from the infirmary. A memorial (statement and petition) signed by 504 out of the 550 male medical students was presented to the infirmary urging it *not* to admit women to instruction there. It was clear that male medical students from the university would continue to harass the women, with the apparent blessing of much of the faculty.

There was strong condemnation of the students and of the university itself from many newspapers and periodicals. Even the *Lancet* praised the 'brave and resolute women'.[113] However, Sophia Jex-Blake recorded how certain papers made indecent allegations about the women's motives, 'as if a general signal had been given for an attack from all the powers of evil'.[114] The worst of these, described by her as 'too filthy to quote', were circulated to the infirmary board by opponents in an attempt to discredit the women, but it appears that this also had the effect of stirring up some members in their defence. One of the contributors to the infirmary, described by Sophia Jex-Blake as 'a total stranger to us', wrote to *The Scotsman* to express his disgust: 'I have scarcely ever met anything so bad, so gratuitously nasty.'[115] The women students also received direct support from Henry Kingsley, the editor of the *Daily Review*. His wife sat in on their classes to show her solidarity with the cause.

In December further attempts were made to exclude the women from extra-mural lectures when a memorial signed by 66 students was presented to the Royal College of Surgeons, Edinburgh, complaining that their presence constituted a breach of contract between the lecturers and the male students, and that their studies had been suffering. The memorial about the extra-mural school was greeted with approval by the *Lancet* and the college passed a resolution by 27 votes to 4 against mixed classes.[116] However, the college was unable actually to *stop* mixed classes because it simply rented out the rooms at Surgeons' Hall to independent lecturers who only needed a licence from the college if their students wanted to go forward for professional examinations.

Elizabeth Garrett marries

Meanwhile in London important events were occurring in Elizabeth Garrett's life. In March 1870 she became the first woman doctor to hold a hospital post when she was appointed visiting Medical Officer at the East London Hospital for Children. This had been founded in 1868 by Dr Heckford, an old friend from her London Hospital days. In October a deputation made up of men who were husbands and fathers of her women patients at the St Mary's Dispensary approached her with the proposal that she stand for the London School Board elections in the local area of Marylebone.

A report in the *Lancet* called upon the medical profession to support her candidature, saying that Elizabeth Garrett was so exceptionally able that support for her would *not* imply support for medical women generally.[114] The *Lancet* was now having to tread a very fine line. It was not possible to dismiss Elizabeth Garrett, who by now was clearly a serious and respected practitioner, although it wanted to persist with their implacable hostility to the entry of women to the profession generally. This also points to the limitations of Elizabeth Garrett's personal success for the campaign. She was essentially a *pioneer*, carving out a career for herself, rather than a *campaigner*, with the central purpose of opening up the medical profession for women generally.

After two busy months of canvassing, with support from old friends such as Barbara Bodichon, Octavia Hill, and her brother-in-law Henry Fawcett, she came top of the poll in Marylebone with more votes than anyone in London. The *Englishwoman's Review* attributed her success to her hard work and popularity at the dispensary.[115] Her election was obviously of great importance to the women's movement: one of their main aims was for professional women to have a say in the administration of government legislation which directly affected girls and women, for instance on schools, prisons, and workhouses. As an indication of the issues on which Elizabeth Garrett worked very hard while on the board, she voted in favour of the regulation that schoolgirls should only be taught by women.

This was a time of important developments in her personal life too. In December she was engaged to J.G.S.Anderson, a businessman who was on the board of the East London Hospital and whose older sister Mary Anderson had recently joined the women medical students in Edinburgh. In a letter in December to her sister Millicent Fawcett, Elizabeth Garrett set out her views on marriage and career:

> I am sure that the woman question will never be solved in any complete way so long as marriage is thought to be incompatible with freedom and with an independent career.[119]

They were married very quietly, with only family and Emily Davies present, at 8.30 a.m. on 9 February 1871, at the Scottish Presbyterian Church in Upper George Street. She chose to omit the word 'obey' from her wedding service, and she ensured that her earnings were legally secured to her, under the provisions

of the new Married Women's Property Act. Apparently Anderson was hurt by her decision to do this.[120]

The *Lancet* had claimed that Elizabeth Garrett would have
to resign from the London School Board once she was married
and that married women could not be legally qualified medical
practitioners. In reply, she made it clear she had no intention of
resigning from the board.[121] She announced she would continue
practising medicine under the name Elizabeth Garrett Anderson.
After their marriage, they set up home above her surgery at 20
Upper Berkeley Street.

The Royal Infirmary elections

Edinburgh had been divided into two opposing camps by the
events of the autumn. In January 1871 the public meeting at
which subscribers to the infirmary elected the board of managers
had to be transferred to St Giles' Cathedral because of the
unusually large attendance. Elections to the board were a direct
way in which lay middle-class people could actively participate
in debates over the question of medical women. The female
subscribers used their right to vote for the first time ever and
all 16 supported the women. A petition was sent from 956
Edinburgh women asking that women be allowed into the
infirmary to study. There was also a petition to the meeting
from 22 male students asking that the women be admitted to
the infirmary and expressing their outrage at the behaviour of
their fellow students.

At the infirmary meeting the women got strong support from
Elizabeth Pease Nichol. Her father, Joseph Pease, a Quaker
manufacturer from Darlington, had been closely involved in the
abolition of slavery in India. Elizabeth had become involved in
this work too, as his secretary and also as a member of the
Women's Abolition Society of Darlington. She had corre-
sponded with the Grimké sisters in the United States and had
attended various international congresses in the 1840s and
1850s on issues such as abolition and world peace. At the
age of 46 she had married John Nichol, Regius Professor of
Astronomy at Glasgow University, and on his death in 1859
had moved to Edinburgh, where most of her close friends lived.
These included the MP Duncan McLaren and his wife who both

strongly supported medical women. She was a member of the Edinburgh Committee for Women's Suffrage, which had been set up by Mrs McLaren. She was also on the executive committee of the Ladies' National Association for the Repeal of the Contagious Diseases Acts and had taken part in a public meeting in Edinburgh the previous September attended by Josephine Butler. A recurring entry in her diary at this time gives an indication of the importance she attached to the repeal of the Acts: 'Writing all day on *the* subject.'[122] Unfortunately none of her other writings have survived.

Given the friends she had, and her lifelong commitment to radical causes, it is not surprising that she came out strongly in public in support of women's entry to the medical profession at the infirmary election meeting. In her speech she attacked the double standard which on the one hand denounced mixed classes as immoral but on the other hand insisted that it was better for women to be treated by men. She insisted that she was *not* speaking in the interests of the women students but instead 'on behalf of those women who looked forward to see what kind of men were they who were to be the sole medical attendants of the next generation of women, if women doctors are not allowed'.[123] She questioned the fitness of the students to be future doctors for women if they were unable to study alongside female students. She asked how they could possess 'either the scientific spirit or the personal purity of mind which alone would justify their presence in female wards during the most delicate operations on and examination of female patients'.[124] Her speech was greeted with 'laughter, hisses, and applause'. In a letter to Sophia Jex-Blake after this meeting in which she gave her written support for the campaign, she compared it to the anti-slavery work of women in the United States.

In contrast to this support from women contributors, 25 of the 30 men on the medical staff were opposed to women studying at the infirmary. One of these opponents, Professor Muirhead, said that women students should be excluded from the infirmary because of the delicacy of the male students. Unfortunately the effect was somewhat spoilt by a roar of laughter from male students in the gallery in response to this. Sophia Jex-Blake gave a long speech in which she claimed that the rioters at Surgeons' Hall had been positively encouraged by 'bitter partisans' from within the faculty and had been made 'to dance as puppets on such ignoble strings'.[125] She also made allegations against Professsor Christison's assistant, Mr Craig, accusing him of playing a leading part in the 'riot', being drunk, using foul language, and being there with the professor's approval.

On 3 January *The Scotsman* reported that an infirmary board unsympathetic to the medical education of women had been elected by the narrow margin of 100 votes to 98. On 11 January the paper reported that a recount had taken place but that the result had been upheld by 94 to 88. These managers voted against female entry in mid January and, after postponing the matter at four subsequent meetings in February and March, voted again in March against the women. Two of the three medical men on the board had voted in favour of the women in January but now voted against. A third supporter was unseated by the medical body he represented when he refused to alter his views. The *Lancet* reported this as a final defeat for the women and blithely stated that the only course left to them was to open their own infirmary.[126] Both the *Lancet* and those campaigning in Edinburgh knew this was impossible.

Support committee formed

The Lord Provost of Edinburgh called a meeting on 26 January at which supporters of the women set up the Committee for Securing Complete Medical Education to Women in Edinburgh, which included such influential men as the Lord Provost himself, the editor of *The Scotsman*, and Duncan McLaren, the MP for Edinburgh (Town). It also included Elizabeth Pease Nichol, who had spoken out in support of the women students at the infirmary elections. The affair of Edith Pechey being denied the Hope Scholarship had first alerted the public to the tactics of the faculty and since then the women students had enjoyed growing outside support, especially financial help. According to Sophia Jex-Blake, this support was 'crystallised' by further evidence of medical obstructiveness in the 'riot' at Surgeons' Hall and over the infirmary elections. What had previously been only a vague interest in women doctors or mild sympathy for the seven students was now replaced by an explicit support campaign.

The formation of the committee had an important effect on

the women students as they now became 'no longer a few isolated women struggling for our own object, but the pioneers of an important movement...'[127] Sophia Jex-Blake later paid tribute to the committee's 'fidelity and ... chivalrous readiness to help, which was never marred by officiousness or needless interference'.[128] By the end of its third week of existence the committee numbered over 300. It took on the task of publicising the cause, and letters of support began to flood in. One of its first actions was to call on women to sign petitions to Parliament to prove the demand for women doctors, a tactic used repeatedly throughout the campaign. It also suggested that middle-class women, who could wield a measure of social influence, should refuse to be attended by a male doctor, at least in childbirth. Another of its stated objectives was to raise funds to support women medical students through their degree course.

On 10 February *The Scotsman* printed a heavily sarcastic poem entitled 'The Charge of the Five Hundred; A Lay of Modern Athens' about the 'defence' of the university by 500 medical men against seven women.[129] The following lines give a flavour of the poem:

> Then marked the bard who stood afar
> The gallant leaders of the war —
> The plumed crest of Andrew Wood,
> Who for his sons in battle stood,
>   A Christison hard by!
> A Turner, Laycock, Lister too,
> All met for deeds of derring-do;
> Gillespie, Douglas (Oh, that shame
> Should fall on that time-honoured name!)
> Dun-Edin's chivalry.

Around this time five women competed for the scholarship set up by Lady Amberley for women medical students. According to a letter to *The Scotsman* from Professor Kelland, the standard of examination papers was exceptionally high.[130] The five women presented a total of 28 papers between them, with an average mark of 70 per cent.

The committee now approached the infirmary to gain access for the women students. It proposed to the board a scheme which entailed no disruption of existing arrangements, but this was defeated by nine votes to seven. An approach to Leith Hospital, near Edinburgh, was refused on the now familiar grounds of inexpediency and the women eventually had to settle for an unsatisfactory arrangement for clinical instruction at St Cuthbert's Poorhouse. In April Sophia Jex-Blake was invited to speak at a suffrage meeting in London which she did with great success.

Sexual harassment

At this point Professor Christison's assistant, Mr Craig, brought an action for damages against Sophia Jex-Blake for the allegedly slanderous remarks she had made during the infirmary meeting in January. The trial was held in June. In her diary Sophia made fun of the obsession of the press with the appearance of the students:

> That female medical students should dare to be good-looking, dare to be married, dare to be dressed in good taste is, of course, an unpardonable crime.[131]

She was found guilty by the jury but with damages of only a farthing. However, the judge was unsympathetic to the cause of medical women, as the plaintiff has the right to choose the judge in Scottish libel cases. He awarded costs of £915 11s 1d against her, an enormous sum of money in 1871. As a very rough guide, prices have risen by a factor of 40 since then, which puts the penalty Sophia was expected to pay at over £35,000!

The Scotsman, which had been reporting all events to do with the struggle in great detail, published a verbatim account of the trial in June, and in July printed letters in support of Sophia.[132] In separate letters, two members of the jury explained that they had been split exactly equally in their views and had reached their verdict on an assurance from the clerk that such a verdict would not allow the judge to award costs against her. 'A Lawyer' then advised her to appeal against the decision because the clerk had technically interfered. This was followed by a letter from Edith Pechey, pointing out the extreme injustice of a woman being insulted and then saddled with the enormous costs from a court case. The message, she said, was clearly that women must put up with being insulted. Male students had taken this to heart, continuing 'to shout after her all the foulest epithets in their voluminous vocabulary of abuse'.[133]

One of the most striking features of the struggle in Edinburgh was the repeated, and often extreme, sexual harassment the women students had to put up with. Towards the end of this period Sophia Jex-Blake wrote:

> For the sake of the women who long for the medical
> services of their own sex, we have borne to be pelted with
> street mud, and with far fouler names by the 'perfect
> gentlemen' who desire to keep in their own hands
> exclusively the medical care of all women.[134]

Edith Pechey referred to being followed home at night by men who used medical terms in their abuse 'to make the disgusting purport of their language more intelligible to me'.[135] Sophia Jex-Blake's front door bell-pull was wrenched off and her name-plate damaged five times. On one occasion a firework was attached to the door. Paint was burnt off but luckily no one was injured. Several of the women also received 'the filthiest possible anonymous letters' by post.[136] In Sophia Jex-Blake's diary, she referred to 'the constant hisses and rudeness even on the streets . . . those two scamps shouting 'whore' after SMM . . .'[137] There was further unrest in the autumn during the elections for the rector (a university officer chosen annually by the students) at which a supporter of medical women was elected. His inaugural address was completely disrupted and a crowd of students laid siege to 15 Buccleuch Place, where many of the women students lived.

The determination of Sophia Jex-Blake and Edith Pechey that women must gain entry to the profession was greatly strengthened by these personal experiences of opposition and overt hostility in Edinburgh. In her letter to *The Scotsman* following the libel trial, Edith Pechey explained how she had been radicalised by the events of the last one and a half years and in particular by the verbal and physical violence she and the others had faced from male medical students. She also made the point that the students who were harassing them would become less successful members of the profession and would therefore not have their behaviour policed by the 'rich husbands and fathers' of their patients but instead have 'the treatment of unprotected servants and shop-girls'.[138] It would be working-class women who in their relative social powerlessness would be particularly vulnerable to the verbal and sexual abuse of these medical men.

In her account of the struggle, published in 1886, Sophia Jex-Blake gave her own description of the process of radicalisation:

> We had begun to study simply because we saw no reason why women should not be the medical attendants of women. When we came in contact with such unexpected depths of moral grossness and brutality, we had burnt into our minds the strongest possible conviction that if such things were possible in the medical profession, women must, at any cost, force their way into it, for the sake of their sisters, who might otherwise be left at the mercy of such human brutes as these.[139]

Sophia Jex-Blake tried to explain the harassment they faced by saying that the Edinburgh medical students included 'boys of low social class, of small mental calibre, and no moral training' and that there would have been little problem if all the male students had been 'gentlemen'.[140] This can be seen simply as an example of middle-class prejudice. It could possibly also have been an attempt on the part of Sophia Jex-Blake to avoid generalising from the experience of the women students about the behaviour of all men. To believe that opposition is coming only from a certain section of an oppressing group can be a comfort, particularly in situations of physical threat.[141]

The Craig decision did have its compensations for the women as it attracted stronger support than ever for them. Around the time of the trial, Sophia wrote to Lucy Sewall in the United States, 'People are getting wild for women doctors here . . .'[142] Letters of support arrived from Frances Power Cobbe and Harriet Martineau, among others, and one from 'a few working men', in favour of 'women's rights to a liberal education and remunerative employment'.[143]

On 27 July a meeting was held from which another committee was formed specifically to raise funds to pay the court costs. Sophia Jex-Blake initially rejected the proposal to collect money for her but then realised the propaganda value of the exercise in which the fund would be 'in reality but a form of appeal to the bar of public opinion'.[144] Donations poured in and on 19

August *The Scotsman* published two lists of susbscribers.[145] This was a common practice for middle-class fundraising events in Victorian Britain. The paper reported that the appeal had closed after only one month, by which time over £1000 had been raised, mainly in small donations from 265 individual contributors. These donations included some from medical men and some from working-class men. All the court costs were paid and the balance of £100 was set aside for a future hospital for women.

In July the *Englishwoman's Review* reported that the committee in Edinburgh was now inviting supporters to join a national committee.[146] Members of this latter committee included a number of prominent feminists, such as Josephine Butler, Emily Davies, Harriet Martineau, Barbara Bodichon, Jessie Boucherett, Frances Power Cobbe and Elizabeth Wolstenholme, and a few important male supporters of medical women, such as the Earl of Shaftesbsury, James Stansfeld, Russell Gurney, Dr Anstie and Dr King Chambers.

During 1871 Elizabeth Blackwell was continuing her work in the field of preventive medicine. She gave a speech at St George's Hall on 'The Religion of Health' in which she condemned pollution, bad housing and lethal working conditions. She insisted that 'we now possess enough sanitary knowledge' to prevent a wide range of common diseases.[147] This same year the National Health Society was formed at a meeting held in Elizabeth Blackwell's drawing-room. The society had the motto: 'Prevention is better than cure.'[148]

She also gave a lecture at the Working Women's College on 'How to keep a household in health', in which she set out principles of hygiene and advocated sex education for children. This lecture had unfortunate consequences for her. Somebody sent what she described as a 'slanderous account' of it to the *Pall Mall Gazette*. As a result she was deluged with anonymous letters asking her for 'advice on the most important and delicate subjects', some even enclosing fees. On advice from the Reverend Charles Kingsley, a close friend, she decided to ignore the letters.[149] The experience must, nevertheless, have proved very unsettling for her.

11 Final Defeat

Blocking tactics

On 30 June 1871 the women students received a second blow with the extra-mural lecturers deciding to rescind their previous resolution and not even allow separate classes. This did not affect those who were lecturing to the women elsewhere and so some classes were able to continue. But the responsibility for arranging classes and paying fees fell back on the women students.

This decision to stop lecturing to women students at the extra-mural school may have been influenced by the action in March of the Presidents of the Royal Colleges of Physicians and Surgeons, Edinburgh, in boycotting the annual prize-giving at Surgeons' Hall, clearly an attempt to intimidate those who gave lectures there. Many commentators noted that they lacked any sense of how ridiculous they were being. *The Scotsman* attacked the tactic with typical sarcasm:

> . . . the delicacy of these gentlemen who cannot
> contemplate with equanimity the distribution of prizes to
> an audience of both sexes, must really be so very
> transcendental that most common-sense people will give
> up the attempt even to follow their line of honour.[150]

In a memorial (petition) to the Senate of the university the women then proposed that special arrangements be made to enable them to finish their degrees, but the Senate rejected this by one vote. Sophia Jex-Blake consulted legal opinion in the hope that the university might be legally obliged to let them finish but received conflicting advice from two lawyers.

In October the faculty notified the women at the last minute that they could not sit the preliminary arts examinations which had to be passed before degree examinations could be attempted. *The Scotsman* reported the exchange of letters and decisions in full and accused a minority of trying to block the women by 'underhand' methods.[151] The committee sent a letter to the Senate stating that they had been advised by lawyers that the university *was* legally empowered to allow the women to graduate. They also collected a petition with the signatures of 9127 women from all parts of the country in the space of four days. Under this pressure, the Senate agreed to let the women sit the preliminary examinations.

This was the beginning of three months of wrangling in the various university bodies. The issue turned largely on whether or not the university regulations of November 1869 implied that women were to be allowed to enter the university for the study of medicine with a view to graduation and entry to the profession.

In his history of the university, Alexander Grant, who was the Principal at this time, said the real mistake had been to admit women in the first place before checking the legal position about the granting of degrees to them.[152] He said the only solution to the impasse of 1871/72 would have been for the constitution of the university to have been changed. The implication of this remark is that this would have been possible and would therefore have solved any legal problems. But, he said:

> they had learnt by experience that there were great
> practical difficulties in the way of carrying out the medical
> education of women in the University.[153]

Presumably the 'practical difficulties' to which he is referring here are the obstructiveness and hostility of the medical professors and male medical students and the overall reluctance of the university to let women graduate.

The Medical Faculty claimed that the women had been allowed in as a limited experiment, which had not worked, and so permission to enter should be withdrawn, as it was a 'trap for the unwary'.[154] The opponents of women's graduation were probably also influenced by the important fact that all graduates had a right to vote on major university issues through membership of the General Council. For women to aspire to become medical practitioners alongside men and possibly provide extra competition was bad enough, but for women to be in a position where they could have any influence, however limited, on the education of men was undoubtedly seen as intolerable.

During the autumn of 1871 three of the women students married. Mary Anderson became Mrs Marshall, Matilda Chaplin married William Ayrton, a professor at the university, and Helen Evans married Alexander Russel, the editor of *The Scotsman* and strong supporter of the women students from the first. Sophia Jex-Blake received a letter from a woman who was worried about these developments:

> I do hope you and Miss Pechey will remain firm to the end, for really, three marriages within six months is quite alarming![155]

Growing support

The Scotsman maintained detailed, and at times daily, reporting of the events of these three months. It published verbatim texts of statements made by those involved and complete lists of subscribers to appeal funds. This is characteristic of the detailed coverage of the issue of medical women in the local and national press during the years of the campaign. All the major issues, such as mixed versus separate classes, the demand for women doctors, and the scope of female medical practitioners, were debated fully in leading articles and in letters to the editor in various newspapers and periodicals.

The struggle over women's entry to the university gripped the attention of the middle-class community in Edinburgh. Here, as elsewhere, the issue of medical women became caught up in other conflicts. There was a background of tension between 'Town' and 'Gown', that is, between the city and the university. In 1855 the Town Council had won a long-running legal struggle with the Medical Faculty over the recognition of extra-mural lectures. But, with the Universities Act of 1858, the council lost overall control of the university which it had founded in 1582 and run since then.

The city was critical of any action which went against the

Scottish tradition of free access to education for all. Supporters of medical women insisted that the university was meant for the general benefit of the community and not for the benefit of the professors. In October the suggestion was first made that the revenues raised annually for the university be reduced by the exact amount of the medical professors' salaries. This was greeted with indignation by the *Lancet*. It defended the right of the professors to act on their opinions and predicted that such tactics would result in the cause being abandoned by all but the 'extreme left'.

The depth of support in Edinburgh for the women students is apparent from the number of people involved in the committee set up in January 1871. In her book, Sophia Jex-Blake remarked on the strength of support from the 'municipal element'.[157] The Lord Provost was an active member of the committee and let it hold its meetings in the City Council Chambers. David McLaren, MP for the City of Edinburgh, was also a strong supporter of campaign, both in the House of Commons and in Edinburgh itself.

Supporters were increasingly insistent that the university must not by itself have the power to make it impossible for women to be able to consult doctors of their own sex. They also spoke very plainly about the nature of the opposition the women had faced and accused the Medical Faculty of not letting the 'experiment' proceed fairly. The committee and much of the national press saw the issue of graduation as a matter of the university keeping faith with the women and being morally obliged to allow them to graduate.

Even the *Lancet* was finding it very difficult to support the blatant tactics of the Edinburgh Medical Faculty. Presumably it was acutely aware of the bad publicity the campaign there was giving to the profession. Without shifting from its complete opposition to women doctors *in principle*, it called on the university to let the women graduate.[158] It was careful to be seen to separate the issue of graduation for the 'Edinburgh Seven' from the wider issue of medicine as a profession for women. In reply to Sophia Jex-Blake's claim at the lecture at St George's Hall that even the *Lancet* supported medical women, the journal insisted that it was only in favour of the seven at Edinburgh being allowed to finish.[159] As with its response to Elizabeth

Garrett, it found itself in a position where it could not comfortably maintain a stance of complete opposition and so proposed that *certain* women be allowed into the profession without that creating a precedent for women generally. In any case it considered that it was safe to allow the Edinburgh students to continue as it believed that they would ultimately fail.

Immediately after the Senate decision to let the women sit the examinations, Dr Wood proposed a motion to the General Council that they be allowed to complete their studies and graduate. Although Professor Christison apparently said that he thought everything possible should be done to find a solution, he and other medical opponents continued to block every practical suggestion. *The Scotsman* condemned the professor's claim that he would do anything to help the women as 'farcical'.[160] The General Council voted 107 to 97 against allowing women to complete their medical studies. There were allegations in a letter to *The Scotsman* from 'A Member of Council' that the voting had been unregulated, with medical *under*graduates and others swelling the ranks of those graduates opposed to the women.[161]

Three days later the Senate refused an offer from the committee to guarantee the costs of setting up separate classes and in mid November voted to rescind the 1869 regulations allowing matriculation of women students. In December David Masson took an appeal against this to the General Council, again referring to the committee as evidence of widespread support for the cause, and the regulations were confirmed. The University Court had already agreed to relax the rules about extra-mural classes, which meant that recognised classes in all subjects were open to the women.

However, in early January the University Court refused the committee's proposals for a final solution and said that they would only continue negotiations if the women dropped all talk of graduation. It seems that the issue of *graduation* was the key to opposition. The following summer it was revealed in *The Scotsman* that Professor Crum Brown, who had refused Edith Pechey the Hope Scholarship and had later been implicated in the 'riot', had continued to give lectures to *non*-professional women while refusing to allow his assistant to lecture to the women degree students.[162]

Sophia Jex-Blake was by now something of a celebrity in

Edinburgh. She resigned herself to this fact but consistently refused to give any interviews or to allow herself to be photographed. At Christmas this year her name occurred repeatedly in the pantomime in Edinburgh. In one scene a card game was played on stage with Edinburgh dignatories as the cards. 'Miss Jex-Blake' took the trick.[163]

In January *The Scotsman* published a witty poem lamenting the divisions which had been created in middle-class society in Edinburgh:

> When can I again invite
>   Friend of mine
>   To come and dine,
> Without danger of a fight,
> Without danger that the party
> Change its tone from frank and hearty
> To the angry tone of strife,
> As the theme so quarrel-rife
> Croppeth up amidst the talk
> (As weeds crop up across a walk)
>   Of the doctors and the ladies?
>
> When Christison resigns his chair,
> And Andrew Wood is with the blest;
> When the doctors cease from troubling,
> And the ladies are at rest.
>
> When can I again subscribe
>   Gold or note,
>   And buy a vote,
> Without danger that a tribe
> Of canvassers will call on me,
> To talk of the Infirmary,
> Of female student *versus* male,
> Of classes mixed, a horrid tale,
>   And beg my vote against the ladies?
>
> When Christison resigns his Chair,
> And Andrew Wood is with the blest;
> When the doctors cease from troubling,
> And the ladies are at rest.[164]

Infirmary elections again

The committee once again canvassed vigorously for the infirmary elections, this time with the guarantee that they would pay for lecturers and separate rooms. It is clear that this was an important step. In a letter to *The Scotsman* from 'A student who won't sign', the writer explained that many students, like himself, were still opposed to women in the profession and saw mixed classes as a threat to their medical education. However, they were not prepared to sign a petition being circulated at the time against entry to the infirmary, now that they were assured there was no possibility of mixed classes.[165] The petition had to be abandoned for lack of support.

A board of managers favourable to medical women was elected, supported by a majority of the firms who contributed to infirmary funds and all but two of the women contributors. Most doctors voted against this board. After the opposition departed *en masse* from the election meeting, a motion was unanimously passed that all registered students be allowed into the infirmary, regardless of sex. However, blocking tactics were once again used against the women. A challenge to the vote was made on the basis that the firms had no right to vote. This demonstrates the blinkered determination of those opposed to women's entry, as the firms were by far the largest financial contributors to the infirmary and therefore crucial to its survival. In May the women had one small victory. Their initial application to the Royal Dispensary had been refused the previous October but they now managed to persuade one of the medical officers there to give them instruction.

The rest of the year was taken up with a long legal wrangle over the right of firms to vote at infirmary elections. The women's side won the initial court case and the appeal. On 30 October Peter Bell, the clerk to the managers, wrote to all 18 members of the medical staff asking whether they were in favour of women students being admitted on the same terms and at the same times as the men.[166] They were asked to suggest alternative arrangements if they were not in favour. Professor Heron Watson, Professor Balfour and Professor Hughes Bennet replied that they could see no reason why women should not be admitted and that they would be happy to see this either at the same time as the male students *or* at different times.

All of the other 15 members were strongly opposed to the women students. Recurring objections were that there were too many male students already, that mixed classes would be 'repugnant' to the patients, and that they would inhibit teaching of the male students. William Sanders and Douglas Maclagan referred specifically to the problem of students being exposed to patients with illnesses connected with venereal disease, which would lead to a 'violation of propriety'. Dr Maclagan asked what would happen if a woman with a 'blunted' moral sense were to study at the infirmary: she would be a 'very dangerous neighbour' to the male students. The only alternative suggestion put forward was that women form their own hospital, although Dr Maclagan was even worried that this might attract funds away from the infirmary.

In December 1872 the women were at last issued with tickets of admission, although only for wards to which they had been invited by the three sympathetic members of staff and at times when the male students were not present. Dr Balfour gave clinical instruction to the women three days a week and Dr Heron Watson gave surgical instruction from 9 to 10 a.m. on Sunday mornings, the only time available. They continued to face harassment, however, even over this meagre instruction. There were protests that male students were present as clerks and dressers and that these sessions therefore constituted mixed classes.

At this point a letter appeared in *The Scotsman* from 'A Woman on Woman Doctors', which reiterated that the debate should not focus on issues of mixed classes or practical difficulties but rather on the need for women doctors:

Men have little idea how much prolonged and increased suffering is often borne by their mothers, wives, sisters and daughters, just because they have not been able to consult physicians of their own sex. Nay, death itself has often prematurely cut down women, whose reluctance to seek advice from a man was only overcome by extreme pain when it was too late.[167]

Appeal to law

Meanwhile deadlock had been reached with the university. The committee refused the offer of certificates instead of graduation and the University Court made no moves to make any proposals for an alternative solution. So the women decided to go to court to bring an 'Action of Declarator' against the Senate in an attempt to use legal pressure to force the university to let them graduate. The Senate decided by a majority to defend the action, a decision welcomed by some friends of the movement as they believed a legal confrontation would resolve the issue once and for all. At the court case in July, the Senate claimed that it had never promised graduation. It also said that the decision to agree to matriculation was itself *ultra vires*, that is, outside its legal powers. It is ironic that the membership of the University Court which passed these supposedly illegal regulations in 1869 included the Lord Advocate and the Lord Justice-General, two of Scotland's top lawyers.

These arguments were rejected by Lord Gifford, Lord Ordinary, who was the judge presiding over the case in the Court of Session. He said the university was not established for the education of male students *only* and that it was unfair to let the women study but not to graduate. He supported the claim that certificates of proficiency and foreign degrees were no solution, as neither led to registration and so this condemned any woman thus qualified to practising without legal recognition or protection. Although he was not able to force the university to let women into all classes, he could at least make them recognise the extra-mural classes for the purposes of graduation.

He stated clearly that, although the point at issue was whether the regulations of November 1869 were *ultra vires* or not, the real conflict was over the desire of these women to practise medicine. He also took the opportunity while delivering his judgment on the regulations to assert his belief that certain branches of medicine were particularly suited to women and *not* to men:

> . . . nothing but the deadening effect of habit would ever reconcile the community to that anomaly in name and in reality, 'A Man-midwife'.[168]

In the midst of these struggles in Edinburgh a public meeting on female suffrage was held at St George's Hall in London, with the Earl of Shaftesbury in the chair. Elizabeth Garrett Anderson was one of the major speakers at the main meeting and Sophia Jex-Blake addressed the overflow. There was strong support for medical women from leading figures, the Earl of Shaftesbury in particular, and there was wide coverage in the press. *The Times*, for instance, showed clear sympathy for the cause.[169]

Sophia Jex-Blake was busy revising her essay on medicine as a profession for women and writing an account of events at Edinburgh, which were published together as a book in mid 1872.[170] The issue of medical women continued to be reported regularly in the newspapers and numerous letters were published about the suffering of women as a result of their lack of opportunity to consult a woman doctor. In the appendix to the 1886 edition of her book Jex-Blake quoted at length from a number of these letters.

One letter from 'A Sufferer' contrasted the supposed injury to the feelings of male medical students resulting from the presence of the seven women at Edinburgh with the real mental agony of being examined in front of these same male students:

The question, however, arises — which evil is the greater, — that five hundred youths, in full health and vigour, should be made a little uncomfortable by the presence of seven women, or that seven times five hundred women, unnerved by suffering, should be subjected to the very trial they shrink from? That women do truly shrink from this trial, the number of wretched, broken-down sufferers from chronic disease but too clearly proves . . . This objection, looked at fairly, is a case of the delicacy of five hundred men versus that of all suffering women.[171]

Another correspondent, 'A Catholic Wife and Mother', insisted that it should be women and not men who should decide on this issue:

Then, again, how can any man, medical or not, know what agonies of shame and outraged modesty women can and do undergo, when submitting to male medical and surgical treatment.[172]

One letter from 'A District Visitor' to *The Scotsman* in December 1870 reported cases of women refusing to go to the doctor for treatable illnesses unless they could go to a woman doctor, as they had heard this was now possible in some places.[173]

In the new section of her book in which she gave an account on events at Edinburgh Sophia Jex-Blake talked about the dual pressures they were under of studying *and* defending themselves from attack. She said of this period:

> I doubt whether any written record can place fully before those who know nothing of Edinburgh at the time all the bitterness of the last four years of the struggle.[174]

She also quoted a lecture which she herself gave in Edinburgh in 1872 in which she said that the opposition had themselves proved that women were strong enough for the medical profession by putting them through such a test. A number of articles sympathetic to medical women appeared in the press in the autumn in response to the book, and in particular to the sections on the nature of the opposition in Edinburgh.

Sophia Jex-Blake was under personal pressure from these and other commitments. In the summer she had written to Lucy Sewall: 'I think when the fight is won, I shall creep away into some wood and lie and sleep for a year.'[175] There were constant requests from journalists for interviews with her. She was also approached by James Stansfeld MP, who was active in the anti-vivisection campaign, about the possibility of legislation. At the same time she was trying to study and was finding the strain intolerable, as entries in her diary show at this time:

> Rather out of heart . . . My head seems tired . . .
>
> Things seem to *crowd* on me so.
>
> I nervous and shaky again, – feeling strength go out of me drop by drop.[176]

However, she did have a supportive network of female friends around her: a letter from Agnes McLaren to Ursula Du Pre in November assured Ursula that she would be with Sophia as much as possible during this difficult time.

Not surprisingly, in November Sophia failed her university examinations. This was reported with glee by the *Lancet*:

> The tables have been turned, and an inexorable band of examiners have had the audacity to reject a fair examinee, who has found 'too late that men betray', and that scientific knowledge is not acquired in courts of law.

Four years later she finally gained a medical degree from the University of Berne, a licence from the Irish College, and her place on the Medical Register. For the moment, however, the disappointment was bitter.

The New Hospital for Women

In November 1871 *The Times* published a series of letters from Alice Westlake, the honorary treasurer of a committee set up to found a new women's hospital in London, staffed by women.[177] In this she set out reasons why a hospital was needed and appealed for funds. The committee included a number of familiar names: Lady Amberley, the Earl of Shaftesbury, John Stuart Mill, Mrs Gurney, Miss Cobbe, Henry Fawcett, Mrs Stansfeld, and Newson Garrett. They proposed to convert rooms above the St Mary's Dispensary into a temporary hospital while collecting funds for a new hospital big enough to house 20 patients, to be known as 'The Women's Hospital'. All the medical and surgical staff would consist of qualified women.

The work of the dispensary under Elizabeth Garrett Anderson had grown steadily, with 40,000 outpatient visits from women in the five years since it had opened. This was despite the fact that a small fee was charged at the dispensary while free treatment by male doctors was available at a nearby hospital. In March 1871 Elizabeth Garrett Anderson had been joined in her work at the dispensary by Frances Morgan (later Hoggan). However, the nature of the practice had changed in these five years. Whereas originally her patients had primarily been local working-class women with a variety of illnesses, women, presumably middle-class, were now coming from all over London with mainly gynaecological problems.

In general the proposal for a women's hospital met with a good public response. For instance, the *Daily Telegraph* described it as an 'admirable enterprise'.[178] In a letter to *The Times*, Elizabeth Blackwell gave an account of the successes of the New York Infirmary for Women. She declared that there would be no question of opposition in England if the public could hear 'the pathetic appeal which comes constantly to the woman physician, "Do help me; I shall not mind the operation if you will be the surgeon." '[179] She reported that the infirmary had had almost 60,000 patients in the previous ten years.

However, medical opponents questioned the need for the hospital. They insisted that there were adequate facilities for women and that experienced male surgeons could offer better medical treatment than inexperienced women. There was also some debate in the press about the competence of the proposed female medical staff. One fellow of the Royal College of Physicians wrote to *The Times* to condemn the venture as an attempt by the women who had graduated from Paris and Zurich to take a short-cut to fame, whereas male surgeons had to work their way up from the bottom over a number of years.[180] It was a common complaint during this period that the founders of the many specialist hospitals set up in the 1860s and 1870s were medical profiteers. Opponents refused to recognise the different motives behind the setting up of a hospital for women by women.

The New Hospital for Women was opened in rooms above the dispensary in Seymour Place in February 1872, only three months after the appeal was launched. Elizabeth Garrett Anderson started performing a variety of surgical operations during the following year. Frances Hoggan resigned her post at the hospital in protest at her performing an ovariotomy (removal of the ovaries), as it conflicted with her opposition to vivisection. There was a great deal of controversy among doctors over this operation and death rates were very high during the early years. It was attacked by feminists as medically unnecessary and a mutilation of women's bodies. The committee insisted that the operation be conducted elsewhere for fear of the reputation of the hospital being damaged if it failed. Elizabeth Garrett Anderson rented a room in a private house and had it disinfected in preparation for the operation. For 20 years she was the only woman on the staff who could perform major surgery, which must have been a considerable burden on her.

The hospital continued to rely on constant fundraising, for instance through charity concerts and individual donations. In its first two and a half years the hospital had 302 patients, 149 of whom had been suffering from gynaecological problems. Women were now able to give personal testimony about how their suffering had been greatly lessened because they had been operated on in a women-only environment.

In September the Committee of the Birmingham Medical Hospital for Women appointed to its medical staff Louisa Atkins, who had just graduated along with Eliza Walker from the University of Zurich. This appointment was made despite the fact that Atkins' name was not on the Medical Register. She worked under the surgeon Robert Lawson Tait, who had four other women working under him in the 1870s at a time when most hospitals refused to employ women doctors. He was strongly opposed to animal vivisection. He was also, however, a major proponent of experimental surgery techniques in gynaecology such as ovariotomy.

In October *The Times* carried a report about a donation to the Edinburgh committee of £1000 from a Mr Walter Thomson, whose address was given in different reports as London and Shahabad.[181] It was to be used for furthering the cause of medical women, particularly for legal and other expenses incurred in the campaign for a medical education at Edinburgh and to assist women students who had had to pay high fees for separate classes. In a letter to her mother, Sophia Jex-Blake described how she had received a visit from Walter Thomson, 'a Scotchman resident in India', during which he had offered this donation to the campaign.[182] According to Sophia, he 'cares simply for the principle'. His name does not appear elsewhere in accounts of the campaign. £1000 was a very substantial sum of money in 1872 and such a donation is perhaps an indication of the indignation of the lay public in response to newspaper reports of the medical profession's behaviour.

Walter Thomson seems to have been turned into a supporter of medical women by the extreme hostility, and often unfair tactics, of the medical profession. In a paper printed in *The Scotsman* he laid out his reasons for the donation:

Because I feel that the *right* of women to the higher as

well as to the lower branches of medical education is a matter of simple justice and fair-play. Because . . . I feel utterly ashamed of the conduct and opinion in this matter of some of my own sex . . . [183]

He called on others to follow his example and give donations to the cause as 'an essential aid to all who have to contend against monopoly and prejudice'.

However, the *Lancet* tried to use the donation against the campaign. It declared that soon there would be no need for women to demand entry to existing medical schools as they would be able to found one of their own.[184] From this period on, it was a recurring theme in the pages of the *Lancet* that women should stop asking for special arrangements to be made for them, but should go off and set up their own hospitals and schools.

In November *The Times* reported an attempt by male medical students to disrupt the meeting of the Female Medical Society which opened the ninth annual session of the college, now renamed the Obstetrical College for Women.[185]

Registration of midwives

By 1872 the issue of the seven at Edinburgh was spilling over into discussions within the medical profession about the training and registration of midwives and nurses. During a debate at a meeting of the General Medical Council over whether the council should register qualified midwives and nurses, one member remarked that 'the Council had enough to do without bothering itself about women.'[186] Despite the fact that Dr Acland, the proposer, insisted that the motion had nothing to do with women doctors, constant references were made throughout the debate to the situation at Edinburgh. One contributor said he 'declined to have anything to do, directly or indirectly, with the question of the admission or rejection of Jex-Blake'. In its characteristic way, the *Lancet* went over the top in its reaction to this episode: 'Dr. Acland will be canonised when we get a lady-Pope, which, of course, must follow in the wake of lady-doctors.'[187] By now the profession seems to have had a knee-jerk reaction to any issue involving women and medicine.

In 1872 the London Obstetrical Society (made up of registered medical men) set up its own set of examinations in midwifery, to a mixed reaction from the medical profession. Some saw it as reducing the risks of infant mortality while others saw it as unnecessarily raising the status of midwives. The society was clearly proposing that midwives should only get a yearly renewable licence and so would remain subordinate to and policed by the profession. An article in the *Lancet* came down in favour of educating women as midwives because doctors suffer from 'the drudgery of very cheap midwifery' and this was harmful to the health of rural doctors.[188]

However, many medical men saw the proposals as dangerously close to those coming from the Female Medical Society. The system of registration envisaged by the Female Medical Society was one which would ensure a measure of independence for midwives and thereby constitute a threat to the profession. The *Medical Times* said midwives should only work under close supervision of a medical man and dismissed the Female Medical Society as made up of 'hopeless spinsters' and 'sterile matrons'.[189] One of the key issues over which the medical profession and the radical midwives disagreed strongly was whether midwives should be considered competent to attend abnormal births without necessarily calling in a doctor.

Many within the profession were trying to secure obstetrics as the sole preserve of medical men and were particularly opposed to any proposal which made it easier for women to specialise in the treatment of women and children. According to Dr Aveling, the outspoken opponent of all independent female practitioners, midwives should be seen 'compared with the skilled obstetrician . . . as the organ-blower to the organist'.[190] In December 1872 the short-lived Obstetrical Association of Midwives asked the Royal College of Surgeons to set up a hospital-based course, under the supervision of the association, and to open its midwifery licence to women. The college refused. One response to this proposal was a letter to the *Lancet* from a doctor who stated:

It should be the steady aim of every man engaged in obstetrical practice to discourage – the time has scarcely arrived when we can abolish – midwifery practice.[191]

Women themselves were not united on the best approach to this issue. Many feminists were opposed to proposals even from women for the registration of midwives as independent practitioners, because they feared that these proposals could be subverted by the medical profession to further restrict yet another area of female employment.

Eventually, the registration of midwives was brought in on government, not medical, initiative in 1902, at least 50 years later than in other European countries. The long delay was due to the general opposition from the medical profession towards the registration of ancillary medical professions such as dentistry and chiropody and their particular determination to exclude *all* female practitioners from any legal recognition. It is clear that the profession saw a midwifery qualification as the thin end of the wedge, leading to full registration of women as doctors, and that it agreed that the safest course was to exclude women from all diplomas and licences.

Defeat at Edinburgh

In Edinburgh events were now moving towards a final stalemate. The situation was still unsatisfactory, despite Lord Gifford's judgment and the infirmary decision, since the women students had to rely on the extra-mural lecturers and were excluded from surgical operations at the infirmary. In September 1872 the Senate announced its decision to appeal against Lord Gifford's ruling. In the elections for the infirmary board the following January, the women's side was narrowly defeated. It was only through the intervention of the Lord Provost that the new board was prevented from withdrawing even the very limited access to the wards which had been granted in December. The *Englishwoman's Review* reported a meeting held on 24 February at which Sophia Jex-Blake insisted that a radical solution must be found, either to let women into all classes on equal terms or to change the law to allow registration of those women ready to enter practice.[192]

According to the *Englishwoman's Review* the women students were frantically busy trying to study, attend lectures, defend lawsuits, plead their case, and 'engage . . . in defeating the last new dodge of the Medical Faculty'.[193] They started looking into possibilities elsewhere, at St Andrews, Newcastle and Dublin, but met with no success, despite promises to provide enough women students and to pay any extra expenses. The journal also reported that Edith Pechey had agreed to a request from the Ladies' Educational Association in Leeds for lectures on physiology over the winter and had then been asked to repeat the lectures in York and Halifax.[194] The classes were larger than usual, and larger than when a medical man taught them. This was seen by the *Review* as proof that women *did* want to learn about their own bodies from doctors of their own sex.

The final blow in Edinburgh came in June when the Court of Session upheld the Senate's appeal against Lord Gifford's judgment. One argument used by the university in court pursued the following dogged logic: women are excluded from the franchise but university graduates have the right to vote and therefore women cannot be allowed to graduate. In its ruling, the Court of Session declared that the 1869 regulations had been *ultra vires* and awarded costs of £848 6s. 8d. against the women. As supporters were quick to point out, however, only seven out of the 12 judges ruled in the university's favour. The *English-woman's Review* bitterly criticised this decision and declared that it 'inflicts a monopoly of male medical attendance on every Englishwoman' [sic]. It was particularly outraged that the women were to be financially penalised for the university's supposedly illegal actions.[195]

On July 22 the executive committee in Edinburgh put out a statement, giving a summary of the events of the past two years and details of the ruling.[196] They also put out a general appeal for funds for a variety of purposes: paying lecturers, hiring rooms for classes, seeking legal advice, and daily campaign expenses. Once again the legal costs were covered by public donations. They also started discussing long-term plans for founding a medical school and dispensary for women and children and invited donations for this too. They decided not to appeal against the judgment and, although a few women continued their medical studies at the extra-mural school, the four-year struggle at Edinburgh was over.

PART 4

Rights Which Can No Longer Be Reasonably Denied

12 The Tide Turns

In July 1873 Sophia Jex-Blake and others approached St Andrews for permission to study there but, despite support from some professors, they were refused. In September two of the original 'Edinburgh Seven' went to Paris to continue their studies, with credits for the courses they had taken at Edinburgh. In the end three of the seven emerged with a degree from Paris. Emily Bovell graduated in 1877, but never went on the Medical Register and thus did not practise as a doctor. Both Mary Marshall and Matilda Chaplin Ayrton graduated in 1879 and were accepted on to the register the following year. Although most of the women (including for a while Sophia Jex-Blake) returned to Edinburgh in October 1873 to continue classes with the extra-mural lecturers, the full-scale campaign at the university was for the moment abandoned.

Tactical disagreements

Among various public reactions to the decision at Edinburgh were letters to *The Times* from Elizabeth Garrett Anderson and Sophia Jex-Blake, in which they put forward two conflicting proposals for future strategy.[1] In her letter on 5 August, Elizabeth Garrett Anderson said that there would be little chance of legislation until women had the vote. It was commonly believed by feminists at this stage that women would get the vote after only a short struggle and that *other* reforms (which in fact preceded by a number of years the granting of limited female suffrage in 1918) would follow as a direct result. She argued that the medical corporations and schools were unlikely to change their minds about admitting women, because of the conservatism and trades-unionism of the profession. She opposed the setting up of separate schools for women, because she believed this would lead to separate diplomas and registration, and women would be seen as an inferior section of the profession.

Her solution was for women to study and graduate in Paris and to return to England to set up in practice unregistered. She said that the problem of practising while not on the register had been greatly exaggerated: she herself was of course on the register but other unregistered women such as Eliza Walker Dunbar, Lousia Atkins and Frances Hoggan had been practising in Britain from the early 1870s on a foreign degree alone. She dismissed as groundless fears that women would agree to accept lower fees. Opposition would disappear, she said, 'if we could point to a considerable number of medical women quietly making for themselves the reputation of being trustworthy and valuable members of the profession'. It is very tempting to interpret this comment, and in particular the word 'quietly', as an implicit dig at Sophia Jex-Blake.

In her reply, Sophia Jex-Blake said that going abroad was the worst possible alternative, since very few women could afford this solution. Moreover, she said, practising on a foreign degree would give women doctors no legal standing or protection and it would seem to their opponents an admission of defeat. This point echoes the strong conviction of her American friend, Dr Lucy Sewell, that it was a bad idea for unregistered medical women in Britain simply to set up in practice because there would be no differentiation in the public mind between properly trained and other women practitioners. This view must have come out of her own experience of the medical women movement in the United States. It was, Sophia said, too much to assume that the Scottish universities were closed for ever and that legislation was impossible. She wanted aspiring medical women to join the classes at the Edinburgh extra-mural school, and called for continuing pressure to be put on Parliament to legislate for admission.

One of the central features of the medical women movement of these decades was the fundamental disagreement over tactics between Sophia Jex-Blake and Elizabeth Garrett Anderson. Alongside other pioneering women of this period, these women were exploring new territory. They had no role model for their own personal or professional behaviour and could not draw on the experience of women gaining entry to professions on a large scale to help them formulate strategies for this campaign. Apart from a few individuals, professional women were not an established part of Victorian society and consequently those who were attempting to make a career for themselves, and open the way for others, were operating in a vacuum. With no established support system, yet, for women involved in feminist campaigns, there was an underlying conflict between the individualistic pioneer approach of someone like Florence Nightingale and various collective attempts to gain rights for women as a group.

These differing approaches can be seen quite clearly in the campaign for women doctors. Whereas Sophia Jex-Blake advocated confrontation and a full-scale political campaign in order to force the medical profession to accept female entry as an indisputable right, Elizabeth Garrett Anderson believed in quiet persuasion and the example of a few respectable and respected women practitioners. She saw her own career, with its many personal successes, as paving the way for general acceptance of women doctors. She was all the time conscious of her responsibility as a pioneer: 'It is my business to become a great physician, nothing else I [could] do [would] help women so much as this.'[2] She saw her membership of the British Medical Association and her work on the London School Board as important steps towards winning the respect of the medical profession and the general public.

It had of course been her experience that a sufficient number of medical men had been prepared to support her in her solo attempt at a medical education and career. In the early days she was the *only* woman seeking a medical education in Britain and therefore seen as less of a threat by the medical profession. Once she was well launched on her education, even the *Lancet* had been forced to give grudging recognition of her ability and reconciled this with its overall hostility to medical women by seeing her as an exceptional case. In 1870 the journal had called on the medical profession to support her in the election for the London School Board, saying that she was so able by the standards of either sex that support for her did *not* imply general backing for women doctors.[3]

However, the contribution she made to opening the medical profession to women by establishing securely her own professional career was of only limited value. Other women did not find it so easy to follow in her footsteps in the new climate of outright medical hostility towards the campaign for women doctors. Nor did other women necessarily have the access to money and influence which Elizabeth Garrett Anderson enjoyed: throughout her career she was supported financially and in other important ways by her father.

There were other ways in which Elizabeth Garrett Anderson and Sophia Jex-Blake did not see eye to eye. Elizabeth was always at pains to avoid any suggestion of a conflict of interests between the sexes. Although she did believe that women doctors 'would make war, perhaps more successfully than men, against chronic ill-health in women', she questioned the view that they would be better at treating female complaints simply *because* they were women, and asserted that this would depend on their medical knowledge and intelligence.[4] All along she was insistent that the most important thing was that women should be as thoroughly trained as men and have equally high professional standards.

She also stressed the importance of behaving 'like a lady' and presenting an overall impression of femininity, for the good of the cause.[5] There was obviously a fundamental difference in the attitudes of Elizabeth and Sophia towards men and a wider personality clash between the two women. Throughout the years of the campaign Elizabeth was worried that Sophia's abrasive manner and confrontational tactics would only harm the interests of medical women and alienate the support of men. It is interesting that Elizabeth Blackwell, whose personal experience of medical attitudes was fairly close to that of Elizabeth Garrett Anderson, seems to have held similar views. For instance, at one point she declared that she did not want to have anything to do with 'an anti-man movement' because she herself had had so much support from individual men. She believed that education had 'nothing to do with women's rights or men's rights, but only with the development of the human soul and body'.[6]

Elizabeth Garrett Anderson also believed that professional women should be able to marry and have children without having to give up their career. She herself had a daughter, Louisa, named after her sister, in July 1873 and a second one, Margaret, in September 1874. At the age of 37 she worked hard in the New Hospital to within days of Louisa's birth. However, in the autumn of 1873 she did resign from the school board and her post at the East London Hospital, presumably because of the new baby. Sadly, her second child, Margaret, died of meningitis when she was a year old.

Sophia Jex-Blake saw combining marriage and a career as trying to 'serve two masters' and she herself never married.[7] In the second edition of her book she stated that 32 out of the 50 registered women in 1886 had never married.[8] Of the 18 who had married, three began study while already married, five were already widows, and 10 married during or soon after studying. She also asserted that out of 160 to 170 women who had studied medicine in Britain since 1869 she knew of only eight or 10 who had abandoned their studies in order to marry. By 1911 the figures were even more striking: 80 per cent of all women doctors were unmarried.

Over the summer of 1873 a woman attempted to enrol as a medical student at Queen's College in Birmingham. The professors agreed to her entry on the condition that separate classes were set up but, although a group of women said they would guarantee fees to these professors, the council of the college said it was not possible to make separate arrangements. A 'meeting of ladies' was held at the beginning of June, at which an all-woman local association was formed to promote the medical education of women and specifically to gain entry to the college. The meeting decided to approach the council and the professors to propose either that arrangements be made for separate classes or that women be admitted to all existing classes. However, this local support for medical women failed to persuade the authorities to allow women into the college as medical students.

During this summer too a proposal to elect Eliza Walker Dunbar as house surgeon at the Hospital for Sick Children and Outdoor Treatment of Women in Bristol was met with threats of resignation from the existing male surgical staff. However, a meeting of subscribers passed a motion by 72 votes to 12 to admit women to medical appointments at the hospital and in July Eliza Walker Dunbar joined the staff. According to a report in the *Englishwoman's Review* in January 1874, two members of the medical staff resigned immediately after her appointment.[9] Tension continued between her and the other doctors and, following an argument between her and one of the honorary physicians, the entire male staff resigned before any attempt to resolve the matter had been made. For five days Eliza Walker Dunbar was left to cope single-handedly with the running of the medical affairs of the hospital. Then two doctors agreed to fill in until new staff were chosen. As a result of these events, she decided to resign and set up in private practice in Bristol. The incident was reported fully in *The Times* and the *Lancet*.[10] The *Lancet* attributed the problem in Bristol to the fact that the hospital was well established and a woman doctor was being 'forced' on *existing* staff. This, they said, was entirely different from the situation in Birmingham where Louisa Atkins was appointed to a post at the Birmingham Medical Hospital for Women, which was a *new* institution. In a letter to *The Times* Eliza Walker Dunbar accused the doctors of unfair treatment towards a fellow professional.[11]

In September another correspondence was published in *The Times*, this time over the interpretation of the past four years' events at Edinburgh. According to Alexander Grant, the Principal of the university, the professors had all wanted women to be admitted to medical education, as far as the existing structure allowed, and denied that any barriers had been put in their way![12] He said the 1869 regulations allowing professors to lecture to the women were only permissive and experimental and the experiment had simply failed.

In her reply, Sophia Jex-Blake completely rejected this account of events.[13] She said the 1869 regulations had not been seen by either side as experimental but that the university had agreed specifically to 'the education of women for medicine'. By declaring that this very decision had been beyond the university's constitutional powers, the appeal judges in June 1873 effectively confirmed that this had indeed been the agreement. She reasserted the claims that there had been both open and hidden hostility from Medical Faculty staff and students and denied that the university had done all in its power to let the women continue.

First attempts at legislation

The women were now actively seeking legislative solutions to the deadlock. In July 1873 Sir David Wedderburn MP agreed to introduce a bill to enable the Scottish universities to educate women in medicine and grant them degrees, since Edinburgh University seemed to regard the supposed constitutional problem as the main barrier. This proposal was met with informal promises of support. It also received a favourable response from the Home Secretary, Robert Lowe, who as MP for the University of London had just received a petition from 470 London graduates (about one third of the total) which contained the statement that they were in favour of opening all degrees to women. This petition had been started by a Dr Alfred Shewen and the signatories included 60 other medical men. But, soon after, Parliament was dissolved and this initiative was lost.

In the new Parliament Sir David Wedderburn was no longer an MP and so Sophia Jex-Blake approached Russell Gurney about the possibility of introducing new legislation. He refused, on the grounds that he was too busy and in bad health. She then tried James Stansfeld, who replied that the doctors hated him and it would be better if someone else proposed the bill. David Masson dismissed this objection: 'We can't expect anyone who takes up the cause to be a darling of the doctors or to remain one.'[14] In the end William Cowper Temple MP, the brother-in-law of Shaftesbury and head of Louisa Twining's Workhouse Visiting Society, agreed to introduce a similar bill. He had been among those who expressed support for the proposed hospital for women in 1859. It is ironic that he had also been responsible for piloting the 1858 Medical Act (which set up the register) through the House of Commons. The bill was immediately 'hot news' in Scotland, with every university professor and medical man keen to find out what it contained.

In April 1874 the bill had its second reading and a debate took place in June. In the course of this debate William Cowper Temple ridiculed the opposition of the profession:

> Most corporations, as well as individuals, were not averse to having additional powers given to them; particularly powers which they previously believed they had, and which they had proceeded to exercise.[15]

The committee had already started to mobilise public support. By the summer, 65 petitions in favour of the bill had been submitted, including one from 16,000 women, one from all nine of the extra-mural lecturers based at Surgeons' Hall, and one from the University of Glasgow. A memorial in favour of the bill was received from 26 Scottish professors, including 14 from Edinburgh and eight out of the 14 professors at St Andrews. In this memorial they said that 'a cruel hardship and injustice has thus been inflicted on the ladies' and added the following comment on the court decision of 1873: 'They consider that, by that decision, the Scottish Universities are poorer institutions, and less truly Universities . . .'[16] Support was forthcoming also from the town councils of Edinburgh, Aberdeen and Linlithgow, who were motivated by their belief in the Scottish tradition of freedom of access to education for all.

Petitions against the bill were received from the University Court, the Senate and the Medical Faculty at Edinburgh, as well as one from the University of Glasgow in favour of the bill. However, the one from the Senate had been signed by only 12 of its 37 members at a meeting when most non-medical professors were out of town. In May a letter appeared in the *Lancet* urging medical graduates from Edinburgh to sign a petition against this legislation, despite the fact that it would give the university *greater* freedom of action.[17] Furthermore, it was only *permissive* and thus carried no power of compulsion. During the debate in the House of Commons the MP for Edinburgh declared that the city:

> had no sympathy with the bigotry of a small section of
> the professors and that, if this were a question to be settled
> by the intelligent inhabitants of Edinburgh, nine-tenths of
> them would vote in its favour.[18]

He went on to say:

> If two or three of the professors would only take a voyage
> round the world, the whole question would be
> satisfactorily settled before they returned.[19]

During the debate in the Commons William Cowper Temple declared that Parliament must be the final arbiter on medical issues since the profession itself could not be objective on matters concerning their interests.[20] Supporters of the medical women movement believed that the profession had distorted the intentions of the 1858 Act and that their resulting monopoly must be challenged in Parliament and in the courts. This appeal to authority outside the profession was a threat to medical men. At a time when they were fighting to establish professional autonomy and self-regulation they were very sensitive about intervention in medical affairs from outside the profession. In June the bill was postponed for a year, at the request of Lyon Playfair, the member for the Universities of Edinburgh and St Andrews.

Medical scaremongering

In April 1874 the *Fortnightly Review* printed an article called 'Sex in Mind and in Education' written by Dr Henry Maudsley, a well-known psychiatrist who ran a private mental hospital for women and after whom the Maudsley Hospital was named.[21] In this article he summarised his recent book of the same title. He claimed that over-education would harm the health of girls, and in particular that mental and physical exertion after the onset of puberty would result in menstrual disorders and sterility. Allegations of women's intellectual inferiority made during the 1860s were increasingly giving way in this decade to warnings about the possible harmful effects of secondary and higher education on women's health. There was a general belief that ovulation occurred during menstruation and that women and girls should therefore rest at this time in their cycle. It is perhaps significant that University College, London, where Dr Maudsley taught, had just agreed to grant certificates to women.

Dr Maudsley's claims in England were mirrored in the United States by Dr Edward H. Clarke, in a work entitled 'Sex in Education: or, A Fair Chance for the Girls' which was published in 1873.[22] Dr Clarke had initially been a cautious supporter of medical women but had changed his mind shortly after Harvard agreed to admit women to examinations and after women started to apply to the university with enthusiasm. He had recently been elected to the board of overseers at Harvard. Not only did this book affect debates about female education but it also had a very personal effect on those women who were pioneering university education for women. M. Carey Thomas, the first President of Bryn Mawr, a women's college in the United States, recalled the fear among women students themselves:

> We did not know when we began whether women's health could stand the strain of education. We were haunted in those days by the clanging chains of that gloomy little specter, Dr Edward H. Clarke's 'Sex in Education'.[23]

One response, however, to Clarke's book took the offensive. A feminist suggested that women should go on strike during menstruation and refuse to perform any household tasks during that time of the month. It is significant that many medical justifications for separate spheres which were being developed during the 1870s in the United States originated with medical men from Boston. The city was one of the main arenas for the struggle of women to be fully accepted as medical students and practitioners in America.

Maudsley's article created a crisis for those campaigning for secondary education for girls. On behalf of the recently founded Girls' Public Day School Trust, Emily Davies and Frances Buss asked Elizabeth Garrett Anderson to challenge his claims publicly, and as a result an article appeared in the next issue of *Fortnightly Review*.[24] In this article she maintained that it was intellectual frustration and lack of exercise, rather than the strain of education, which caused ill-health among middle-class women. She pointed out that working-class women carried on working at often physically demanding jobs all through their cycle and so women could not, and should not, be seen as being incapacitated by menstruation.

From the first, women doctors were committed to proving the normality of female physiology and thus using their professional knowledge and status to counter pronouncements about women's biological inferiority. For instance, in the United States in 1874 Mary Putnam Jacobi conducted a survey of 286 women in which she discovered that 54 per cent experienced no menstrual problems and most of the rest had only moderate pain.[25] In establishing the normality of menstruation a further aim was to make identification of *real* menstrual problems clearer and to explore improved treatments.

In May the Senate of the University of London declared that it wanted to extend educational opportunities to women in all subjects. There was opposition to this from within the university and from outside, for instance in the *Lancet*.[26] In July the Senate declared that this offer of entry to courses did not include the granting of degrees. In June there was success for the cause in the preliminary examinations at Apothecaries' Hall. Five out of the six women candidates did well, compared with only 11 of the 50 male candidates. Edith Shove was in first place.

In June news also came that Sophia Jex-Blake had again failed her examinations, a misfortune made much of in those sections of the press which were hostile to the cause. The *Lancet* declared that she should not 'appear in public as a martyr to a doubtful cause' if she herself could not show herself capable of academic success.[27] In a letter to *The Times* Isabel Thorne declared that it was 'devotion to our cause' which had led to her failure, as she had been busy with campaigning right up to the day before her examinations.[28] In reply, Sophia Jex-Blake claimed that her preparation *had* been adequate and made allegations that she had been unfairly discriminated against by the examiners.[29] However, she was unable to offer concrete evidence in support of these allegations. Despite the fact that he was sympathetic to medical women and to the higher education of women generally, T. H. Huxley refused to back her claim. Whether or not she was justified in her claim, it was undoubtedly a grave tactical error as it gave adverse publicity to the cause. She had had to cope with intense pressure for a long time and had faced a number of disappointments over the past year. Perhaps this accusation was the result: it is possible she had simply 'cracked' under the strain.

In August she went to London to approach medical schools there but met with no success, although she received various offers of support from individual lecturers. At around this time she, Isabel Thorne and Edith Pechey wrote to the General Medical Council saying that they had had a full medical education but had been refused by all licensing bodies and asking what course they should take. The only reply they received was an acknowledgement of receipt of their letter.

'Establishing the fort'

At this point in the summer of 1874 Sophia Jex-Blake decided that the schools would not give way under present circumstances and that women must fall back on their own resources and take up the long-standing suggestion that they form their own school. In devoting herself to this task over the next two years, she was sacrificing her own studies for the moment. She provided the main driving force and financial backing for this project and gathered a body of distinguished supporters around her. At a meeting held in the house of Dr Anstie on 22 August a provisional committee was formed, with membership confined to qualified medical practitioners in order to establish the school's professional credibility. This committee included Elizabeth Blackwell, Elizabeth Garrett Anderson, T. H. Huxley, and Dr Billing, an elderly and respected member of the profession. It did not include Sophia Jex-Blake, who was not yet on the register, and instead she took on the work of secretary. At this stage the school had a temporary office in Wimpole Street.

Active support also came from Dr King Chambers and Dr Anstie, who were strongly opposed to the profession's exclusion of women. They were prominent medical men and were both Fellows of the Royal College of Physicians. Dr Anstie remarked to Sophia Jex-Blake: 'I wonder that the public do not rise against the medical profession and stone us with paving-stones?'[30] A supporter of medical women later referred to the 'old-world chivalry' of Dr Anstie, although he was in fact only 40 years old.[31] Sadly for medical women, he died in September. His place as Dean of the school was taken by Dr Arthur Norton, who had been a consultant at the New Hospital for Women almost from the start. King Chambers, who was honorary physician to the Prince of Wales and senior consultant physician and lecturer at St Mary's Hospital, continued to teach at the school until 1879 and also acted as trustee. It was at this stage that supporters of the Female Medical Society and its renamed Obstetrical College for Women transferred over to working for the school. The Society and College subsequently folded.

In September Sophia Jex-Blake signed the lease on a building at 30 Henrietta Street, Brunswick Square, London WC. A friend of hers remembered the first few days of the school: 'You stood there alone in almost bare walls, establishing the fort.'[32] On 12 October the London School of Medicine for Women opened with 14 students, 12 of whom had been studying in Edinburgh. In its first year 23 women enrolled as students. Prospective students had to take a rigorous preliminary examination: only very able women were allowed to try for a medical education out of the fear that failure would damage the movement. They also had to find £200 per annum for personal and academic expenses and no scholarships were available at this stage.

The school assembled a staff of qualified lecturers (including Elizabeth Blackwell in the Chair of Gynaecology) and was able to offer the same curriculum as any other medical school. Most of these lecturers were also teaching at one or other of the eleven prestigious hospital medical schools and they faced opposition from within the profession for supporting the medical education of women. As the lecturers were not teaching at the hospital where their medical practice was based, as was the normal arrangement, the school had to guarantee a fixed fee to each one, which was obviously an added financial burden. Thirteen people contributed £1000 each to launch the school. These included 'Mrs Jex-Blake of Brighton', presumably Sophia's mother or sister-in-law, 'Mr Edward Pease of Darlington', a relative of Elizabeth Pease Nichol, Augustus Thorne, Joseph Thorne and Isobel Thorne herself.[33]

The newly opened school was met with hostility and ridicule from the opposition. The response from the *Lancet* was predictable.[34] It referred to the school as a 'dead letter' and implied that the lecturers were second-rate. It also asked whether they should be allowed to carry on in their posts at other hospitals and medical schools. These comments were made despite the fact that medical opponents had been telling women for years to set up their own colleges and hospitals!

The Earl of Shaftesbury gave out the prizes at the end of the first term and Lord Aberdare presided at the first meeting of the governing body. William Shaen, a radical lawyer, agreed to act as solicitor to the school. He had assisted in the foundation of Bedford College and was connected with the campaign for women's entry to Cambridge University. He had taken the chair at a meeting in 1858 held to discuss the medical education of women and had helped Elizabeth Garrett Anderson in her early career. He was a leading member of the campaign against the Contagious Diseases Acts and was also involved in issues such as anti-vivisection, anti-slavery and temperance.

Mary Putnam Jacobi wrote from the United States to congratulate Sophia Jex-Blake on the impressive list of supporters she had already compiled and compared this with the situation in the United States:

> You at least have had the advantage attaching to a
> conspicious battle with real and dignified forces engaged
> on each side; whereas here, – this question, as so many
> others, has rather dribbled into the sands.[35]

However, two major problems remained. First, the school still needed to find a hospital which would admit the women students to clinical instruction, in order to be able to provide a complete medical education. Secondly, all 19 examining and licensing boards refused to recognise the school, and so anyone who completed the course would still be unable to have her name put on the register. It also faced hostility from the landlord who was not entirely happy about his property housing a medical college for women.

Elizabeth Garrett Anderson had always disagreed with the tactic of opening a medical school for women but did agree at the last minute to join the provisional committee. In her book *Medical Women* Sophia Jex-Blake recounted how she had personally persuaded her, and Elizabeth Blackwell, to join:

> I begged her to join the Committee which we were about
> to form, and after some hesitation, she kindly agreed to
> do so, as did also Dr. Elizabeth Blackwell.[37]

The school brought back Elizabeth Garrett Anderson's old fears of women being hived off into a separate and second-rate qualification. She was worried that the school might be tempted to issue its own diploma and that graduates 'would at once be marked as a special class of practitioners, subordinate and inferior to the ordinary doctor.'[32] The old antagonism between her and Sophia Jex-Blake also played a part. In a letter to Elizabeth Garrett Anderson, Sophia accused her of listening to 'cock and bull stories' about what had happened in Edinburgh and of blaming her unfairly for the failure there. The letter ended:

> I never said it did not signify whether you joined the Council, though I did say that I believed the School was already tolerably certain of ultimate success. I think it is of very great importance, both for *your* credit and ours, that there should be no appearance of split in the camp, and I should greatly prefer that your name should appear on the Council.[38]

The opposition of Elizabeth Garrett Anderson and Elizabeth Blackwell hinged on what they saw as a very real danger to medical women. By the early 1870s it was clear that women would settle for nothing less than full entry to the profession and the tactics of the medical opposition shifted from outright exclusion to an attempt to buy women off with a separate medical qualification. Throughout the 1870s Elizabeth Garrett Anderson resisted strongly the recurring threat of women being fobbed off with what would be seen by the public as an inferior education.[39] Elizabeth Blackwell too was unsure whether opening a medical school for women was tactically the right move at this time.[40]

With hindsight we can now see that their fears of women being bought off were not justified. The London School of Medicine for Women not only filled a great need for medical education for women at a time when all other courses in Britain were closed to them, but also operated as a valuable centre where medical women could come together as students, teachers and practitioners.

In June 1874 the New Hospital for Women moved to a new and better site at 222/4 Marylebone Road, where it remained until the final move to Euston Road in 1889. Despite the desperate need for expansion, it still had only 24 beds. In July 'A Surgeon' wrote to *The Times* explaining that the move had become necessary because the demand for beds was so high and pointing out that this was still the case after they introduced, and later increased, a charge for treatment. Elizabeth Garrett Anderson and Frances Hoggan were the visiting physicians. In July they were joined by Louisa Atkins as house surgeon, who was replaced as house surgeon at the Birmingham and Midlands

Hospital for Women by Edith Pechey. Edith Pechey's appointment was treated very favourably in an article in the *Birmingham Daily Post*:

> Public sympathy will be with the Committee in their conviction that it is a great advantage to the Hospital for women to have a lady for its House Surgeon.[41]

In April 1880 Mary Marshall, Elizabeth Garrett Anderson's sister-in-law and one of the original 'Edinburgh Seven', was added to the staff of the hospital, shortly after receiving her degree from Paris and having her name added to the register.

Despite the remaining impasse over medical degrees and registration, those women who had managed to get a good medical education were being accepted in some places, mainly provincial hospitals for women and children, as qualified practitioners. There was also a fresh approach to Queen's College in Birmingham, with a deputation led by the Mayor, Joseph Chamberlain. However, the medical staff of the two teaching hospitals demonstrated their continuing opposition and this approach was rejected by the council. A limited concession was made the following January when one of the hospitals admitted women into instruction on the wards.

The radical connection

Many prominent male supporters of medical women were committed to a wide range of radical causes. Familiar names crop up in expected places in connection with a variety of other campaigns. For example, there were obvious connections between anti-vivisection and the medical women movement.[42] There was an unusually high percentage of women in this campaign and the *Englishwoman's Review* publicly supported it. It attacked the medical profession and this must have struck a chord with the widespread anti-medical feeling among many middle-class women.

There was also an extensive overlap of personnel in the two campaigns. The following supporters of medical women were also all involved in the campaign against vivisection and in the anti-vaccination movement: William Cowper Temple, the Earl of Shaftesbury, James Stansfeld, William Shaen, Frances and

George Hoggan, Duncan MacLaren, and Russell Gurney. Similarly, opponents of medical women appear on the other side in these campaigns: Professor Christison was one of the group of medical scientists who used experiments on live animals as part of their research; Lyon Playfair, who was MP for the Universities of Edinburgh and St Andrews and had been a lecturer at Edinburgh University, was the parliamentary spokesman for the vivisection lobby.

The friendship network between those involved in radical causes in the mid-Victorian period was extensive. Individual connections within this radical community were often a great help to medical women. For example, Elizabeth Garrett Anderson had been introduced to Dr John Chapman (proprietor of the radical *Westminster Review*) by the feminist Bessie Rayner Parkes in 1861, and had got a letter of introduction from him to Professor Day of St Andrews University. Similarly, Sophia Jex-Blake's approach to Edinburgh University in 1869 had been made easier by personal connections.

As in other radical campaigns such as anti-vivisection, lawyers and clerics were prominent among the supporters of medical women. Radicals and liberals from other professions were keen to take every opportunity to attack what they saw as the dangerously increasing power of the medical profession. As part of this inter-professional hostility, many lawyers and clerics were eager to support the entry of women into the medical profession. They sought to deflate the profession's claim to status by making remarks which portrayed medicine as a skilled craft rather than a scientific profession. For example, at the meeting to elect the infirmary board in Edinburgh in January 1872, the respected Reverend Dr Guthrie asked why 'women should not be trusted with administering a dose of physic or preparing a blister'.[43]

Whereas medical men saw self-regulation as vital to the establishment of their profession, others saw this as 'trades-unionism'. Throughout the campaign the accusation of 'trades-unionism' was levelled at the medical profession by supporters of medical women, particularly by men. It was used interchangeably with 'monopoly', a term associated with capital rather than labour. This confusion of terms reflects the ambiguous class position occupied by the profession at this time. Doctors were characterised both as jumped-up craftsmen or, what was considered to be even worse, tradesmen, but were also condemned as 'aristocratic'. What supporters were clear about was their distaste for any legal or institutional barrier which hindered the operation of 'free trade' in the field of employment. They saw both 'trades-unionism' and 'monopoly' as opposed to the 'spirit of the age'.

They also saw the growing public authority of medical men and the encroachment of materialist and utilitarian social values as politically and morally worrying. They believed that the application of purely scientific and medical criteria to questions such as vivisection, vaccination and venereal disease would lead to government policies which paid little regard to morality or to the rights of the individual. Also, lawyers were alarmed at the claims made by doctors, particularly psychiatrists, that medical evidence in certain cases could override legal notions of motivation and responsibility.[44]

Despite the undoubtedly genuine and much-needed support given to medical women by leading members of the liberal/radical community, it is not clear that this was not prompted in the first instance by *general* hostility to the medical profession, as described above. Support for women's issues in this period often came from men such as these as a logical extension of their liberal politics. A survey of those sympathetic to feminists in this period shows that women often devoted their whole lives to women's politics but that this was not true for any of the men, who tended to commit their time and energy to a number of causes.[45] Many of them served these causes through their professional work, as MPs, lawyers and journalists. Their involvement in feminism was often as *spokesmen* on women's issues, at a time when certain public arenas were closed to women. As women's participation in public life increased, the need for men to speak for them decreased.

Male support for feminism was often rooted more strongly in their hostility towards *other men* than in a fundamental belief in women's rights. For example, for many men the campaign against the Contagious Diseases Acts was more a struggle *between men* on the question of sexual morality than a fight for women's rights. On a more personal note, it seems that Elizabeth Garrett Anderson's father, who was initially strongly opposed to her plans to study medicine, was won round by what he saw as the prejudice and exclusion tactics of the male medical profession.

Where there was a conflict between support for women's rights and adherence to strict liberal principles, the male response was often to abandon their feminist commitment. For example, J.G.S. Anderson resigned from the committee of Emily Davies' Girton College over its heavy involvement with the Church of England. In a letter to Emily Davies, Elizabeth Garrett Anderson remarked that whereas *they* were both interested first in women's rights, *he* was primarily committed to liberalism.[46]

Despite the common political ground between the medical women movement and campaigns such as those against vivisection and the CD Acts and the extensive overlap of individuals involved, full-scale alliances were never formed. Frances Power Cobbe was horrified by pro-vivisection medical women whom she saw as women taking on male 'vices'.[47] Certain individual doctors, such as Elizabeth Blackwell, Frances Hoggan and Anna Kingsford, were actively involved in one or more of the other campaigns but these were women who had particular religious or political reasons for doing so. Anna Kingsford, who gained her MD from Paris in 1880, in fact decided to get a medical qualification specifically for the purpose of campaigning more effectively against vivisection. Although she did practise as a doctor in England from 1880 to 1887, she was mainly involved in spiritualism.

These campaigns were characterised by such a high level of hostility towards the medical profession as a whole that most medical women probably felt themselves unable to support them openly, for fear of jeopardising their own careers. The London School of Medicine for Women decided to play it safe over this issue. No animal experiments were conducted at the school but it avoided any direct contact with the campaign against vivisection, and pro-vivisectionists had quite a lot of influence in its affairs.

Both Marie Zakrzewska in the United States and Elizabeth Garrett Anderson in Britain made conscious decisions not to be seen to be publicly in favour of other radical causes, for the sake of medical women generally. Also, they both came into direct conflict with Elizabeth Blackwell over what she saw as their excessive use of surgery on women, an issue which particularly concerned women anti-vivisectionists. Elizabeth Blackwell even made veiled accusations that Elizabeth Garrett Anderson was carrying out experimental ovariotomies (the removal of ovaries) at the New Hospital in 1894, although she withdrew her accusation after receiving a protest from Elizabeth Garrett Anderson.[48] Frances Hoggan's resignation from the New Hospital in 1872 was said to have been over the same issue. It is interesting that it was those women doctors who most stressed adherence to (male) professional values, and who came into direct conflict with Blackwell over experimental surgery, who also achieved greatest professional success. It was not possible to be politically active *and* have a successful career.

The failure of most women doctors to come out in public against vivisection and the CD Acts did not deter all of those involved in these other campaigns from supporting women doctors. For instance, James Stansfeld seemed quite philosophical about their opposition and took an optimistic long-term view:

> I foresaw the danger of their becoming at first, in majority, our opponents on the CD question but, I saw, it is their right and must ultimately tell for us.[49]

Medical women in India

In March 1875 public attention was drawn to the medical education of women in India. *The Times* reported that the government of Madras wanted to encourage women to study medicine in order to be 'useful practitioners to look after women in childbirth and to attend them in everyday ailments'.[50] They agreed to let Mary Scharlieb and three other white European women start a full degree course at the medical college there.[51] Five years earlier an American doctor, Clara Swain, had gone to India with the Women's Foreign Missionary Society of the Methodist Episcopal Church. She had started training girls at an orphanage in Bareilly in physiology and hygiene and opened a dispensary there in 1873 and a hospital in 1874.

Mary Scharlieb's mother had died of puerperal fever ten days afer Mary was born. She had been brought up by her aunt who had sent her to a succession of boarding schools because she believed she needed to be able to earn her own living. In 1865

Mary had moved to India with her barrister husband. In her autobiography, *Reminiscences*, she spoke of hearing stories of a young Indian woman barricading her door with her body to stop the doctor seeing her, despite being in considerable pain from a difficult labour.[52] Under the influence of this and similar examples of the sufferings of other Hindu and Moslem women, Scharlieb decided that some European women should qualify in order to help them. She did not, however, suggest that it should be *Indian* women who should receive a medical training.

She started studying privately and got instruction in midwifery from Mrs Secluna, the matron of the local lying-in hospital, despite facing opposition from the male superintendent. She then decided a full education in medicine and surgery was needed. Her husband had supported her so far in her medical training but refused to let her go to Britain to join Elizabeth Garrett Anderson and Sophia Jex-Blake. Instead she set out to persuade the authorities in India of the need for medical women. In contrast to what was happening in Britain, arrangements for the students were made in a 'generous spirit'.[53] They did not have to pay fees and they were provided with books and a study room. They went to most lectures with the male students and to separate classes in midwifery and surgery. They could either follow the full curriculum, leading to a degree, or take a more limited midwifery course. In 1878 all four women received the Licence of Medicine, Surgery and Midwifery from the college.

After the London School of Medicine for Women opened, some women missionaries left their work in India in order to take medical degrees and return as qualified doctors to their work with Indian women in dispensaries and the zenanas. In 1878 Mary Scharlieb herself returned to England and approached Elizabeth Garrett Anderson about entry to the London School of Medicine for Women. She was advised to wait until her health improved on the grounds that she needed to be physically strong to commence studies at the school, which she did later that year. At this time she made contact with Florence Nightingale who was interested to hear about the position of Hindu and Moslem women in India and gave her help and encouragement in her studies. She returned to India in 1883. Among the first graduates of the school were other younger women who then went out to India for the first time.

No doubt the ease with which white women entered medicine in India, and the support for this in Britain, can be largely explained by racist and imperialist attitudes. It was far easier for white middle-class Englishmen to accept the idea that Indian doctors were offering inadequate medical care than to accept the same criticism of their medical counterparts in Britain. Similar racism was seen in the anti-vivisection movement in which doctors in Britain were happy to condemn the practices of doctors in other countries while hotly denying that experiments involving live animals were ever carried out by British doctors. Also, approval for the work of white female medical missionaries, despite the supposed 'handicap' of their sex, was probably forthcoming because it fitted in with the imperialist scheme of imposing all aspects of western culture on India.

By 1880 there was general acceptance that women with a full medical education were needed in India. References were often made to the existence of this need by supporters of medical education in Britain during the 1870s, at public meetings and during debates in the House of Commons in 1875 and 1876.[54] The undeniable fact that women doctors were needed in India provided important material for the arguments of the campaign in Britain. Similarly, women doctors in the United States were already proven to be competent and in great demand. Claims by medical and other men that women did not possess the abilities to pursue a medical career, and that no one would want to consult them if they did, were thus constantly being undermined.

13 Victory at Last

In early March 1875 William Cowper Temple reintroduced his Universities of Scotland (Degrees to Women) Bill. Although this proposed that the Scottish universities be legally empowered to open *all* degrees to women, the debate focused almost entirely on the medical education of women. He and another MP both stated that, even if all degrees were open to women, most would choose to study medicine.[55] After a long debate, fully reported in *The Times*, the bill fell by 196 votes to 153, despite general acceptance of women's suitability for medicine and their right to higher education.[56]

Three weeks later he tried a different tack with a proposal to allow women with foreign degrees on to the register since at that time there was no means of registration for women. The *Englishwoman's Review* remarked that this would test the sincerity of those MPs who had opposed the Scottish Universities Bill on the grounds that it interfered with the universities' liberties.[57] Opposition to the bill came instead from another male institution: it was greeted with indignation by the *Lancet*. It protested that it would mean registering practitioners over whom the General Medical Council had no examining powers. It also seemed deeply concerned that this would discriminate against *men* who held foreign degrees![58] The proposed bill got no government support and was shelved. However, it seemed that the government now decided that the issue could not be continually put off and promised to make a statement in the next session.

Next came a crucial move, with a request from the Privy Council that the General Medical Council state its position on medical women. It is interesting to note that the wording of the question in fact made it very difficult for the General Medical Council to return an unfavourable judgment. They were asked, 'Shall women be excluded by law' from the practice of medicine.[59] The debate lasted for three days and, according to the *Englishwoman's Review*, 'a desperate struggle took place'.[60] In the course of the debate Dr Turner, a familiar figure of opposition from the Edinburgh days, raised the issue of women's smaller brain size as an argument against entry. A contribution also came from Dr Wood, another of the Edinburgh professors, who declared that women were discredited by women doctors and that men must stand up chivalrously for women and stop this happening. Shortly afterwards, the *Englishwoman's Review* published a letter from a woman signing herself 'A Convalescent', who had recently received treatment at the New Hospital for Women in which she protested against the views of Wood:

> How low and sordid it must be to prescribe medicines and receive handsome fees as a *physician* – how grand and magnanimous to perform the ill-paid drudgery of a nurse.[61]

After the debate, the General Medical Council issued the following statement:

> The Medical Council are of opinion that the study and practice of Medicine and Surgery, instead of affording a field of exertion well fitted for women, do on the contrary, present special difficulties which cannot be safely disregarded; but the Council are not prepared to say that women ought to be excluded from the profession.[62]

Although the *Lancet* insisted that this did *not* mean that the General Medical Council was in favour but was leaving it to the government to decide, the declaration was definitely seen as favourable and was a crucial turning point in the struggle for women's entry to the profession.[63] According to James Stansfeld, from this point on 'the position of the opponents of medical women became untenable, and the legalised admission of women to the ranks of the profession only a question of time'.[64] The *Englishwoman's Review* declared: 'We have entered upon the last phase of the long contest.'[65]

Rearguard action by the medical profession

In late 1875 a new idea emerged that women medical students should try for the licence in midwifery of the Royal College of Surgeons, which would enable women to have their names put on the Medical Register. Edith Pechey said the certificate would be a 'sorry thing to practise on' and Sophia Jex-Blake was worried that, if the idea worked, opponents might use it to refuse any further demands.[66] But, along with Isobel Thorne, Edith and Sophia decided to go ahead and apply for examination.

However, certain sections of the profession did not want women to be channelled into the profession via the midwifery licence and tried to block this move. In her book *Medical Women* Sophia Jex-Blake wrote amusingly of the reaction of the Obstetrical Society. She reported that they 'were at once in a flutter when the mere idea got wind' and immediately set up a committee to monitor the proposal.[67] She went on to say that this committee 'evidently passed into a condition of grievous trepidation' and sent a letter to the Royal College of Surgeons urging them not to let women on to the register by this route.[68]

After consulting legal opinion, the college was forced to agree to examine the women. Then, when the three women sent in their applications, the entire board of examiners resigned and, according to Sophia Jex-Blake, 'the greatest possible pressure was exercised to prevent any leading man-midwife' from replacing them thus making examination impossible.[69] A letter from one of the examiners declared that he had been motivated by a desire to protect women, 'feeling deeply the injustice and danger of making women and children the subjects of inferior medical skill'.[70] At a meeting of the Obstetrical Society soon afterwards, a vote of thanks to the examiners was passed by 'universal acclamation'. This train of events effectively closed off this side door to the profession.

Supporters of the medical women movement constantly remarked on the particular hostility from those doctors who earned a living by treating women. In 1874 Elizabeth Garrett Anderson's application for membership of the Obstetrical Society was refused. The response of *The Scotsman* to this refusal was scathing:

The Society gave its formal adhesion to the most advanced principles of medical trade unionism by deciding that no woman could ever be allowed, with its sanction, to join in the discussion concerning the treatment and relief of those sufferings which women alone have to endure.[71]

The exclusion of Elizabeth Garrett Anderson also drew from Sophia Jex-Blake a typically sarcastic response in her book. She noted with amusement that the society's librarian had had to apply personally to Agnes McLaren for a copy of her thesis on the uterus. Her comment on this was that the society was happy 'to avail itself of women's brains, if it can do so without making any return for their services'.[72] In 1877 Sophia Jex-Blake herself was refused entry from the Hospital for Women, Soho Square, which had been the first of its kind in the world when it was founded in 1842. She wrote twice to the secretary of the medical committee, but with no success.

In a leading article in the *Lancet* already quoted, it was claimed that obstetrics had been 'rescued from the midwives and "sages femmes" '.[73] This 'rescue' of women from medical treatment by women seems to have been of paramount importance to the male medical profession. Although the bulk of midwifery work was exhausting and unprofitable, an important part of a doctor's income came from attending their middle- and upper-class women patients in childbirth. Doctors also often used midwifery cases as a way of establishing a practice and then later handed over all but the remunerative cases to a midwife. In 1861 the *Lancet* had stated that midwives were by then employed only by those people who could not afford male doctors. Otherwise:

in civilised communities midwives have long given way to the superior energies, calmness of judgement, and acquirements of their male competitors.[74]

In an article published in 1877, James Stansfeld made the following observation:

But it is curious to notice how persistent hostility still finds its stronghold in the ranks of those practitioners who have devoted themselves to the special treatment of the diseases of women, and to the practice of midwifery. Can it be that they, more than others, tremble for their monopoly.[75]

As well as seeking to protect their own professional interests, they were also reacting as men to the threat of female solidarity. The professionalisation of nursing and proposals for the greater independence of midwives were seen as equally threatening: their acquisition of medical skills and authority was dangerous precisely because they were women. If women were not only handing down information from one generation to another about such things as birth control but could also call on the support and knowledge of independent professionally-trained women, their chances of controlling their own fertility and by extension their own lives would be greatly increased. One argument used against medical women in a General Council debate in Edinburgh in November 1869 was that women doctors would enter upon 'very improper practices', such as abortion.[76]

The particular concern of the medical profession to keep women away from treating women seems ironic, since these branches of medicine are among the most male-dominated areas of the profession today. In 1986 women made up only 11.5 per cent of consultant obstetricians and gynaecologists in England and Wales, and there was only one woman elected to the council of the Royal College of Obstetricians and Gynaecologists.[77] This may be the result of a successful rearguard action by medical men or of women's fear of becoming ghettoised in the area of women's medicine, or both.

At this point in late 1875 Sophia Jex-Blake was strongly tempted to rush off to work in a hospital in Sarajevo: 'It would be an intense relief to break right away into half savage parts and to hard rough work – and breathe.'[78] She was clearly feeling the strain of having campaigned non-stop for six years, but decided against this move. As well as having fears about her mother's health, she was worried about the possible implications for the campaign: 'Also I should hurt "the cause" by doctoring men.'[79]

Success in parliament

In February 1876 William Cowper Temple reintroduced his Foreign Degrees Bill and once again supporters tried to exert their influence. The Duke of Richmond at the Privy Council received a deputation made up of lecturers and students from the London School of Medicine for Women and other sympathisers, including the Earl of Shaftesbury. They pointed out that the 1858 Medical Act had *not* been drafted so as to exclude women but that it had been used for that purpose by opponents of medical women. Clarification that medical bodies were not legally prevented from educating and licensing women was needed from the government.

The deputation was led by James Stansfeld MP, one of the staunchest supporters of medical women. He was a barrister and a close friend of William Shaen, who was involved in feminist and other radical politics. He was married to Shaen's daughter, Caroline, who was herself a feminist. He was also a supporter of women's suffrage. He had first contacted the campaign about the possibility of legislation in 1873 while he was still President of the Local Government Board, but he was now out of office following the fall of the government in 1874. Since then he had devoted his time (and sacrificed his political career) to reviving the campaign against the Contagious Diseases Act, which had rather lost its momentum during the early 1870s.

The bill had its second reading in July. Shortly afterwards Russell Gurney introduced his Enabling Bill whose main purpose was to permit licensing bodies to examine women. It was promised government support so William Cowper Temple withdrew his bill. An interesting feature of debates about Gurney's bill was that one MP, John Roebuck, supported the medical education of women while being opposed to female suffrage. Apparently he believed that women would not need the vote if Parliament fulfilled what he considered its proper function of looking after the interests of all members of society, whether or not they had the vote.[80] *The Scotsman* held the same contradictory views. Perhaps both positions can be seen as arising out of a desire to control female sexuality: preventing intimate contact between male doctor and female patient, on the one hand, and keeping women out of the (male) public sphere on the other.

At a meeting of the General Medical Council in June members expressed worries about any legislation 'which would interfere with the free action of the Universities and Corporations . . . in respect of the medical education, examination, and licensing of women'.[81] However, the bill was only *permissive*, stating that there were no legal barriers to the medical examining boards granting licences to women. The exclusion of women from any medical school or licensing body continued to be perfectly legal. The meeting was also assured that any licensing body which did choose to admit women as members could still continue to exclude them from the *privileges* of membership. The Enabling Bill passed through Parliament surprisingly quickly and became law on 12 August.

During the same period, from May to August, an important episode in the battle over vivisection was taking place. A bill had been introduced which would restrict the carrying out of animal experiments. An amended version of this bill was passed in August after intense pressure from the medical profession, both from the scientific researchers who would be directly affected by such legislation and from the medical profession as a whole which perceived it as a general threat to its authority.

Although opposition had not yet lessened among the die-hards, the debates over legislation in the mid 1870s showed a marked change in general attitudes towards the question of women doctors. The public success of those women who had already set themselves up in practice in Britain (despite the unregistered status of all but Elizabeth Blackwell and Elizabeth Garrett Anderson) and the flood of letters and petitions to newspapers, journals and MPs made it virtually impossible to claim there was no demand for women doctors. According to the report in the *Englishwoman's Review* of the debate on Gurney's Enabling Bill, women's rights to be attended by a female doctor 'was almost universally acknowledged' by MPs.[82] Contrast this with the derision for such an assertion in the pages of the *Lancet* during the 1860s. Although the opposition from the University of Edinburgh had not lessened, Lyon Playfair, the MP for the Universities of Edinburgh and St Andrews, was forced to concede that public opinion was increasingly in favour of medical women. He said he had had no letters of protest against the Enabling Bill from medical men in his constituency or petitions from either university. In 1878 a leading article in *The Times* accepted female qualification and registration as 'privileges and rights which . . . can no longer be reasonably denied'.[83]

Following this victory, in the winter of 1876–7, Edith Pechey and Sophia Jex-Blake travelled to Berne, with Annie Clarke, a student from the London School of Medicine for Women, to complete their studies. In January Sophia Jex-Blake and Edith Pechey passed the degree examinations and Annie Clark graduated the following year. They returned to London for more clinical experience and then went to Dublin to sit the examinations which would at last place their names on the Medical Register. It seems that the first breakthrough came in Ireland because London was still in the grip of the conservative consultant elite and Scotland had too recently been a battleground for either to be ready to open their doors to women at this stage. The two women passed these examinations and became Licentiates of King's and Queen's College of Physicians, Ireland, (LKQCPI). At this point Sophia finished a letter to her mother with the triumphant signature: 'S.J.B.M.D.L.K.Q.C.P.I.'[84] Edith Pechey then moved to Leeds and set up in private practice there. Annie Clark set up in practice in Birmingham. Around this time, Eliza Walker Dunbar and Louisa Atkins also gained the qualification from the college. So, after a wait of 12 years, four more women had joined Elizabeth Blackwell and Elizabeth Garrett Anderson on the register, and other women joined them at frequent intervals from now on.

Continuing struggles

However, there were still major barriers to women seeking a medical education in Britain. The persistent refusal of the medical schools to let women in to ordinary classes meant that female students were faced with the prospect of paying very high fees to complete the necessary courses by means of separate classes and individual instruction. Commenting in 1882 on a similar situation in the United States, Mary Putnam Jacobi talked of 'the severe struggle with practical and pecuniary necessities' which faced women students and damaged their concentration.[85]

Women were able to gain a medical education in Britain at this time only if they had access to personal wealth, as Elizabeth

Garrett Anderson and Sophia Jex-Blake had, or with help from scholarships set up, for instance, by Elizabeth Garrett Anderson, Lady Amberley and the Edinburgh committee. This meant that entry to the profession was confined to upper- and upper-middle-class women. Also the reliance on large donations, for campaigning and for setting up the New Hospital for Women and the London School of Medicine for Women, ensured that it was a campaign controlled by upper- and middle-class people. As with so many radical campaigns of this period, working-class women (and men) had very little chance of influencing the issue of medical women.

There was still nowhere where women students could receive clinical instruction. The London School of Medicine for Women approached all the London hospitals for clinical instruction but was met with refusal at each. At the London Hospital in Whitechapel the committee at first agreed to having women medical students study there but was forced to withdraw the offer after objections from the male medical staff. The New Hospital for Women, the only one willing to take female students, was considered too small by examining body regulations. It seemed that the school's very existence was threatened.

However, in March 1877 the school council was able to strike a hard bargain with the managers of the Royal Free Hospital in Grays Inn Road under which women students were able to use its facilities from October as a five-year experiment. The managers were worried about the effect this decision might have on the reputation of the hospital and the school had to agree to pay £315 to the hospital and £400 to the medical staff each year to compensate them for a potential fall in public subscriptions and fees from male students. J.G.S. Anderson (Elizabeth Garrett Anderson's husband), James Stansfeld, and another MP, Frederick Pennington, agreed to act as financial guarantors. Despite this agreement the medical staff remained hostile.

Once the agreement was reached, the number of students at the school immediately increased, as a full medical education could now be provided. However, £715 was an enormous sum, and a public appeal was launched to raise it. By August donations were starting to come in. £1000, half the school's annual expenditure, was raised from subscriptions each year for the next five years, with the other half coming from students' fees.

There was a similar episode in the course of the campaign in the United States for women doctors. Women were eventually able to enter a university medical school by buying their way into Johns Hopkins. Mary Putnam Jacobi's comment on this would have been equally appropriate to the Royal Free agreement:

> It is astonishing how many invincible objections on the score of feasibility, modesty, propriety, and prejudice will melt away before the charmed touch of a few thousand dollars.[86]

Also in March, the Senate of the University of London (made up of the academic staff of the colleges) decided to admit Edith Shove to medical examinations by 14 votes to 7. The following month they received a petition from 230 male medical graduates protesting against this decision and the matter was suspended. The medical graduates claimed that female graduation would render their degrees valueless, as in this letter to the *Lancet*:

> I, as one of the medical graduates, having been put to much expense and trouble to procure my degree, consider that it is an extremely dishonourable thing that my degree should be by that vote rendered to me practically valueless.[87]

During this period medical women were continuing to do exceptionally well in various examinations. It was clear, therefore, that these men were objecting to the very *fact* of women students rather than questioning their ability.

The debate now turned into a clear conflict between medical and non-medical graduates. According to the *Englishwoman's Review*, it was the 'self-interested and unjust exclusiveness' of the medical contingent at the University of London which turned otherwise neutral graduates into strong supporters of the women, out of a sense of fairness.[88] After an opposing circular from three of the non-medical graduates, the issue was brought before Convocation, a meeting open to all graduates of the university, which voted 140 to 129 against the admission of women. The two sides almost exactly represented a split: only nine medical men voted for admission, and only 35 non-medical men voted against.

The medical graduates deeply resented the interference of non-medical men and insisted that medical men alone were qualified to make this decision. A Dr Wilkes asked whether or not the arts graduates believed the medical graduates when they said that women have babies! One medical graduate apparently supported women's entry to *all* degrees in the hope that this would meet with opposition from non-medics and hold up their entry to medical degrees.

On June 25 the Senate voted again in favour of the women and refused to go back on its decision. Opponents continued to protest to the Senate and to write letters to the *Lancet* but in January 1878 the university adopted a new charter under which women were admitted to all degree courses. Again, the vote at Convocation on the charter showed the majority of medical graduates to be against women's entry while the majority of arts graduates were in favour.

Although the barriers were now falling rapidly and registered medical women were an acknowledged fact, hostility from the profession itself showed no signs of lessening. Throughout the 1870s the *Lancet* kept up close reporting of events and a steady stream of leading articles which denied the need for and the competence of women doctors. By August 1878 it was still referring to medical women as a 'conceit contradictory to nature'.[89]

Women and the British Medical Association

Hostility towards medical women was also surfacing in the deliberations of the British Medical Association, the largest medical association in Britain which drew its membership largely from general practitioners. In early 1874 Elizabeth Garrett Anderson had been elected to the association through the efforts of friends within the profession. It is likely that most members were unaware of this for a year or so. Shortly after her election, an Edinburgh doctor had written a letter to the *British Medical Journal* in which he set out the reasons why he believed women should be excluded:

The British Medical Association is not only a very
distinguished medium and arena for the display of
advancing science, but it is also a body of professing, and
acquiring still more largely, a great measure of public
influence beyond the limit of its own members – an
influence which has weight, and will yet have more, with
many governing local bodies in their charge of the public
good, and even with the supreme governing powers of
the country. This influence, which we ought by all means
to promote, I think, the admission of female practitioners
to membership, whatever may be their excellence or their
attainments in the study of medical science, will derogate
from and harm.[90]

Medical men were enjoying a new sense of corporate identity
and political power as professional men and saw women doctors
as a direct threat to these interests.

Elizabeth Garrett Anderson attended the Annual General
Meeting in Edinburgh in August 1875. She managed to obtain
a ticket quite easily but her sister-in-law's application for a
student ticket was refused. She was allowed to give her paper
on obstetrics only after a protest against her speaking had been
made. It is clear from correspondence between her and her
husband that she believed that the British Medical Association
would not be able to support *her* membership and keep other
women out. She was delighted when her speech was well
received: 'I do hope it will be useful in a solid way to the
cause.'[91]

In March 1878 the British Medical Association held a special
meeting to discuss the membership of women, after receiving a
two to one vote against admitting women in a postal ballot
of all members. During the summer another woman, Frances
Hoggan, was elected to the association and a second special
meeting was held in September to discuss the issue.

During the debate members claimed that their 'feelings of
comfort and independence' would be 'trespassed on' if women
were present at meetings and that they would be unable to
express themselves freely.[92] Elizabeth Garrett Anderson answer-
ered these claims by stating that the advancement of medical
knowledge would be hindered if women were excluded. She

also pointed out that if the profession was worried about their corporate identity and the effect of women practising medicine on the level of fees, it was far safer to allow entry rather than fostering 'an antagonism and self-seeking spirit' among medical women.[93]

Following this debate, the meeting decided to uphold Elizabeth Garrett Anderson's membership but to elect no more women. The elections at which Frances Hoggan became a member were declared void and all the male doctors elected at the same time as her were duly re-elected. This decision to allow Elizabeth Garrett Anderson to remain a member but to exclude all other women was symbolic of her isolated position as a successful professional woman. It also raises further doubts about her belief that she was carving a way for women by her individual success. She was the only woman member of the British Medical Association for 19 years.

Despite the passing of the Enabling Act, there was still only very limited access to the register for women. In March 1878 the Royal College of Physicians voted 68 to 16 against admitting women to the licence. The opening up of university education to women also moved forward only very slowly. The 1878 Royal Commission on Scottish Universities refused to hear a submission from women about the medical education of women and this important issue merited only a passing reference in their four volume report. The growing numbers of medical women felt the need to bond together as a minority within a hostile profession. One result of this was the setting up of the Medical Women's Federation in 1879, with Edith Pechey as one of the founding members.

More dangerous than these petty attempts to exclude women from professional bodies and meetings were certain clauses of the government bill introduced in 1878 to amend the 1858 Medical Act. This proposed that the Royal Colleges be allowed to form a conjoint board to grant a single medical and surgical licence to medical practitioners. The bill was in fact part of a struggle between different factions of medical men. It received only lukewarm support from the *Lancet* and the *British Medical Journal*, who believed it did not go nearly far enough in challenging the power of the General Medical Council. Luckily for medical women the bill was dropped in August 1878.

In a long letter to *The Times* in May, Elizabeth Garrett Anderson pointed out that the demand that all registered practitioners have a diploma in both medicine and surgery endangered the medical women movement, as their only means of access to the register at that time was via a *medical* diploma from the Irish College, with all surgical bodies still refusing to examine women. Also, the General Medical Council was proposing amendments which would require all women candidates to prove they had attended no mixed classes and to have their names placed on a separate register. Again, she said, this was an attempt to relegate women doctors to a separate and inferior category of practitioners.

In February 1879 the Committee for Securing a Complete Medical Education for Women, which now changed its name to the National Association for Promoting the Medical Education of Women, declared that there was still much work to be done in giving financial support to individual women who wanted to study medicine and in resisting moves such as this proposed bill. Constant vigilance was needed to preserve the gains already made.[95]

The movement had its internal problems too. In June 1878, Sophia Jex-Blake and Elizabeth Garrett Anderson were both put forward as candidates for the post of organising secretary of the London School of Medicine for Women and it looked as if the old antagonism would resurface. A compromise candidate was finally chosen in Isabel Thorne who gave up her own medical career to take up the post. In February 1879 the school was formally accepted by the Secretary of State as one of the medical schools qualifying for the University of London examinations. In September Edith Shove, Mary Scharlieb and two other women passed examinations which formed part of the medical degree at the university, all in the first division. The *Englishwoman's Review* continued to publish more and more reports of women graduating and having their names placed on the register.

Epilogue

In August 1880 the *Englishwoman's Review* published a list of names and addresses of the 20 women on the register: Elizabeth Blackwell, Elizabeth Garrett Anderson, Sophia Jex-Blake, Eliza Walker Dunbar, Frances Hoggan, Louisa Atkins, Edith Pechey, and 13 others who had all been educated at the London School of Medicine for Women.[1] All but Elizabeth Blackwell and Elizabeth Garrett Anderson had entered the register via the Irish College of Physicians. Women could now acquire a complete medical education in England, have their names placed on the register, and graduate from an English university. All the major barriers had fallen and the campaign *for entry* was over. However, the struggle for complete professional equality for medical women has continued ever since and could fill another book.

For a number of years after the victories of the 1870s women were still denied access to many hospitals, institutions and medical societies. The first generation of medical women were forced to build their careers in private practice, particularly in working-class areas where the demand for their services was highest. In 1881 women doctors were excluded from the scientific meetings of the International Medical Conference in London, and members of the Medical Women's Federation sent a letter of protest. The British Medical Association did not reopen its membership to women until 1892. Medical men were fighting a rearguard action to preserve the profession, as far as possible, as a male club.

Even today, the medical profession retains many of the characteristics of a male club. In her book about her fight against suspension from her medical post, Wendy Savage mentions two clubs to which only *male* members of the Royal College of

Obstetricians and Gynaecologists are invited. She goes on to say:

> Excluded from the cosy male get-togethers where, it is rumoured, all the consultant posts are 'fixed', women have formed their own club but it does not seem to be an effective pressure group for women, either as obstetricians or as patients.[2]

There is still a long way to go before women can be seen as equal members of the profession, particularly, it seems, in areas of medicine devoted to women's health.

By 1887 only seven of the 19 examining bodies which gave access to the register were open to women. King's and Queen's College of Physicians, Ireland, had been joined by the College of Surgeons, Ireland, and the Royal University of Ireland in Dublin. In 1885, under no pressure from campaigners, both the Royal College of Physicians, Edinburgh, and the Royal College of Surgeons, Edinburgh, opened their licences to women. The Faculty of Physicians and Surgeons, Glasgow, decided to follow suit, so all three medical corporations in Scotland were now open to women. The only English licensing body, and the only other university besides Dublin, to allow access to women was the University of London. Edith Shove became the first woman graduate from a university in Britain when she gained her MB at London in 1882.

In 1895 the London School of Medicine for Women wrote to the Royal College of Physicians, London, and the Royal College of Surgeons, England, asking for a change of policy. They pointed out that there were now 200 women on the register, women doctors held appointments in hospitals and other institutions, and were admitted to membership of the British Medical Association and other medical societies. But the colleges refused to budge, and it was not until 1910 that the then conjoint board opened its examinations to women. The Royal College of Physicians did not allow women in as fellows until 1925!

Women doctors continued to have some involvement in women's politics. Sophia Jex-Blake was active in suffrage politics in Edinburgh in the 1880s and 90s. The Women's Suffrage Declaration, published in the *Fortnightly Review* in July 1889, contained 30 names in the 'medical and nursing' section, including Elizabeth Garrett Anderson, Elizabeth Blackwell and Mary Scharlieb.[3] In her seventies Elizabeth Garrett Anderson was drawn into militant suffragette activities by her daughter, Louisa, and on one occasion only narrowly escaped arrest through the intervention of her sister Millicent Fawcett. Elizabeth Blackwell remained a strong supporter of the anti-vivisection and anti-vaccination movements to the end of her life, and continued her efforts to persuade the medical profession to play a more responsible role over the issue of prostitution.

In 1889 the New Hospital for Women moved to larger premises on the Euston Road. A sum of £21,000 had been raised for the new building and the Prince of Wales laid the foundation stone. Other small hospitals and dispensaries with female medical staff had opened, for instance in Bristol, Leeds and Manchester, but for many years the New Hospital was the only place where women students could get clinical experience in gynaecology. Then in 1912 Maud M. Chadburn started an appeal for another major hospital for women. After a letter hostile to her venture was published in *The Times*, she received an anonymous donation of £100,000, on condition that the hospital be staffed by women and treat women and children only.[4] The South London Hospital for Women opened two years later. In 1917 the New Hospital was renamed the Elizabeth Garrett Anderson Hospital on her death.

The London School of Medicine for Women, which Sophia Jex-Blake had done so much to build, continued to prosper in the years after the split between her and Elizabeth Garrett Anderson in 1878. When the agreement with the Royal Free came to an end in 1882, it was renewed automatically at a greatly reduced fee. The experiment had been entirely successful.

In 1883 Dr Arthur Norton resigned after nine years as Dean. Most people believed that the opportunity should now be taken to appoint a woman to this post, and that Elizabeth Garrett Anderson was the obvious choice. However, Sophia Jex-Blake's bitter memories of the many disagreements they had had over the years, in particularly over whether or not to open a medical school for women, had not dimmed and she travelled down from Edinburgh on a rare visit to London to oppose Elizabeth's nomination. At the meeting to elect a new dean, Sophia put forward Edith Pechey's name but could not find a seconder for this nomination. When it came to the election, Sophia's was the only dissenting vote and Elizabeth was duly elected.

Elizabeth Garrett Anderson held this post from 1883 until retiring in 1903, at which point she became president. These years saw a steady increase in the number of students at the school and a piecemeal expansion of its facilities. The 'Iron Room' was built in the garden to relieve pressure on space, although the landlord objected when he heard that it was to be used for the study of anatomy.

By 1896 there were 159 students and an urgent need to move to larger premises. By 1898 £12,000 had been collected in a special fund for this purpose and the new building was opened that year by the Prince and Princess of Wales. Relations between the school and the hospital continued to improve and the school was renamed the London (Royal Free Hospital) School of Medicine for Women. In 1900 the school was accepted as one of the medical schools officially recognised by the University of London.

Jex-Blake in Edinburgh

After her defeat at the school in spring 1878, Sophia Jex-Blake decided to move back to Edinburgh to set up in practice there. It has been suggested that she made a mistake in moving to Edinburgh, where the image of the fiery campaigner could not easily be replaced by that of the sober, respected professional.[5] Also, because of the rift at the school, she had now cut herself off from the support of other medical women. She did, however, receive promises of help from medical men who had supported the campaign at the university in the early 1870s, particularly Dr Balfour and Dr Heron Watson. Her choice of where to settle was, of course, limited by the fact that it had to be in a large town so that she could find enough women who wanted to consult a woman doctor. She set up in practice at 4 Manor Place in June 1878 and reported to friends that she had had a total of 100 visits from 23 patients in her first two and a half months.[6] As the first woman doctor to practise in Scotland, she had to treat a number of women with advanced medical problems who had refused up to then to consult a man. She also occasionally took in patients to care for them in her own home, for instance a governess who was staying in miserable lodgings. Her private practice continued to grow and in the first year she saw a total of 574 patients.

Shortly after moving up to Edinburgh, the following entry appeared in Sophia's diary:

> My life is full and complete again, if somewhat greyer for the past pain; and, if I can have J. [Ursula Du Pre], the former things may abide in shadow.

However, it was to be another three or four years before Sophia was joined by Ursula and her 'past pain' could start to fade.

She had first met Ursula Du Pre in January 1869, and their friendship had developed very quickly into something deeper. Already by February Ursula had wanted to go with Sophia to Edinburgh to help her in her attempt to enter the university. However, until the early 1880s Ursula seems to have been unable to leave the south of England because of family ties. This meant that they were apart while Sophia was pursuing her medical career in Edinburgh, and later in Berne and Dublin. The two women obviously found separation from each other difficult. During the struggle at the university Ursula wanted reassurances that Sophia was being looked after well by her friends in Edinburgh, as she could not be with her herself. After Sophia moved up to Edinburgh again in 1878 Ursula travelled north at regular intervals to spend time with her, and in October 1879 gave her a horse to go with a brougham (carriage) her mother had given her. At some point in 1881 or 1882 Ursula was finally free to join Sophia in Edinburgh, and in 1883 they moved to Bruntsfield Lodge, where they lived together until Sophia's retirement.

Female friendships were central to Sophia Jex-Blake's life, and she also had relationships of a more intimate nature with women. In her early twenties she had what seems to have been a passionate and stormy relationship with Octavia Hill, sharing a flat with her for ten months until they found it impossible to continue living with each other. Some 50 years later Sophia wrote to Octavia to say she would love to see her again, although it is not clear whether this reunion ever took place. She seems to have been very close to Lucy Sewall while in the United States in the mid 1860s, living with her and working alongside her at the hospital in Boston. The two women maintained a close correspondence for years, with Sophia, at least, confiding in Lucy at all the most stressful points in her life. Sophia dedicated the 1886 edition of her book, *Medical Women*, to her.

Feminist historians have warned about the dangers of defining close female friendship of the past in terms of lesbianism, as the category was not formulated explicitly until the beginning of the twentieth century. Emotional and physical intimacy between women friends in Victorian Britain was not seen as unusual. There are problems, therefore, with describing Sophia Jex-Blake as a lesbian. However, it is clear from her life and her writings that she never envisaged marrying, that she had intimate relationships with at least two women, and that a network of female friends provided crucial support for her in her political work and her medical career.

In August 1878 she organised a meeting on the subject of female medical care for women at which the following resolution was passed: 'That it is desirable to afford to poor women the opportunity of consulting medical practitioners of their own sex.'' A dispensary was opened soon after, administered by 'a Committee of Edinburgh ladies', at 73 Grove Street. Although it was open only twice a week and, unlike other dispensaries in Edinburgh, charged 3d for medicines, it was soon over-attended. It had visits from 2464 patients in the first year.

In 1885 the dispensary moved to larger premises where there was space for five beds. It was opened officially by the Lord Provost of Edinburgh on 23 September. When Sophia Jex-Blake moved away from Edinburgh in 1899 she left her property in trust for the purpose of opening a hospital. By the following year the committee had managed to raise sufficient funds to open the Edinburgh Hospital and Dispensary for Women and Children at Bruntsfield Lodge, where Sophia Jex-Blake and Ursula Du Pre had lived together. In 1899 a small hospice was opened by Elsie Inglis in George Square and in 1904 moved to larger premises in the High Street. In 1910 the two hospitals amalgamated, with the hospice becoming the maternity department of the hospital.

In 1886 Sophia opened the Edinburgh School of Medicine for Women in premises in Surgeon Square which had been bought years ago by herself, Lucy Sewall and Ursula Du Pre. She managed to gather together a committee and a band of lecturers. Ursula Du Pre acted as honorary treasurer. However, the school was always on shaky foundations. There was constant friction between Sophia Jex-Blake and the students, and there was a major incident in the summer of 1889 known as the 'Action of the Lady Medical Students' in which one of the students, Elsie Inglis, rebelled against what she saw as Sophia's dictatorial approach.[8] With support from her father, she founded the Scottish Association for the Medical Education of Women and the Medical College for Women, a rival to Sophia's school. Then in 1890 Queen Margaret College in Glasgow started offering a medical education to women. In the face of opposition, but also the existence of other opportunities for women, Sophia Jex-Blake decided to close the Edinburgh school. She became the first woman lecturer at the extra-mural school when she agreed to accept an invitation from Dr Balfour to teach midwifery there.

She was closely involved in women's politics in Edinburgh. She was one of the organisers of two large suffrage meetings in the early 1880s and active in the campaign for the election of women Poor Law guardians. In 1886 she gave a lecture to a packed audience of over 2000 women as part of a series being given in Edinburgh on the subject of 'Health'. She had insisted that it be free and women-only so that her dispensary patients could come. She had been urged by Mrs Traynor, one of the committee members organising the series, to withdraw her insistence that there should be no charge, on the grounds that this would only alienate the male doctors. Her reply was as follows:

> Pray thank Lord Traynor warmly for his kind interest in me and the medical women generally. I think, however, that he somewhat overestimates the importance of what the men doctors may think one way or the other. You and he will remember that all that we have gained has been gained in the teeth of nearly all of them, and if they have failed to hinder me hitherto, they are certainly powerless to hurt me now.[9]

She had certainly not lost any of her talent for scathing prose.

She also continued to campaign for the medical education of women. In 1884 she was asked to write a memorial to the Privy Council to say that the proposed Charter of Incorporation for the Edinburgh Extra-Mural School must include women on equal terms. She also wrote to *The Times* asking women who were interested in the extra-mural classes to write to her.[10] However, these remained closed to women as the charter granted to the school did not in the end specify women. In an article she wrote in 1887 entitled 'Medical Women. A Ten Year Retrospect', she said the need for scholarships for women medical students would continue until the universities let women in freely.[11] In 1888 she tried to get a clause on women included in the Universities (Scotland) Bill. Three years later she was invited to give evidence in front of the university commissioners for Scotland. They concluded that it was 'desirable and necessary' to give medical degrees to women.[12]

The final breakthrough came in October 1894 when the University of Edinburgh at last agreed to open medical degrees to women. On 3 November, at a meeting organised by survivors from the National Association for Promoting the Medical Education of Women, an address of thanks was delivered to Sophia Jex-Blake in recognition of her central role in the struggle at Edinburgh. The following year she was guest of honour at the ceremony marking the entry of women to the university medical school.

Conclusion

The campaign for women doctors in Britain achieved its immediate goal of winning entry to the Medical Register within 16 years of Elizabeth Garrett enrolling at the Middlesex Hospital as a student. In this time a hospital and a medical school, both run entirely by women for women, were also established. Few people in 1860 would have believed that so much would have been achieved in so short a time. They assumed that women would be given the vote years before women gained entry to the medical profession. As it turned out, it was to be another 42 years before the vote was finally won.

This early victory was due in no small part to the strength and determination of Elizabeth Garrett Anderson, Sophia Jex-Blake, and other pioneering medical women. They achieved what they did in the face of extreme hostility, especially from the male medical profession, even extending to verbal and physical violence. They also had to cope with great isolation, as the first women in Britain to carve out a career in a male-dominated profession. It is difficult to imagine what the strain of dealing with this degree of opposition and isolation must have been like.

There were great differences of opinion over how these achievements had been won. There were recurring tactical disagreements between Sophia Jex-Blake and Elizabeth Garrett Anderson over the best and quickest way to establish women's undisputed right to enter the medical profession. Elizabeth Garrett Anderson was dismayed by the confrontational tactics used by Sophia Jex-Blake. She was convinced that the greatest contribution she could make to the cause was steadily to pursue her own professional career and to build up her reputation as a respected medical practitioner.

In contrast, Sophia Jex-Blake believed that the only way to open the profession fully to women was to wage a campaign of confrontation, and win. In the preface to the 1886 edition of her book *Medical Women*, she explained her conviction that it had been absolutely necessary to stir up strong feelings on *both* sides in order to secure entry:

> I am very anxious to submit to the public as full a narrative as possible, and am content to abide by their judgement whether or no the so-called 'failure in Edinburgh' was due in whole or in part (as some have endeavoured to maintain) either to the errors, or to the 'lâches', of those who carried on the warfare. My own opinion is that, properly speaking, there was no 'failure'; I believe that it was the seed sown in tears in Edinburgh that was reaped in joy elsewhere. It is my firm conviction that, in view of the then prevalent attitude of the profession and the undeveloped state of public opinion at large, it was absolutely requisite that the battle should be fought out somewhere, and that no more passive policy would have secured (at any rate for many years) the results that have now been won.[1]

The fatal flaw in Elizabeth Garrett Anderson's approach was that it relied on the goodwill of the medical profession. From coverage of the medical women question in the pages of the *Lancet* it is clear that the determined opposition from male doctors to female entry was showing no signs of abating even by the mid 1870s, despite growing acceptance in Parliament and many other influential sections of society. The conclusion she should have drawn was that victory would come only if fought for as a *right* by a group of women rather than as a *favour* by individual women. However, the political value of what Elizabeth Garrett Anderson achieved must not be underestimated. Perhaps it was a *combination* of Elizabeth Garrett Anderson's strategy of campaigning by personal example and Sophia Jex-Blake's strategy of confrontation which ultimately brought about victory. It is possible that neither strategy on its own would have been successful, or at least not for many years.

One key factor in the success of the medical women movement of these two decades was the absolute determination felt by many women that all women should have the choice to consult doctors of their own sex. They insisted that women suffered mental agony when consulting male doctors and, in many cases, preferred to endure continuing ill-health, leading even to death. They were very clear that there were reasons other than simple prudery why women would rather consult a female physician. First, a man can never *fully* understand the complexities of female ill-health from a personal point of view. Secondly, women experience medical examination by a man as sexually invasive, a feeling heightened by the behaviour of many male doctors.

Campaigners for women doctors were very clear that arguments of modesty should not be used to prevent women's entry to the profession. Any unpleasantness suffered by women in the study of medicine was bearable because of the benefit to all those women who would thereby be saved the far greater unpleasantness of having to consult a male doctor. Anyway, the embarrassment felt by women medical students was usually the result of sexual innuendo from the lecturers or the male students rather than their own reluctance to discuss certain matters. As was eloquently explained by Edith Pechey and Sophia Jex-Blake, the treatment they received at the hands of many of their teachers and fellow-students only served to make women even *more* determined to qualify as doctors in order to be able to rescue women from the care of men such as these.

As with other areas of Victorian women's history, this issue raises the whole question of the relationship between separate spheres, a social system imposed on women by men, and separatism, a strategy chosen by women for fighting their oppression. On the one hand, the desire for women doctors could be seen as arising out of a society in which, according to conventional morality, intimate contact between adults of the opposite sex was regarded with horror. The main function of this sexual segregation was to maintain men's power by excluding women from the public sphere. On the other hand, this desire could also be seen as a strong woman-identified impulse and part of a drive for female autonomy. We shall never know how far women made use of 'delicacy' arguments for their own ends. I am sure that a political operator like Sophia Jex-Blake was at least aware of the strategic value of concentrating heavily on such arguments, as she and others did.

However, what is clear is that the campaign for female entry to the medical profession did not arise out of a Victorian notion of prudery but rather was the result of women's clear and rational preference, based on real experience, for doctors of their own sex. The determination to provide female medical care for women was further strengthened by the consciousness of the fact that women's exclusion from medicine was a relatively recent phenomenon. Women insisted that they were not asking for women to be allowed into a *male* occupation but were demanding women's reinstatement to the central place in medicine which had been theirs before the rise of the modern male profession.

There is extensive written evidence for the strong desire by middle-class women to be treated by doctors of their own sex. Although evidence of this kind is not available for working-class women, their views on this issue are clear from their actions. Dispensaries run by women doctors – for example, by Elizabeth Blackwell in New York, Elizabeth Garrett Anderson in London, and Sophia Jex-Blake in Edinburgh – were all supported enthusiastically by local working-class women, even though in many cases a charge was made for treatment and there were free medical services available nearby. However, the issue of class is not as uncomplicated as this support for women doctors from working-class women might suggest. There are many examples of stereotypes of working-class men and women creeping into the writings of early medical women. Also, in common with other middle-class women of the period, early medical women did not see the need to question the basic assumption of the campaign that it would be middle-class women only who would train to be doctors. Working-class women were to get doctors of their own sex but not of their own class.

Male paranoia and hysteria provided constant background noise during the campaign. An exclusively male preserve was supposedly being invaded by 'Amazons' and the very survival of the male doctor was seen to be threatened. This attack by women was deemed to be so dangerous (and unnecessary) that medical men, in particular, felt they had the right to use dirty tricks and even violence in order to defend themselves. What they were so afraid of was not simply that their job security and levels of income would be jeopardised by women doctors but also, and perhaps more importantly, that the nature of the profession would be fundamentally altered by women's entry.

Recent events have made it clear that this paranoia is alive and well in Britain today, with the hounding of Wendy Savage for her woman-centred perspective on obstetrical care, and Marietta Higgs for her child-centred priorities in relation to child sexual abuse.[2] It is interesting that in both these cases the perspectives of the two women were not directly challenged. Instead both women were unfairly accused of gross professional incompetence. It is difficult to see quite how these women could have reached such positions of responsibility within the profession if they were even mildly incompetent!

I recently re-read Wendy Savage's account of her battle for reinstatement as consultant obstetrician in Tower Hamlets and was amazed at the many parallels with the campaign for women doctors in the 1860s and 70s. Throughout the inquiry into her suspension she was backed by a support group and an appeal fund committee who between them collected petitions, organised marches and public meetings, and raised money. She was faced with the frightening prospect of having to pay heavy legal costs if she was to clear her professional name and have the suspension lifted. Partly as a result of this high-profile support campaign, there was regular coverage of events and a vigorous debate in the national press.

The whole story of the months leading up to her suspension is one of manipulation and secrecy on the part of certain male doctors. Medical men, it seems, are still happy to resort to a 'dirty tricks' campaign when faced with a woman who threatens their professional power. Wendy Savage had to endure malicious gossip among medical colleagues about her 'sexual inclinations and marital history'.[3] At the inquiry Professor Grudzinskas, from the medical school, delivered a subtle insult by referring to her as 'Dr Savage': obstetricians are generally considered to be surgeons and have this status confirmed by being addressed as Mr, Mrs, Miss or Ms.[4] Although the issue behind her suspension was clearly one of a difference in attitude towards maternity care, strenuous attempts were made to brand her as incompetent and a danger to her patients.

Wendy Savage herself summed up the whole affair with the comment: 'Fundamentally, the issue was power.'[5] Her only 'crime' had been to put the needs and feelings of women patients first. She believed that every woman should have access to contraception and abortion 'on her terms' and should play a major part in making decisions about her own pregnancy and labour:

> The role of the doctor is that of counsellor rather than
> that of an authoritarian, trained professional, and this is
> very hard for some doctors to accept – especially the
> majority of male obstetricians.[6]

Her view is that pregnancy is not an illness and that rising rates of medical intervention during labour are not backed up by solid scientific evidence. For instance, the rate of Caesarians has risen dramatically in the United Kingdom (although it has not reached the frightening level of the United States), despite the fact that it is safer for the woman to deliver vaginally. Throughout her medical philosophy runs the thread of giving power back to the woman patient. I am sure she would have been cheered on enthusiastically by the pioneer generation of women doctors in her battles for her own professional survival and for women's control over her own fertility. They would have been delighted to see her final victory and reinstatement by the health authority.

In contrast, they would have been shocked to see the major battles during the last 15 years over the survival of three of the women's hospitals set up during the late nineteenth and early twentieth centuries. In 1975 the government declared its intention to close the Elizabeth Garrett Anderson Hospital. After a desperate four-year struggle, during which staff at the hospital campaigned for its survival, the Garrett Anderson eventually won a reprieve in 1979. In 1983 a similar threat faced the South London Hospital for women. This time the threat was carried out swiftly and the hospital closed within a year. Despite a vigorous campaign, involving lengthy occupation of the hospital by local women, the decision was never reversed. Then in 1987 a campaign was launched in Edinburgh to 'Save Elsie's', the Elsie Inglis Memorial Hospital at Bruntsfield. The issues here were again those of medical power and women's freedom of choice: Elsie's was liked by women because of its size, friendly atmosphere and special facilities, like the birthing room, but the health board claimed that it was less safe than a maternity unit in a general hospital because there were no emergency services on site. Once again, however, the battle to save a local medical resource for women was lost. It is horrifying to see these hospitals, set up *by* women *for* women in the face of great practical difficulties and strong opposition from the medical establishment, being closed down. The principles for which early medical women fought so hard have become submerged in a drive to 'rationalise' NHS resources and save money.

We must not forget the history of radical campaigns such as the campaign for women doctors. Nor must we lose sight of how many of the gains of the nineteenth century have since been lost through a blind pursuit of sexual equality through the supposedly progressive principle of integration. I hope that this book will be a source of strength to women today who are fighting battles for women-only and women-orientated medical care.

Medical Women:
a Chronology, 1835–1879

1835	Harriot Hunt starts practising.
1842	Soho Square Hospital for Women opened.
1848	Boston Female Medical College opened.
1849	Elizabeth Blackwell gets medical degree from Geneva College, New York.
1857	New York Infirmary for Women and Children opened.
	First issue of the *English Woman's Journal*.
1859	Medical Register set up.
	Blackwell visits London and gives lectures through England.
	Blackwell accepted on to the register.
1860	Florence Nightingale's training school for nurses opened at St Thomas'.
Aug.	Elizabeth Garrett enters the Middlesex as unofficial student.
1862	Garrett tries to enter Edinburgh and St Andrews Universities.
1864	'Ladies Medical College' opened by the Female Medical Society.
1865	Zurich University admits women to medical degrees.
Oct.	Garrett becomes LSA.
	Sophia Jex-Blake at the New England Hospital for Women and Children.
1866	Garrett accepted on to the register.
1867	Isabel Thorne passes Female Medical College and Society of Apothecaries preliminary exams.
	Paris University admits women to medical degrees.

1868		Jex-Blake enrols at the Women's Medical College of the New York Infirmary.
1869		Jex-Blake's essay 'Medicine as a Profession for Women' published.
	Mar.	Jex-Blake travels to Edinburgh to seek entry to the university.
		Blackwell returns to London for good and attends the Social Science Congress in Bristol.
	Oct.	Five women begin medical studies at Edinburgh University.
1870	Jan.	'Ladies' Manifesto' to Parliament against the CD Acts.
	Mar.	Edith Pechey denied the Hope Scholarship.
		Garrett joins the medical staff of the East London Hospital for Children.
	Jun.	Garrett graduates MD from Paris. Frances Morgan graduates MD from Zurich.
	Jul.	The women students enter the Edinburgh Extra-Mural School.
	Oct.	First approach to the Edinburgh Royal Infirmary.
	Nov.	'Riot' at Surgeon's Hall and hostile memorials from male students.
1871	Jan.	The women's candidates are narrowly defeated at the infirmary elections in Edinburgh.
		The Committee for Securing a Complete Medical Education for Women in Edinburgh is set up.
	Feb.	Garrett marries J.G.S. Anderson.
	Jun.	The Craig trial.
	Oct.	Attempt to exclude the women from Edinburgh University exams.
	Nov.	Appeal for New Hospital for Women launched.
1872	Jan.	Action of Declarator against the University won by the women.
		Jex-Blake lectures at St George's Hall and has her book, *Medical Women: a Thesis and a History*, published.
		Louisa Atkins and Eliza Walker Dunbar graduate from Zurich.
	Nov.	Jex-Blake fails her degree exams.

1873 Jan.   The women's candidates are defeated in the infirmary elections again.

Jun.   Meetings in Birmingham and Bristol on the medical education of women.

Jul.   Eliza Walker Dunbar appointed to the Bristol Hospital for Sick Children but resigns soon after. First proposals for legislation.

Aug.   Garrett Anderson and Jex-Blake debate the implications of the June decision in the letters column of *The Times*.

Sept.   Alexander Grant and Jex-Blake debate the implications of decision made by Edinburgh in autumn 1869.

1874 Apr.   Second reading of William Cowper Temple's Scottish Universities' Bill. Postponed for a year. Debate takes place in June.

Garrett Anderson refused entry to the Obstetrical Society. Elected to the British Medical Association.

Jun.   New Hospital moves to Marylebone Road.

Oct.   London School of Medicine for Women opens.

1875 Mar.   Cowper Temple's bill falls. He proposes a Foreign Degrees Bill.

General Medical Council statement on the admission of women to the profession.

Mary Scharlieb and three other women admitted to the Madras Medical College.

Oct.   Queen's College, Birmingham, refuses to admit women to medical degrees.

Examiners at the Royal College of Surgeons resign after three women apply for midwifery licence.

1876 Feb.   Cowper Temple's Foreign Degrees Bill introduced.

Jul.   Cowper Temple withdraws and Russell Gurney's Enabling Bill made law.

1877 Jan.   Jex-Blake and Pechey graduate MD from Berne.

Mar.   Bargain struck between the London School of Medicine for Women and the Royal Free Hospital.

May   Jex-Blake and Pechey become LKQCPI. Soon joined by Atkins and Walker Dunbar.

Oct.   Clinical instruction for women medical students starts at the Royal Free.

1878 Jan.   University of London opens all degrees to women. Proposal for conjoint board and separate register for women.

Jun.   Thorne voted secretary of the London School of Medicine for Women. Jex-Blake moves to Edinburgh.

Sept.   British Medical Association decides to uphold Garrett Anderson's membership but not to elect any more women.

1879 Feb.   National Association for Promoting the Medical Education of Women formed.

London School of Medicine for Women recognised for purposes of University of London medical degrees.

Medical Licences and Degrees

1 Corporations

Royal College of Physicians, London (RCP): FRCP, MRCP, LRCP

Royal College of Surgeons, England (RCS): FRCS, MRCS, Lic. Mwy.

Society of Apothecaries (SA): LSA. (Closed to women in 1865–6)

Royal College of Physicians, Edinburgh (RCP Edin.): FRCP Edin. MRCP Edin. (Open to women in 1885)

Royal College of Surgeons, Edinburgh (RCS Edin.): MRCS Edin., FRCS Edin. (Open to women in 1885)

Faculty of Physicians and Surgeons of Glasgow (FPSG): FFPSG, LFPSG (Open to women in 1885)

King's and Queen's College of Physicians, Ireland (KQCPI): FKQCPI, LKQCPI (Open to women in 1878)

Royal College of Surgeons, Ireland (RCSI): FRCSI, LRCSI (Open to women in the early 1880s)

Apothecaries' Hall, Dublin (AH): LAH

(Key: F = Fellow, M = Member, L = Licentiate e.g. FRCS = Fellow of the Royal College of Surgeons)

2 Universities

Oxford, Cambridge, London (open to women in 1878), Victoria, Durham; Edinburgh (open to women in 1895), Aberdeen, Glasgow, St Andrews; Dublin (open to women in early 1880s): MB (Bachelor of Medicine), MD (Doctor of Medicine), BCH (Bachelor of Surgery), MCH (Master of Surgery), Lic. Med.

(Adapted from table in Jeanne Peterson, *The Medical Profession in Mid-Victorian London*, University of California Press, 1978, Appendix A, p. 289.)

Registered Medical Women

The following is a complete list of the women who had their names on the Medical Register by 1882, with their year of registation, medical degree (if any), address, and post, as at November 1988.

1858   Dr Elizabeth *Blackwell* (MD Geneva, New York),
Rock House, Hastings.
Consultant Physician, New Hospital for Women, London NW.

1866   Dr Elizabeth *Garrett Anderson* (MD Paris, LSA),
4 Upper Berkeley St, London W.
Consultant Physician, New Hospital for Women; Lecturer on Medicine and Dean of the London School of Medicine for Women.

1877   Dr Eliza *Walker Dunbar* (MD Zurich),
9 Oakfield Road, Clifton, Bristol.
Medical Officer, Dispensary for Women and Children.

Dr Frances *Hoggan* (MD Zurich),
Monaco.

Dr Sophia *Jex-Blake* (MD Berne),
Bruntsfield Lodge, Edinburgh.
Attendant Medical Officer, Edinburgh Hospital for Women and Children; Dean of Edinburgh School of Medicine for Women; Lecturer on Midwifery in the Extra-Mural School of Edinburgh.

Dr Louisa *Atkins* (MD Zurich),
37 Gloucester Place, London W.
Lecturer on Gynaecology, London School of Medicine for Women.

Dr Edith *Pechey* (MD Berne),
Senior Medical Officer, Kama Hospital, Bombay, India.

1878   Dr Annie *Clark* (MD Berne),
       4 Calthorpe Road, Edgbaston, Birmingham.
       Physician, Birmingham and Midland Hospital for Women.

       Dr Agnes *McLaren* (MD Montpellier),
       Bruntsfield Lodge, Edinburgh, (June to October); Cannes,
       Riviera, (October to June).

       Dr Annie *Reay Barker* (MD Paris),
       The Mount, Aldershot.

       Dr Anna *Dahms* (MD Paris),
       17 St Ann's Square, Manchester.
       Medical Officer, Dispensary for Women and Children.

1879   Dr Alice *Ker* (MD Berne),
       Birmingham, Liverpool.

       Dr Eliza F *McDonagh Frikart* (MD Zurich),
       Zofingen, Aargau, Switzerland.

       Dr Jane E *Waterston* (MD Brux.),
       Medical Missionary, 61 Plein St, Capetown, Africa.

1880   Dr Mary *Marshall* (MD Paris),
       16 Stanley Gardens, London W.
       Physician, New Hospital for Women; Medical Officer,
       Provident Dispensary, Notting Hill.

       Dr Matilda *Chaplin Ayrton* (MD Paris),
       died July 19, 1883.

       Mrs *Foggo*,
       Medical Officer, Lady Dufferin's Dispensary, Calcutta.

       Mrs *Grant*,
       5 Sion Villas, Richmond, Surrey.

       Miss Alice *Vickery*,
       333 Albany Road, London SE.

       Miss Fanny *Butler*,
       Medical Missionary, Srinagar, Kashmir, India.

       Mrs *Rushbrook*,
       25 Upper Phillimore Place, London W.
       Medical Officer, Provident Dispensary for Women and
       Children.

1881   Miss Edith *Shove* (MD London),
       Medical Officer (Female Staff), GPO, London, 25 St Mark's
       Crescent NW.

Mrs *Mears*,
47 Front St, Tynemouth.

Miss Alice *Marston*,
Medical Missionary, India (ZBMM).

Dr Hope *Adams Walther* (MD Berne),
Neue Mainzer Strasse, Frankfurt-am-Main.

Mrs *De La Cherois*,
28 Clifton Gardens, Maida Vale, London W.
Physician, New Hospital for Women.

1882   Mrs Julia *Mitchell*,
45 Sloane St, London SW.

Miss Katherine *Mitchell*,
45 Sloane St, London SW.

Miss Julia *Cock*,
Physician, New Hospital for Women; Medical Inspector,
North London Collegiate School.

Mrs Mary *Scharlieb* (MD and BS London),
149 Harley St, London W.
Physician, New Hospital for Women; Lecturer on Forensic
Medicine, London School of Medicine for Women.

(From Sophia Jex-Blake's, 'Medical Women. A Ten Years'
Retrospect', *Nineteeth Century*, November 1887, reprinted by the
National Association for Promoting the Medical Education of
Women, Edinburgh, 1888, pp. 28–30.)

Short Biographical Notes on Prominent Medical Women

Abbreviations used:

LSMW   London School of Medicine for Women
LKQCPI Licentiate of King's and Queen's College of Physicians, Ireland
NHW   New Hospital for Women

Louisa Atkins (life dates not known)
Louisa Atkins studied at Apothecaries' Hall and at Elizabeth Garrett Anderson's St Mary's Dispensary in 1867. Then she went to the University of Zurich, with Frances Morgan and Eliza Walker, to take a medical degree. She graduated MD in 1872 and was appointed surgeon at the Birmingham and Midlands Hospital for Women and Children in autumn 1872. In 1875 she moved to London and was appointed surgeon at the NHW. In May 1877 she became LKQCPI and entered the register.

Elizabeth Blackwell (1821–1910)
Elizabeth Blackwell was born in Bristol of a nonconformist family which was heavily involved in reforming politics, especially the anti-slavery movement. Throughout her life Blackwell maintained a strong religious faith and a commitment to radical politics. When she was 11 years old her family emigrated to the United States.

In 1847 she enrolled as a medical student at Geneva College in New York and graduated MD in 1849. As part of her instruction she had clinical experience at the Blockley Almshouse, New York, in the Women's Syphilitic Department. In 1849 she visited London and was well received by members of the medical profession there. She then went to Paris to study obstetrics and midwifery at La Maternité where she lost an eye in an accident. While in Paris she became strongly opposed to vivisection and was later in her life involved in campaigns against the practice in England. Returning to England in 1850 she met Florence Nightingale, who introduced her to new ideas about hygiene and preventive medicine and who was to be an important lifelong friend and medical colleague.

In 1851 she returned to New York and set up in private practice, but received little support. In 1852 she prepared and delivered lectures on the physical education of girls which were later published. At this time, never having married, she adopted a daughter, Katharine (Kitty) Barry. She opened a new surgery in a poor part of the city in 1853, which was very successful, and started raising funds for a women's hospital. With her sister Emily and Marie Zakrzewska she opened the New York Infirmary for Women and Children in 1857. In 1859 she visited England again, giving lectures on 'Medicine as a Profession for Women' in London and in other cities. She was accepted on to the Medical Register and in 1859–60 various articles by or about her appeared in the *English Woman's Journal*. She returned to the United States to continue her pioneer work there throughout the 1860s. In 1868 she founded the Women's Medical College of the New York Infirmary and took the Chair of Hygiene.

In 1869 she returned to England to settle permanently in London. She attended the Social Science Congress in September, where she went to the sessions on venereal disease. This marked the beginning of a 17-year involvement with the campaign against the Contagious Diseases Acts. She established herself in practice in London and in 1874 was appointed to the Chair of Gynaecology at the LSMW. In 1879 she retired to Hastings with Kitty Barry.

Elizabeth Garrett Anderson (1836–1917)

Elizabeth Garrett's father was a wealthy self-made businessman, who was originally from east London but moved with his family to Suffolk when Elizabeth was a child. She was sent to the Academy for the Daughters of Gentlemen in Blackheath. In 1854 she met Emily Davies through her schoolfriend, Jane Crow. In early 1859 they became involved in the circle around the *English Woman's Journal* and with the Society for Promoting the Employment of Women. In March they attended Blackwell's lecture and were introduced to her.

In August 1860 she entered the Middlesex Hospital as a nurse and unofficial student but was asked to leave in July 1861. From 1861–5 she pursued her medical studies privately, in St Andrews, Edinburgh and London, with extensive financial backing from her father. She received the Licence of the Society of Apothecaries (LSA) in October 1865 and in September 1866 her name was put on the register. In June she opened the St Mary's Dispensary for Women and Children in Marylebone and her practice grew slowly. In 1866 she was also involved in the first Women's Suffrage Committee but soon after withdrew. She refused to support the campaign against the Contagious Diseases Acts and an article by her in their favour, 'An Enquiry into the Nature of the Contagious Diseases Acts', appeared in the *Pall Mall Gazette*, on 25 January 1870.

In 1869 she started studying for the Paris MD degree and graduated in June 1870. In March 1870 she was appointed visiting Medical Officer to the East London Hospital for Children. She was asked to stand for the new London School Board and came top in the Marylebone poll. She was very involved in the work of the board for three years. In February 1871 she married J. G. S. Anderson, who ran a shipping business in the City and was on the board of the East London Hospital. In July 1873 she had a daughter, Louisa, and in the autumn she resigned from the hospital and the school board.

The NHW had been opened above the dispensary in February 1872 and she started performing operations there. She was elected to the British Medical Association in early 1874 and the following year gave a paper at the BMA Annual General Meeting. In May 1874 she had an article published in the *Fortnightly Review* in answer to one from Dr Henry Maudsley on the effects of education on girls' and women's health. The NHW moved to larger premises on Marylebone Road in June 1874 and in September her second child, Margaret, was born. Also in the autumn, she agreed reluctantly to join the council of the LSMW and accepted a lectureship. She became dean of the school in 1883 and stayed in that post until 1903.

Frances Hoggan (née Morgan) (life dates not known)

Frances Morgan studied at Apothecaries' Hall and at the St Mary's Dispensary in 1867. Then she went to the University of Zurich with Louisa Atkins and Eliza Walker to do the medical degree course. In 1870 she graduated MD and the following year she joined Elizabeth Garrett Anderson at the St Mary's Dispensary and later the NHW. In the early 1870s (exact year not known) she married George Hoggan, a pensioned navy officer who had taken the MB degree at Edinburgh University out of personal interest. They were both actively involved in the anti-vivisection movement in the 1880s. In December 1876 she became LKQCPI and her name was put on the register.

Mary Putnam Jacobi (1842–1906)

Mary Putnam Jacobi received a diploma from the Medical College of Pennsylvania in 1864. She spent a few months at the New England Hospital and in 1866 she enrolled as a student at the Paris school of medicine. In 1871 she returned to New York and started in private practice in her father's house. She was appointed lecturer in material medica at the Women's Medical College in 1871. The next year she was made a professor and remained with the college until 1889. She was also involved in the New York Infirmary itself and active in those medical societies which admitted women. In 1872 she founded the

Association for the Advancement of the Medical Education of Women (later the Women's Medical Association) and was the president from 1874–1903. In 1873 she and another woman founded a paediatric dispensary service at another hospital and in 1886 a separate children's ward at the infirmary. She lectured on the diseases of children at the New York Post-Graduate Medical School from 1882–5. In 1873 she married Dr Abraham Jacobi.

Sophia Jex-Blake (1840–1912)

Sophia Jex-Blake was born in Hastings of very wealthy parents, who had her relatively late in life. Their outlook was deeply influenced by a strong evangelical faith. She was educated by governesses and later sent away to boarding school. In 1858 she persuaded her parents to let her go to Queen's College in London to continue her education. She accepted a salaried teaching post at the college and became involved in the Society for Promoting the Employment of Women. She moved to Edinburgh to pursue her studies and then spent some time in Germany studying women's education there. At this point she was planning to open a training college for women.

In 1865 she went to the United States to look at American women's education and two years later published a book on the subject. She met Dr Lucy Sewall and became involved in the New England Hospital for Women and Children. In September 1866 she enrolled as a medical student there and the following year applied unsuccessfully for entry to Harvard. In 1868, after winning her parents' permission, she entered the newly opened Women's Medical College of the New York Infirmary. But in November her father died and she had to return to England. Over the winter she wrote 'Medicine as a Profession for Women', which was published in 1869 in a collection of essays on feminism, edited by Josephine Butler.

After looking into the possibilities for medical education in England, she travelled to Edinburgh in March 1869 to seek entry to the university. Eventually she and four other women were allowed to matriculate in October. While continuing her medical studies, she became increasingly involved in campaigns within the university over female graduation, especially following the Hope Scholarship affair in April 1870 and the 'riot' at Surgeons' Hall in October. At a meeting to elect the board of managers for the Edinburgh Royal Infirmary in January 1871, she spoke out against the way the women students had been treated. In June she was found guilty of libel for allegations made during this speech. In July 1872 she and the other women students successfully brought an Action of Declarator against the university to force them to allow the women to graduate. However, in November she failed her preliminary exams. Around this time she published her 1869 essay along with a detailed account of events in Edinburgh in a book. In July

1873 the university won an appeal against the previous year's ruling, thus making graduation from Edinburgh impossible.

She moved to London in 1874 and began working on parliamentary campaigns. In the summer she started to plan a women's medical college and in October the LSMW opened.

Following a legislative solution in the form of the Enabling Act of 1876, she went to Switzerland with Edith Pechey over the winter of 1876–7 to complete her studies at the University of Berne. In the spring she gained the MD degree and in May became LKQCPI when her name was put on the register. In summer 1878 there was a power struggle between Sophia Jex-Blake and Elizabeth Garrett Anderson at the LSMW and, following her defeat, Sophia moved to Edinburgh.

She set up in private practice in Edinburgh in June and opened a dispensary in September. She became Honorary Treasurer of the National Association for Promoting the Medical Education of Women. In March 1879, following a two-year internal wrangle, she was admitted to the Medical Society, College of Physicians, Ireland. Throughout the 1880s she was involved in women's politics in Edinburgh, for instance in the organisation of two large suffrage meetings and elections to the Poor Law Board. With the addition of beds to her dispensary in 1885 the Edinburgh Hospital for Women and Children was opened. In 1886 she founded the Edinburgh School of Medicine for Women, with herself as dean, and she was also appointed Lecturer in Midwifery at the Edinburgh Extra-Mural School. In 1886 she produced a new revised edition of her book on medical women. In 1899 she retired to Sussex.

Edith Pechey (1845–1908)

Edith Pechey was the daughter of a Baptist minister from Essex. He had an MA in Greek, Latin and Hebrew from Edinburgh University, which *may* have influenced her decision to join Sophia Jex-Blake there. In early summer 1869 she contacted Sophia Jex-Blake about studying for medicine and, along with her, enrolled as a student in the autumn. In April 1870 she came top in her year in the chemistry exam but was denied the Hope Scholarship. This incident marked the beginning of open hostility at Edinburgh towards the women students.

In July 1875 she replaced Louisa Atkins as surgeon at the Birmingham and Midlands Hospital for Women and Children. Following the Enabling Act of 1876, she went to Berne with Sophia Jex-Blake over the winter of 1876–7 to complete her studies. In the spring she graduated MD, and in May became LKQCPI and had her name put on the register. Then she moved to Leeds and set up in private practice in 1877. During the 1870s she gave a number of lectures to ladies' educational associations in Yorkshire. She was one of the founding members of the Medical Women's Federation of England and was elected president in

1882. She also founded the Medical Women for India Fund in the early 1880s.

In 1883 she went to India to pursue her involvement with the Medical Women for India movement. She was appointed senior medical officer at Kama Hospital in Bombay. In 1889 she married Herbert Phipson, the honorary secretary of the fund. In 1890 she gave a lecture on child marriage and, as well as her medical work, was involved in women's issues in India.

Mary Scharlieb (1845–1930)

Mary Scharlieb's mother died when she was ten days old. Her father was an 'old-fashioned evangelical'. She was sent to boarding school from the age of ten.

In 1865 she married a barrister and moved with him to India. She had two children and then they moved to Madras. She started studying medicine privately in 1871 and received informal instruction at the lying-in hospital. In 1875 the Madras Government agreed to admit women to the degree course at the Madras Medical College and Scharlieb and three other European women enrolled as students. In 1878 all four graduated and received the Licence of Medicine, Surgery and Midwifery.

She travelled to England in 1878 and enrolled at the LSMW. In 1882 she graduated in medicine and surgery (MB and BS) from the University of London and her name was put on the register. A year later she returned to India and continued to work as a lecturer and medical practitioner in Madras. In 1887 she was appointed surgeon at the NHW and lecturer in forensic Medicine at the LSMW. She resigned from the NHW on her appointment as gynaecologist to the Royal Free Hospital in 1902.

Isabel Thorne (life dates not known)

During her early married life, Isabel Thorne lived in Shanghai, China. While out there she lost a child, through inadequate medical care. She also read an article about Elizabeth Blackwell in 1858. After returning to England, she enrolled at the Ladies' Medical College and in 1867 passed the exams with a double first in medicine and obstetrics. In May 1868 she came in the top six in the preliminary arts exams at Apothecaries' Hall. She had been practising as an *accoucheuse* (midwife) but now thought of going abroad for a medical degree. In 1869 she joined Sophia Jex-Blake as a student at Edinburgh University. In 1878, in order to resolve the conflict at the LSMW between Sophia Jex-Blake and Elizabeth Garrett Anderson, she agreed to give up her own medical career and accepted the post of organisational secretary. In 1905 she published the *Sketch of the Foundation and Development of the London School of Medicine for Women*, (reprinted in 1915).

Eliza Walker Dunbar (life dates not known)
Eliza Walker studied at Apothecaries' Hall and at the St Mary's Dispensary in 1867. Then she entered the medical degree course at the University of Zurich, with Louisa Atkins and Frances Morgan, and graduated MD in 1872. In 1873 she was appointed resident medical officer at the Hospital for Sick Children in Bristol but, following extreme opposition from the rest of the medical staff, she resigned in September. She set up in private practice in Bristol and in January 1876 founded a dispensary there. In December 1876 she became LKQCPI and her name was put on the register.

Marie Zakrzewska (1829–1902)
Marie Zakrzewska was born in Berlin. Her father was a Prussian army pensioner. She graduated in 1851 from the school of midwifery in Berlin. In 1853 she and her sister emigrated to the United States. They were introduced to Elizabeth Blackwell and the following October started at the Cleveland Medical Collage. She gained her MD in 1856. She set up in practice in a room in Blackwell's house and worked with her to open the New York Infirmary for Women and Children in 1857, where she spent two years as resident physician. In 1859 she moved to Boston to take up the post of Professor of Obstetrics and the diseases of women and children at the Female Medical College. However, she quarrelled with Samuel Gregory, who had founded the college, and resigned in 1862. In July she set up the New England Hospital for Women and Children where she was resident physician and later attendant physician. She devoted the rest of her medical career to the hospital and its medical school. She retired in 1899.

References

Introduction
1 The *English Woman's Journal*, September 1862, p. 69.
2 *The Scotsman*, 29 December 1872.
3 *The Scotsman*, 14 July 1871.
4 The *Lancet*, 6 July 1861, p. 16.
5 The *Lancet*, 27 November 1869, p. 761.

Part 1
1 Florence Nightingale, 'Cassandra', *Suggestions for Thought to Searchers after Religious Truth* (privately printed in 1859), printed in full in Ray Strachey, *The Cause*, 1978, p. 396.
2 Ibid., p. 401.
3. Ibid., p. 402.
4 Quoted in Martha Vicinus, *Independent Women*, 1985, p. 14.
5 Janet Horowitz Murray, *Strong-minded Women*, 1984, p. 300.
6 Barbara Leigh Smith Bodichon, *A Brief Summary in Plain Language of the Most Important Laws Concerning Women*, 1854.
7 Mrs Jameson, *Sisters of Charity and The Communion of Labour: Two Lectures on the Social Employment of Women*, 1859.
8 Quoted in Vicinus, p. 15.
9 Barbara Leigh Smith Bodichon, *Women and Work*, 1856, quoted in Murray, p. 268.
10 Bodichon, 1856, pp. 35–44; appendix, p. 53–6.
11 Ibid., p. 35.
12 For example, the *English Woman's Journal*, April 1861, p. 133.
13 Sophia Jex-Blake, 'Medicine as a Profession for Women', *Medical Women: A Thesis and a History*, 1886, p. 38.
14 Ibid., p. 6.
15 E. Power, 'Women Practitioners in the Middle Ages', *Proceedings of the Royal Society of Medicine*, 1921, pp. 21, 23, quoted in Margaret Connor Versluyen, 'Old Wives' Tales?

Women Healers in English History', Celia Davies (ed.),
Rewriting Nursing History, 1980, p. 181.
16 Brian Abel-Smith, *The Hospitals, 1800–1948*, 1964, p. 1.
17 Brian Abel-Smith, *A History of the Nursing Profession*, 1960,
p. 5.
18 Jeanne Peterson, *The Medical Profession in Mid-Victorian
London*, 1978, p. 242. This book was a very useful resource
for this whole section.
19 Ibid., p. 232.
20 For example, James Stansfeld in a debate in the House of
Commons on the Universities of Scotland (Degrees to Women)
Bill, reported in *The Times*, 4 March 1875.
21 Peterson, p. 133.
22 For example, comment by Dr Littlejohn quoted in Margaret
Todd, *The Life of Sophia Jex-Blake*, 1918, p. 286; Blackwell,
p. 47.
23 Elizabeth Blackwell, *Pioneer Work in Opening the Medical
Profession to Women*, 1914, p. 172.
24 Mary Roth Walsh, *'Doctors Wanted: No Women Need Apply.'
Sexual Barriers in the Medical Profession, 1835–1975*, Yale
University Press, 1977, p. xvi.
25 Ibid., pp. 14–15.
26 Ibid., p. 2.
27 Ibid.
28 Ibid., p. 26.
29 Ibid., pp. 40–43.
30 Ibid., p. 42.
31 Ibid.
32 Ibid., p. 39.
33 Blackwell, 1914, p. 7.
34 Ibid., p. 22.
35 Ibid., p. 23.
36 Ibid.
37 Ibid., p. 56.
38 Ibid., p. 58.
39 Ibid., p. 64.
40 Ibid., p. 128.
41 Ibid., p. 138.
42 Walsh, p. 30.
43 Ibid., p. 32.
44 Ibid.
45 Ishbel Ross, *Child of Destiny*, 1950, p. 171.
46 Blackwell, 1914, p. 160.
47 Ibid., p. 154.
48 Comment by Janet Martens.
49 Enid Moberley Bell, *Storming the Citadel*, p. 40.

50 Ross, p. 186.
51 Blackwell, 1914, p. 160.
52 Quoted in Bodichon, 1856, p. 37.
53 Walsh, p. 88.
54 Ibid., pp. 89–91.
55 Ibid., p. 180.

Part 2
 1 Bodichon, 1856, p. 54.
 2 Ibid., p. 40.
 3 Blackwell, 1914, p. 173.
 4 The *English Woman's Journal*, January 1860, pp. 329–32.
 5 Ibid., p. 332.
 6 Blackwell, 1914, p. 181.
 7 The *English Woman's Journal*, May 1860.
 8 Ibid., p. 149.
 9 Ibid., p. 154.
10 Blackwell, 1914, p. 177.
11 Quoted in Bell, p. 20.
12 Blackwell, 1914, p. 178.
13 The *English Woman's Journal*, April 1858, pp. 80–98.
14 Ibid., p. 94.
15 Bessie Rayner Parkes, 'Ladies Sanitary Association', the *English Woman's Journal*, March 1859, pp. 73–85; the *English Woman's Journal*, April 1861, p. 140.
16 The *English Woman's Journal*, July 1859, p. 351.
17 The *English Woman's Journal*, July 1860, p. 351.
18 Catherine Beecher, *Letters to the People on Health and Happiness*, New York, 1855; extracts reprinted in Nancy F. Cott (ed.), *Roots of Bitterness*, New York, 1972, p. 263.
19 The *English Woman's Journal*, December 1860, p. 278.
20 The *English Woman's Journal*, April 1861, p. 133.
21 The *English Woman's Journal*, July 1860, p. 319.
22 Cott, p. 269.
23 Angus McLaren, 'Women's Work and Regulation of Family Size: the Question of Abortion in the Nineteenth Century', *History Workshop Journal*, 4, 1977, p. 76.
24 Frances Power Cobbe, 'The Medical Profession and its Morality', *Modern Review*, ii, 1881, pp. 296–328.
25 The *English Woman's Journal*, March 1862, pp. 1–11.
26 Ibid., p. 6.
27 The *English Woman's Journal*, May 1862, pp. 195–200.
28 The *English Woman's Journal*, September 1862, p. 69.
29 The *English Woman's Journal*, May 1862, p. 197.
30 The *English Woman's Journal*, January 1864, p. 337.

31 Ibid., p. 340.
32 The *English Woman's Journal*, April 1862, p. 141.
33 Bessie Rayner Parkes, 'Harriot K. Hunt – A Sanitary Reformer', *English Woman's Journal*, February 1860, pp. 375–86.
34 Ibid., p. 382.
35 Blackwell, 1914, p. 141.
36 Ibid., p. 202.
37 Ibid.
38 Ibid., p. 143.
39 Barbara Stephen, *Emily Davies and Girton College*, p. 55.
40 Emily Davies, 'Female Physicians', *English Woman's Journal*, 1861.
41 Emily Davies, 'Medicine as a Profession for Women', 1863, paper read out by Russell Gurney at the London meeting of the National Association for the Promotion of Social Science, 11 June 1862
42 Elizabeth Garrett to Emily Davies, 15 June 1860.
43 Ibid.
44 Garrett to Davies, 26 June 1860.
45 Garrett to Mrs Richard Garrett, 13 July 1860.
46 Blackwell, 1914, p. 184.
47 Garrett to Davies, (no date), 1860.
48 Garrett to Davies, 17 August 1860.
49 Garrett to Jane Crow, 9 October 1860.
50 Garrett to Davies, 17 August 1860.
51 Garrett to Davies, 19 March 1861.
52 Bell, p. 51.
53 Garrett to Davies, 7 June 1861.
54 The *English Woman's Journal*, June 1861, p. 283.
55 Garrett to Davies, 25 April 1861.
56 Blackwell, 1914, p. 185.
57 The *Lancet*, 6 July 1861, p. 16.
58 Garrett to Davies, 8 October 1861.
59 The *Lancet*, 5 July 1862, p. 17.
60 A. Logan Turner, *Story of a Great Hospital: the Royal Infirmary of Edinburgh, 1729–1929*, Edinburgh, 1937, p. 246.
61 Garrett to Nelson Garrett, 18 June 1862.
62 Davies, p. 6.
63 Jo Manton, *Elizabeth Garrett Anderson*, 1965, p. 127.
64 Manton, p. 134.
65 The *English Woman's Journal*, December 1862, pp. 286–8; the *Lancet*, 13 December 1862, p. 657.
66 Garrett to Mr Burn Murdoch, 3 July 1862.
67 The *British Medical Journal*, 2 February 1867.
68 Josephine Butler to 'Dear Friend', quoted in Jeanne L'Esperance, 'Doctors and Women in Nineteenth-Century Society: Sexuality

and Role', J. Woodward and D. Richards, *Health Care and Popular Medicine*, 1977, p. 120.

69   Manton, p. 172.

70   Garrett to Millicent Garrett Fawcett, June 1867.

71   Brian Harrison, 'Women's Health and the Women's Movement in Britain, 1840–1940', Past & Present Society, *The Roots of Sociobiology*, 1978, p. 20.

72   Garrett to Mrs Richard Garrett, 13 July 1860.

73   The Women's Medical Assocation of New York (eds.), *Mary Putnam Jacobi: A Pathfinder in Medicine*, New York, 1925, p. 354.

74   Margaret Llewelyn Davies, *Maternity: Letters from Working Women Collected by the Women's Co-operative Guild*, 1978.

75   Bodichon, 1856, p. 38.

76   *The Times*, 2 February 1867.

77   The *Englishwoman's Review*, July 1867, p. 255; October 1867, p. 312.

78   The *Lancet*, 23 November 1867, p. 649; 8 February 1867, p. 205.

79   The *Englishwoman's Review*, January 1868, p. 395.

80   Madelyn Holmes, 'Go to Switzerland, Young Woman, if You Want to Study Medicine', in *Women's Studies International Forum*, vol. 7, no. 4, p. 243.

81   Manton, pp. 189–91.

82   The *Lancet*, 30 May 1863, p. 613; 2 September 1865, p. 276.

83   The *Lancet*, 30 May 1863, p. 613.

84   The *Lancet*, 11 October 1862, p. 409; 6 July 1861, p. 16.

85   Ross, p. 226.

86   The *Lancet*, 10 January 1863, p. 45; the *British Medical Journal*, 21 March 1863, p. 302.

87   The *Lancet*, 6 September 1872, p. 268.

88   Bodichon, 1856, pp. 14–15.

89   The *Lancet*, 3 August 1861, p. 117; 7 August 1869, p. 206; 6 November 1869, p. 644; 21 May 1870, p. 740.

90   The *Lancet*, 2 August 1862, p. 123.

91   The *Lancet*, 9 October 1869, p. 511.

92   The *Lancet*, 28 August 1869, p. 329.

93   The *Lancet*, 2 August 1873, p. 160.

94   Eva Gamarnikow, 'Women's Re-entry into Health Care: Medical Reactions to the Nightingale Reforms', paper delivered at the British Sociological Association Annual Conference, 'Gender and Society', Manchester University, April 5–8 1982.

95   The *English Woman's Journal*, June 1862, p. 283.

96   'Female Medical Society', 1864, in Women's Medical Education Pamphlets, Fawcett Library.

97 The *Englishwoman's Review*, July 1867, p. 253, October 1867, p. 312.
98 'Inaugural Address Delivered for the Female Medical Society on October 3, 1864, by James Edmunds, esq. MD', in Women's Medical Education Pamphlets, Fawcett Library.
99 The *British Medical Journal*, 28 October 1865, p. 463.
100 The *Lancet*, 2 June 1866, p. 213.
101 James Edmunds, 'Introductory Address Delivered for the Female Medical Society – Third Session of the Ladies' Medical College', the *Victoria Magazine*, May 1867.
102 Ibid.
103 Report on the Ninth Annual Session, in Women's Medical Education Pamphlets, Fawcett Library.
104 The *Englishwoman's Review*, July 1868, p. 536.
105 Donnison, p. 83.
106 The *Lancet*, 3 November 1866, p. 501.
107 The *Englishwoman's Review*, January 1867, p. 112.
108 Ibid., p. 111.
109 Margaret Balfour and Ruth Young, *The Work of Medical Women in India*, Oxford, 1929.
110 The *Englishwoman's Review*, January 1867, p. 122.
111 The *Englishwoman's Review*, July 1870, p. 233; October 1872, pp. 268–9; April 1875, p. 189.
112 Rita McWilliams-Tullberg, 'Women and Degrees at Cambridge University, 1862–97', Martha Vicinus, *A Widening Sphere*, 1980.
113 The *Englishwoman's Review*, April 1868, p. 446.
114 James Stuart, 'The Teaching of Science', Josephine Butler (ed.), *Women's Work and Women's Culture*, 1869, p. 128.
115 Ziggi Alexander and Audrey Dewjee (eds.), *The Wonderful Adventures of Mrs. Seacole in Many Lands*, 1984.
116 Ibid., p. 56.
117 Ibid., p. 109.
118 Ibid., p. 122.
119 Ibid., p. 141.
120 Ibid., p. 194.
121 *The Times*, 11 April 1857.
122 Isobel Rae, *The Strange Story of Dr. James Barry*, 1958, p. 1. Also reported in the *British Medical Journal*, 2 September 1875, p. 249.
123 The author acknowledges comments by Liz Kelly and Margaret Taylor.

Part 3

1   Todd, p. 64.
2   Ibid., p. 65.
3   Ibid., p. 99.
4   Ibid., p. 118.
5   Sophia Jex-Blake to her mother, 15 September 1862, quoted in Todd, p. 130.
6   Ibid., p. 165.
7   Sophia Jex-Blake, *A Visit to Some American Schools and Colleges*, 1867.
8   Todd., p. 172.
9   Ibid., p. 219.
10 Sophia Jex-Blake, 'Medicine as a Profession for Women', Josephine Butler (ed.), *Women's Work and Women's Culture*, 1869; Sophia Jex-Blake, *Medical Women: A Thesis and a History*, 1886, first published in 1872.
11 Jex-Blake, 1886, pp. 4–38.
12 Ibid., p. 53.
13 Quoted in Todd, p. 223.
14 Ibid., p. 253.
15 Quoted in Josephine Butler, *Memoirs of John Grey of Dilston*, Edinburgh, 1869, p. 326n.
16 Jex-Blake, 1886, p. 42.
17 Ann Oakley, 'Wise Women and Medical Men', in J. Mitchell and A. Oakley (eds.), *The Rights and Wrongs of Women*, 1976, p. 31; Helen Rugen, 'The Roots of Marie Stopes: Ideas about Female Sexuality in Britain, 1900–20', Ph.D., University of Edinburgh, 1979.
18 Manton, p. 178.
19 Garrett to Emily Davies, 23 March 1861.
20 Todd, p. 226.
21 Edinburgh Ladies' Educational Association, in Women's Education Pamphlets, the Fawcett Library.
22 Todd, p. 221.
23 The *Englishwoman's Review*, April 1858, p. 98.
24 Todd, p. 235.
25 Ibid., p. 247.
26 Ibid., p. 287.
27 The *Englishwoman's Review*, April 1871, p. 131.
28 Ibid.
29 Jex-Blake, 1886, p. 72.
30 The *Englishwoman's Review*, January 1870, p. 28.
31 The *Lancet*, 14 August 1869, p. 260; 28 August 1869, p. 329.
32 The *Lancet*, 18 September 1869, p. 421.

33 Sophia Jex-Blake to Lucy Sewall, 26 April 1869, quoted in Todd, p. 247.

34 Sophia Jex-Blake to Lucy Sewall, 6 July 1869, quoted in Todd, p. 259.

35 *The Times*, 28 July 1869.

36 Jex-Blake, 1886, p. 78.

37 Edythe Lutzker, *Edith Pechey-Phipson MD*, New York, 1973, p. 9.

38 Todd, p. 266.

39 Sir Alexander Grant, *The Story of the University of Edinburgh*, 1884.

40 The *Lancet*, 7 May 1870, p. 673.

41 The *Lancet*, 4 December 1869, p. 783.

42 The *Lancet*, 18 September 1869, p. 427.

43 The *Lancet*, 7 August 1869, p. 206; 6 November 1869, p. 644.

44 The *Lancet*, 9 October 1869, p. 511.

45 A classic example of this argument is W.R. Greg, 'Why are Women Redundant?', in *National Review*, April 1862.

46 Blackwell, 1914, p. 47.

47 Jex-Blake, 1886, p. 83; Todd, p. 286.

48 *The Times*, 16 November 1869.

49 See, for example, Judith R. Walkowitz, *Prostitution and Victorian Society*, Cambridge, 1980.

50 Judith R. Walkowitz, 'Jack the Ripper', *Feminist Studies*, 8, 1982, pp. 543–74.

51 Walkowitz, 1980, p. 145–6; see also Dorothy Thompson, 'Women and Nineteenth-Century Radical Politics: A Lost Dimension', Juliet Michell and Ann Oakley (eds.), *The Rights and Wrongs of Women*, 1976.

52 *The Shield*, 6 April 1872, p. 897.

53 Josephine Butler to Mr Edmondson, 13 February 1875, quoted in Harrison, p. 5.

54 Barbara Taylor, 'Female Vice and Feminist Virtue', in the *New Statesman*, 23 January 1981, p. 16.

55 *The Shield*, 13 June 1870, p. 127.

56 Josephine Butler to Mr Edmondson, 28 March 1872, quoted in Harrison, p. 15.

57 *The Shield*, 23 August 1873, pp. 278–9.

58 *The Shield*, 13 September 1873, p. 299.

59 Diary entry, quoted in Bell, p. 39.

60 Blackwell, 1914, p. 162.

61 Ibid., p. 195.

62 Elizabeth Blackwell, 'Rescue Work in Relation to Prostitution and Disease', 1881, Sheila Jeffreys (ed.), *The Sexuality Papers*, 1987.

63 Blackwell, 1914, p. 202.

64 Mary Ann Elston, 'Women and Anti-vivisection in Victorian England, 1870–1900', N.A. Rupke (ed.), *Vivisection in Historical Perspective*, 1987, pp. 268–9.
65 *The Shield*, 29 December 1977, p. 309.
66 Elizabeth Garrett Anderson, 'An Enquiry into the Character of the Contagious Diseases Acts of 1866–69', the *Pall Mall Gazette*, 25 January 1870.
67 Manton, pp. 179–80, 183.
68 Todd, p. 364.
69 Ibid.
70 Frances Hoggan, 'Women in Medicine', in T. Stanton (ed.), *The Woman Question in Europe*, (1884).
71 Bell, p. 86.
72 *The Times*, 25 April 1870; the *Spectator*, 7 April 1870; the *British Medical Journal*, 16 April 1870, in Jex-Blake, appendix p. 58.
73 Jex-Blake, 1886, appendix p. 59.
74 *The Times*, 22 April 1870, 23 April 1870.
75 Ibid.
76 Todd, p. 273.
77 *The Times*, 26 April 1870, 4 May 1870.
78 The *Lancet*, 2 October 1869, p. 496.
79 Jex-Blake, 1886, appendix p. 57.
80 The Women's Medical Association of New York, p. 375.
81 The *English Woman's Journal*, April 1858, p. 90.
82 Garrett to Davies, 23 October 1860.
83 The *Lancet*, 4 December 1869, p. 783.
84 The *Lancet*, 27 November 1869, p. 761.
85 The *Lancet*, 2 October 1869, p. 496.
86 *The Scotsman*, 26 December 1870.
87 Vicinus, p. 98.
88 Letter from 'Medicus' in the *Pall Mall Gazette*, 11 May 1870; letter from 'A Mental Physician' in the *Lancet*, 21 May 1870, p. 751.
89 *The Times*, 14 April 1870; the *Englishwoman's Review*, April 1870, pp. 112–13.
90 *The Times*, 26 May 1870.
91 Jex-Blake, 1886, appendix, pp. 49–56.
92 The *Englishwoman's Review*, January 1871, p. 39.
93 The *Lancet*, 18 June 1870, p. 887.
94 The *Lancet*, 9 July 1870, p. 63.
95 The *Lancet*, 30 August 1873, p. 308.
96 The *Lancet*, 17 August 1878, p. 227.
97 Ibid., p. 226.
98 The *Lancet*, 26 April 1873, p. 618.
99 The *Lancet*, 3 August 1861, p. 117.

100   Lutzker, p. 49.
101   The *Lancet*, 2 August 1873, p. 159.
102   The *Englishwoman's Review*, October 1870, p. 291.
103   Todd, p. 286.
104   Ibid.
105   Jex-Blake, 1886, p. 83.
106   Ibid., p. 90.
107   Ibid., pp. 92–3.
108   The *Daily Review*, 21 November 1870, quoted in Jex-Blake, p. 92.
109   Jex-Blake, 1886, pp. 93–4.
110   Robert Wilson to Edith Pechey, 20 November 1870, quoted in Todd, p. 294.
111   The *Edinburgh Courant*, 17 January 1871, in Jex-Blake, p. 91.
112   Todd, p. 299.
113   The *Lancet*, 26 November 1870, p. 750.
114   Jex-Blake, 1886, p. 95.
115   *The Scotsman*, 23 December 1870.
116   The *Lancet*, 17 December 1870, p. 873.
117   The *Lancet*, 29 October 1870, p. 615.
118   Manton, p. 207.
119   Garrett to Millicent Garrett Fawcett, 25 December 1870, quoted in Manton, p. 211–3.
120   The *Lancet*, 28 January 1871, p. 127.
121   *The Times*, 13 January 1871.
122   Anna Stoddart, *Elizabeth Pease Nichol*, 1899.
123   Todd, p. 300.
124   Jex-Blake, 1886, p. 99.
125   Todd, pp. 298, 299.
126   The *Lancet*, 14 January 1871, p. 62.
127   Isabel Thorne, *Sketch of the Foundation and Development of the London School of Medicine for Women*, 1915, p. 15.
128   Jex-Blake, 1886, p. 103.
129   *The Scotsman*, 10 February 1871, reprinted in Jex-Blake, appendix, pp. 65–6.
130   The *Englishwoman's Review*, January 1871, p. 36.
131   Todd, p. 311.
132   *The Scotsman*, 1 June 1871; 12 July 1871; 13 July 1871; 14 July 1871.
133   Todd, p. 316.
134   Letter to *The Scotsman*, 31 October 1871.
135   *The Scotsman*, 14 July 1871.
136   Jex-Blake, 1886, p. 111.
137   Diary entry, 26 April 1871, quoted in Todd, p. 310.
138   *The Scotsman*, 14 July 1871.
139   Jex-Blake, 1886, p. 161.

140 Ibid., p. 156.
141 The author acknowledges comments by Liz Kelly.
142 Todd, p. 327.
143 *The Scotsman*, 10 October 1871.
144 Ibid.
145 *The Scotsman*, 19 August 1871.
146 The *Englishwoman's Review*, July 1871, p. 214.
147 Ross, p. 246.
148 Ibid., p. 247.
149 Ibid., p. 245.
150 *The Scotsman*, 14 March 1871.
151 *The Scotsman*, 20 October 1871.
152 Grant, p. 161.
153 Ibid.
154 *The Scotsman*, 16 November 1871.
155 Lutzker, p. 24.
156 The *Lancet*, 3 August 1872, p. 236.
157 Jex-Blake, 1886, p. 101.
158 The *Lancet*, 10 February 1872, p. 196.
159 The *Lancet*, 4 May 1872, p. 618.
160 *The Scotsman*, 31 October 1871.
161 *The Scotsman*, 30 October 1871.
162 *The Scotsman*, 17 August 1873; 1 September 1873.
163 Todd, p. 350.
164 *The Scotsman*, 19 January 1872.
165 *The Scotsman*, 2 February 1872.
166 Letter from Peter Bell, 30 October 1872; replies written during November; in History of Medicine and Science Unit, Wellcome Library.
167 *The Scotsman*, 29 December 1872.
168 *The Times*, 30 July 1872.
169 *The Times*, 27 April 1872.
170 Sophia Jex-Blake, *Medical Women: a Thesis and a History*, 1872.
171 *The Scotsman*, 21 November 1870.
172 *The Scotsman*, 27 May 1872.
173 *The Scotsman*, 29 December 1870.
174 Jex-Blake, 1886, p. 59.
175 Todd, p. 378.
176 Diary entries on 6 October 1872 and 11 October 1972, in Todd, p. 382.
177 *The Times*, 14 November 1871; 17 November 1871; 21 November 1871.
178 Quoted in the *Englishwoman's Review*, January 1872, p. 32.
179 *The Times*, 20 November 1871.
180 Ibid..

181 *The Times*, 15 October 1872.
182 Sophia Jex-Blake to her mother, 11 September 1872, in Todd, p. 380.
183 *The Scotsman*, 14 October 1872.
184 The *Lancet*, 21 September 1872, p. 420.
185 *The Times*, 5 November 1872.
186 The *Lancet*, 16 March 1872, p. 365.
187 Ibid.
188 Reported in the *Englishwoman's Review*, July 1873, p. 227.
189 The *Medical Times*, 1872, 1, p. 687, quoted in Donnison, p. 78.
190 The *British Medical Journal*, 22 March 1873.
191 The *Lancet*, 21 December 1872.
192 The *Englishwoman's Review*, April 1873, p. 131.
193 Ibid.
194 Ibid., p. 132.
195 The *Englishwoman's Review*, October 1873, p. 264.
196 In Medical Education Pamphlets, Fawcett Library.

Part 4
1 *The Times*, 5 August 1873; 23 August 1873.
2 Garrett to J.G.S. Anderson, 20 August 1870.
3 The *Lancet*, 29 October 1870, p. 615.
4 Address to the London School of Medicine for Women, in the *Englishwoman's Review*, October 1877, p. 460.
5 Bell, p. 51; Ross, p. 226; Manton, p. 130.
6 Ross, p. 159.
7 Jex-Blake, 1886, p. 212.
8 Ibid., 211.
9 The *Englishwoman's Review*, January, 1874, p. 54.
10 The *Lancet*, 2 August 1873; *The Times*, 12 June 1875, 28 July 1873.
11 *The Times*, 23 September 1873.
12 *The Times*, 1 September 1873.
13 *The Times*, 4 September 1873.
14 Todd, p. 406.
15 Sophia Jex-Blake, 'The Practice of Medicine by Women', in *Fortnightly Review*, March 1875, printed as a pamphlet in Edinburgh, 1876, p. 18.
16 Memorial in favour of William Cowper Temple's Bill from 26 Professors, in Women's Medical Education Pamphlets, Fawcett Library.
17 The *Lancet*, 9 May 1874, p. 679.
18 Todd, p. 414.
19 Ibid.

20 Jex-Blake, 1886, p. 175.
21 Dr Henry Maudsley, 'Sex in Mind and Education', *Fortnightly Review*, April 1874.
22 Dr Edward H. Clarke, *Sex in Education: or, a Fair Chance for the Girls*, Boston, 1873.
23 Walsh, p. 124.
24 *Fortnightly Review*, May 1874.
25 Walsh, p. 130.
26 The *Lancet*, 16 May 1874, p. 705.
27 The *Lancet*, 4 July 1874, p. 27.
28 *The Times*, 18 June 1874.
29 *The Times*, 20 June 1874.
30 Jex-Blake, 1886, p. 177.
31 Robert Wilson, 'Aesculapia Victrix', reprinted from *Fortnightly Review*, January 1886, printed as a pamphlet, 1886, p. 8.
32 Todd, p. 421.
33 Thorne, p. 22.
34 The *Lancet*, 17 October 1874, p. 561.
35 Todd, p. 424.
36 Jex-Blake, 1886, p. 178.
37 Manton, p. 240.
38 Ibid.
39 For example, *The Times*, 5 August 1873.
40 Bell, p. 92.
41 The *Birmingham Daily Post*, 20 July 1875, quoted in Lutzker, p. 50.
42 For the anti-vivisection movement, see R. D. French, *Anti-Vivisection and Medical Science in Victorian Society*, Princeton, 1975; Mary Ann Elston, 'Gender, Medicine and Morality in the Late Nineteenth Century: A Study of the Anti-Vivisection Movement 1870–1904', MA Dissertation, University of Essex, 1984; Mary Ann Elston, 'Women and Anti-vivisection in Victorian England, 1870–1900', in N. A. Rupke (ed.), *Vivisection in Historical Perspective*, 1987.
43 Jex-Blake, 1886, p. 125.
44 See Roger Smith, *Trial by Medicine*, Edinburgh, 1981.
45 Olive Banks, *Becoming a Feminist: the Social Origins of 'First Wave' Feminism*, Brighton, 1986, p. 106.
46 Manton, p. 224–5.
47 Elston, p. 75.
48 Ibid., p. 111.
49 Bell, p. 88.
50 Margaret Balfour and Ruth Young, *Work of Medical Woman in India*, 1929, p. xi.
51 *The Times*, 29 March 1875.
52 Mary Scharlieb, *Reminiscences*, 1924.

53 Ibid., p. 40.
54 For example William Cowper Temple in a debate in the House of Commons reported in *The Times*, 4 March 1875.
55 *The Times*, 4 March 1875.
56 Ibid.
57 The *Englishwoman's Review*, April 1875, p. 165.
58 The *Lancet*, 15 July 1876, p. 91.
59 James Stansfeld, 'Medical Women. An Historical Sketch', in *Nineteenth Century Review*, July 1877, reprinted by The Edinburgh Executive Committee for Securing a Complete Medical Education to Women, 1878, p. 23.
60 The *Englishwoman's Review*, July 1875, p. 317.
61 The *Englishwoman's Review*, August 1875, p. 383.
62 Todd, p. 430.
63 The *Lancet*, 7 August 1875, p. 213.
64 Stansfeld, p. 15.
65 The *Englishwoman's Review*, July 1875, p. 321.
66 Todd, p. 431.
67 Jex-Blake, 1886, p. 196.
68 Ibid.
69 Ibid., p. 197.
70 The *Englishwoman's Review*, May 1876, p. 212.
71 Bell, p. 142.
72 Jex-Blake, 1886, p. 232.
73 The *Lancet*, 2 August 1873, p. 159.
74 The *Lancet*, 3 August 1873, p. 117.
75 Stansfeld, p. 29.
76 *The Times*, 1 November 1869.
77 Wendy Savage, *A Savage Enquiry. Who Controls Childbirth?*, Virago Press, London, 1986, p. 59.
78 Todd, p. 433.
79 Ibid.
80 Jex-Blake, 1876, p. 35.
81 The *British Medical Journal*, 3 June 1876; 10 June 1876.
82 The *Englishwoman's Review*, July 1876, p. 312.
83 *The Times*, 8 May 1878.
84 Todd, p. 402.
85 The Women's Medical Association of New York, p. 381.
86 Walsh, p. 168.
87 The *Lancet*, 24 March 1877, p. 442.
88 The *Englishwoman's Review*, August 1877, p. 366.
89 The *Lancet*, 17 August 1878, p. 227.
90 The *Englishwoman's Review*, December 1875, p. 551.
91 Elizabeth Garrett Anderson to J.G.S. Anderson, 6 August 1875.
92 The *Englishwoman's Review*, September 1878, p. 407.
93 Ibid., pp. 409–10.

94 *The Times*, 8 May 1878.
95 The *Englishwoman's Review*, February 1879, p. 77.

Epilogue
1   The *Englishwoman's Review*, August 1880, p. 364.
2   Savage, p. 59.
3   Harrison, p. 20.
4   Bell, p. 147.
5   Todd, p. 457.
6   Ibid., p. 459.
7   The *Englishwoman's Review*, September 1878, p. 462.
8   Margot Lawrence, *Shadow of Swords*, 1971, p. 52.
9   Todd, p. 494.
10 Ibid., p. 496.
11 Sophia Jex-Blake, 'Medical Women. A Ten Year Retrospect',
    Nineteenth Century, November 1887, reprinted by the
    National Association for Promoting the Medical Education of
    Women, Edinburgh, 1888, p. 18.
12 Bell, p. 133.

Conclusion
1   Jex-Blake, 1886, p. vii.
2   Savage; Bea Campbell, *Unofficial Secrets*, 1988.
3   Savage, p. 72.
4   Ibid., p. 116.
5   Ibid., p. 23.
6   Ibid., p. 177.

Bibliography

Books and articles
Abel-Smith, Brian, *A History of the Nursing Profession*, Heinemann, London, 1960.
—— *The Hospitals, 1800–1948*, Heinemann, London, 1964.
Alexander, Ziggi, and Dewjee, Audrey, *Wonderful Adventures of Mrs. Seacole in Many Lands*, Falling Wall Press, Bristol, 1984.
Allen, Maggie and Elder, Michael, *The Walls of Jericho. A Novel Based on the life of Sophia Jex-Blake*, British Broadcasting Corporation, London, 1981.
Anderson, Louisa Garrett, *Elizabeth Garrett Anderson*, Faber, London, 1939.
Balfour, Margaret and Young, Ruth, *Work of Medical Women in India*, Oxford University Press, London, 1929.
Banks, Olive, *The Biographical Dictionary of British Feminists. Volume One: 1800–1930*, Wheatsheaf, Brighton, 1985.
—— *Becoming a Feminist: the Social Origins of 'First-wave' Feminism*, Wheatsheaf, Brighton, 1986.
Bell, Enid Moberley, *Storming the Citadel: the Rise of the Woman Doctor*, Constable, London, 1953.
Blackwell, Elizabeth, 'Rescue Work in Relation to Prostitution and Disease', in Jeffreys, Sheila, (ed.), *The Sexuality Papers*, Routledge, London, 1987.
—— *Pioneer Work in Opening the Medical Profession to Women*, Dent, London, 1914, first published in New York in 1895.
Bodichon, Barbara Leigh Smith, *A Brief Summary in Plain Language of the Most Important Laws Concerning Women*, 1854.
—— *Women and Work*, 1856.
Joan Burstyn, 'Education and Sex: the Medical Case Against Higher Education for Women in England, 1870–1900', *Proceedings of the American Philosophical Society*, 177, 1973, pp. 79–89.
—— *Victorian Education and the Ideal of Womanhood*, Croom Helm, London, 1980.
Butler, Josephine, *Memoir of John Grey of Dilston*, Edinburgh, 1869.

——(ed.), *Women's Work and Women's Culture*, London, 1869.

Campbell, Beatrix, *Unofficial Secrets*, Virago, London, 1988.

Clarke, Dr Edward C., *Sex in Education: or, a Fair Chance for the Girls*, Boston, 1873.

Cobbe, Frances Power, 'The Medical Profession and its Morality', *Modern Review*, (ii), 1881, p. 296–328.

Cott, Nancy F., (ed.), *Roots of Bitterness: Documents of the Social History of American Women*, Dutton, New York, 1972.

Davies, Celia (ed.), *Rewriting Nursing History*, Croom Helm, London, 1980.

Davies, Margaret Llewelyn, *Maternity: Letters from Working Women Collected by the Women's Co-operative Guild*, Virago, London, 1978, first published in 1915.

Delamont, Sara and Duffin, Lorna, (eds.), *The Nineteenth-Century Woman: Her Cultural and Physical World*, Croom Helm, London, 1978.

Donnison, Jean, *Midwives and Medical Men: a History of Interprofessional Rivalries and Women's Rights*, Schocken, New York, 1977.

Elston, Mary Ann, 'Gender, Medicine and Morality in the Late Nineteenth Century: a Study of the Anti-Vivisection Movement, 1870–1904', unpublished MA dissertation, University of Essex, 1984.

——'Women and Anti-vivisection in Victorian England, 1870–1900', in Rupke N.A., (ed.), *Vivisection in Historical Perspective*, Croom Helm, London, 1987.

Finlayson, Geoffrey, *The Seventh Earl of Shaftesbury*, Eyre Methuen, London, 1981.

French, R.D., *Medical Science and Victorian Society: the Anti-Vivisection Movement*, Princeton University Press, Princeton, 1975.

Gamarnikow, Eva, 'Women's Re-entry into Health-care: Medical Reactions to the Nightingale Reforms', paper at the British Sociological Association Annual Conference, *Gender and Society*, Manchester University, April 5–8, 1982.

Grant, Sir Alexander, *The Story of the University of Edinburgh*, London, 1884.

Greg, W.R., 'Why are Women Redundant?', *National Review*, April 1862.

Gunn, Alistair, 'Maternity Hospitals', in Poynter, F.N.L., (ed.), *The Evolution of Hospitals in Britain*, Pitman Medical, 1964.

Hammond, J.L. and Barbara, *James Stansfeld: A Victorian Champion of Sex Equality*, Longman, London, 1932.

Harrison, Brian, 'Women's Health and the Women's Movement in Britain, 1840–1940', in Past and Present Society, *The Roots of Sociobiology*, 1978.

Hoggan, Frances, 'Women in Medicine', Stanton, T., (ed.), *The Woman Question in Europe*, Low, London, 1884.

Holmes, Madelyn, 'Go to Switzerland, Young Women, If You Want to Study Medicine', *Women's Studies International Forum*, vol. 7, no. 4, pp. 243–5.

Jameson, Anna, *'Sisters of Charity' and 'The Communion of Labour': Two Lectures on the Social Employment of Women*, London, 1859.

Jex-Blake, Sophia, 'The Practice of Medicine by Women', *Fortnightly Review*, March 1875.

——*Medical Women: a Thesis and a History*, Edinburgh, 1886, first published in 1872.

——'Medical Women. A Ten Years' Retrospect', *Nineteenth Century*, November 1887.

Lawrence, Margot, *Shadow of Swords*, Joseph, London, 1971.

L'Esperance, Jeanne, 'Doctors and Women in Nineteenth-Century Society: Sexuality and Role', in Woodwards, J. and Richards, D. (eds.), *Health Care and Popular Medicine in Nineteenth-Century England*, Croom Helm, London, 1977.

Lutzker, Edythe, *Women Gain a Place in Medicine*, McGraw Hill, New York, Maidenhead, 1969.

——*Edith Pechey-Phipson, MD*, Exposition Press, New York, 1973.

McLaren, Angus, 'Women's Work and Regulation of Family Size: the Question of Abortion in the Nineteenth Century', *History Workshop Journal*, 4, 1977.

——*Birth Control in Nineteenth-Century England*, Croom Helm, London, 1978.

McWilliams-Tullberg, Rita, 'Women and Degrees at Cambridge University, 1862–97', in Vicinus, Martha, (ed.), *A Widening Sphere*, Methuen, London, 1980.

Manton, Jo, *Elizabeth Garrett Anderson*, Methuen, London, 1965.

Maudsley, Dr Henry, 'Sex in Mind and in Education', *Fortnightly Review*, April 1874.

Mitchell, Juliet and Oakley, Ann (eds.), *The Rights and Wrongs of Women*, Penguin, Harmondsworth, 1976.

Murray, Janet Horowitz, (ed.), *Strong-minded Women*, Penguin, Harmondsworth, 1984.

Nightingale, Florence, 'Cassandra', in Ray Strachey, *The Cause*, Virago, London, 1978, first published in 1928.

Peterson, Jeanne, *The Medical Profession in Mid-Victorian London*, University of California Press, Berkeley, 1978.

Prochaska, F., *Women and Philanthropy in Nineteenth-Century England*, Clarendon Press, Oxford, 1980.

Rae, Isobel, *The Strange Story of Dr. James Barry*, Longman, London, 1958.

Rosenberg, Charles, 'Florence Nightingale on Contagion: the Hospital as Moral Universe', in Rosenberg, Charles, (ed.), *Healing and History*, Dawson, Folkestone, 1979.

Ross, Ishbel, *Child of Destiny*, Gollancz, London, 1950.

Rugen, Helen, 'The Roots of Marie Stopes: Ideas about Female Sexuality in Britain, 1900–1920', Ph.D, University of Edinburgh, 1979.

Savage, Wendy, *A Savage Enquiry. Who Controls Childbirth?*, Virago, London, 1986.

Scharlieb, Mary, *Reminiscences*, Williams & Norgate, London, 1924.

Smith, Roger, *Trial by Medicine: Insanity and Responsibility in Victorian Trials*, Edinburgh University Press, Edinburgh, 1981.

Stansfeld, James, 'Medical Women', *Nineteenth Century*, vol. 1, no. 5, July 1877, pp. 888–901.

Stephen, Barbara, *Emily Davies and Girton College*, Constable, London, 1927.

Stoddart, Anna M., *Elizabeth Pease Nichol*, Dent, London, 1899.

Strachey, Ray, *The Cause*, Virago, London, 1978, first published in 1928.

Summers, Anne, 'Pride and Prejudice: Ladies and Nurses in the Crimean War', *History Workshop Journal*, 16, Autumn, 1983, pp. 33–56.

Taylor, Barbara, 'Female Vice and Feminist Virtue', *New Statesman*, 23 January 1981, pp. 16–17.

Thorne, Isabel, *Sketch of the Foundation and Development of the London School of Medicine for Women*, Women's Printing Society, London, 1916, privately printed in 1905.

Todd, Margaret, *The Life of Sophia Jex-Blake*, Macmillan & Co., London, 1918.

Turner, A. Logan, *Story of a Great Hospital: the Royal Infirmary of Edinburgh, 1729–1929*, Oliver & Boyd, Edinburgh, 1937.

Vicinus, Martha, *Independent Women: Work and Community for Single Women, 1850–1920*, Virago, London, 1985.

Walkowitz, Judith R., *Prostitution and Victorian Society: Women, Class and the State*, Cambridge University Press, Cambridge, 1980.

—— 'The Politics of Prostitution', *Signs*, 6.1, Autumn 1980.

—— 'Jack the Ripper', *Feminist Studies*, 8, 1982, pp. 543–74.

Walsh, Mary Roth, *'Doctors Wanted: No Women Need Apply.' Sexual Barriers in the Medical Profession, 1835–75*, Yale University Press, New Haven, 1977.

Wilson, Robert, 'Aesculapia Victrix', *Fortnightly Review*, January 1886, pp. 18–33.

The Women's Medical Association of New York, (ed.), *Mary Putnam Jacobi: a Pathfinder in Medicine*, New York, 1925.

Youngson, A. J., *The Scientific Revolution in Victorian Medicine*, Croom Helm, London, 1979.

Other sources
Elizabeth Garrett Anderson letters, held in the Fawcett Library,
Autograph Collection, Volume X: Part A 1860–65; Part B
1867–1909.
Women's Education Pamphlets, held in the Fawcett Library.
Women's Medical Education Pamphlets, held in the Fawcett Library.
The *British Medical Journal*, 1860–66.
The *English Woman's Journal*, 1858–64.
The *Englishwoman's Review*, 1867–80.
The *Lancet*, 1860–80.
The *Scotsman*, 1871–9.
The *Shield*, 1870–80.
The *Times*, 1860–80.

Index

harassment of 135, 136, 202; and Edinburgh's blocking tactics 138; as a celebrity 142–3; fails examinations 149, 166; and Walter Thomson 151; on foreign degrees 157; and marriage 160; rejects account of events at Edinburgh 161; and new legislation 162; refused entry to Hospital for Women 181; tempted to stop campaigning 182; passes MD examinations in Berne 185; becomes LKQCPI 185; joins register 185, 192; and women's suffrage 193, 198; in practice in Edinburgh 195–9; professional isolation 200; and dispensaries 203; biographical notes 218–29

Johns Hopkins University 187

Keiller, Alexander 65
Kelland, Professor 104, 133
Kensington Society 68
King's and Queen's College of Physicians, Ireland 185, 193
King's College, London 5
Kingsford, Anna 111, 174
Kingsley, Henry 128
Kingsley, Rev Charles 137
Kingston, Jamaica 85, 86

Ladies' Educational Association 155
Ladies' National Association 83, 107, 108–9, 116
Ladies' National Association for the Diffusion of Sanitary Knowledge 48
Ladies' National Association for the Repeal of the Contagious Diseases Acts 131

Ladies' Physiological Institute of Boston 30
Laing, Daniel 34
Lancet, the x–xi, 22, 23, 26, 48, 61, 62, 65, 73, 75, 77, 81, 82, 83, 99–100, 103, 106, 108, 117, 118–22, 127–30, 132, 141, 149, 151–3, 158, 161, 163, 166, 168, 178, 179, 181, 184, 187, 188, 190, 201
Latin America 86
Laws of Life in Relation to the Physical Education of Girls (Blackwood) 35
Laycock, Professor 99
'Lectures to Ladies' series 5
Lee, Dr Rebecca 37
Leggett, Mrs 123–4
Leigh Smith, Barbara (later Bodichon) 8–9, 10, 13, 41, 57, 68, 129, 137
Leith Hospital 134
'Letter to Ladies in favour of Female Physicians for their own sex' (Gregory) 49–50, 51
'Letter to Young Ladies Desirous of Studying Medicine' (Blackwell) 43–4
Linlithgow 163
Littlejohn, Dr 124
Local Government Board 183
local medical societies 26, 28, 38
London, University of 73, 191; and technical education 21; and matriculation examination 40, 41; and medical degrees 62, 96; refuses to admit Elizabeth Garrett 64; proposes to extend educational opportunities to women 166; and Edith Shove 187, 193; conflict between medical and non-medical graduates 187–8; recognition of London (Royal